Essential Emeril

Essential Emeril

Favorite Recipes and Hard-Won Wisdom from a Life in the Kitchen

Emeril Lagasse

with Pam Hoenig

Oxmoor House®

Design and Photography ©2015 by Time Inc. Books
1271 Avenue of the Americas, New York, NY 10020

Editorial Director: Anja Schmidt
Senior Editor: Erica Sanders-Foege
Writer: Pam Hoenig
Assistant Managing Editor: Jeanne de Lathouder
Assistant Project Editor: Megan Thompson Brown
Creative Director: Felicity Keane
Art Director: Christopher Rhoads
Junior Designer: AnnaMaria Jacob
Executive Photography Director: Iain Bagwell
Photo Editor: Kellie Lindsey
Cover Photography: Quentin Bacon
Photographers: Cedric Angeles, Becky Luigart-Stayner
Senior Photo Stylist: Mindi Shapiro Levine
Food Stylists: Nathan Carrabba, Victoria E. Cox
Prop Stylist: Mary Clayton Carl
Test Kitchen Manager: Alyson Moreland Haynes
Senior Production Manager: Greg A. Amason
Production Manager: Theresa Beste-Farley
Assistant Production Manager: Diane Rose Keener
Assistant Production Director: Sue Chodakiewicz
Copy Editors: Donna Baldone, Julie Bosche
Indexer: Mary Ann Laurens
Editorial Fellows: Kylie Dazzo, Dree Deacon, Nicole Fisher

Photography Credits: Jim Cooper/AP Photo: 121;
Courtesy of author: 35, 120, 207; Jason Ellis: 165;
David Moir/Bravo/NBCUniversal/Getty Images: 102

ISBN-13: 978-0-8487-4478-6
ISBN-10: 0-8487-4478-0
Library of Congress Control Number: 2015944368

Printed in the United States of America

10 9 8 7 6 5 4 3 2 1

First Printing 2015

in memory of
charlie trotter

friend

colleague

brother

passionate explorer

scholar

perfectionist

genius

missed

contents

introduction

My very earliest food memory—I was probably about eight years old—is of picking vegetables in my family's garden, and then getting up on a step stool so I could reach the kitchen counter, and my mom teaching me how to make vegetable soup. That first time I made it, it was OK, but every time I made it after that, as I gained confidence and a better understanding of what was going on in the pot, the soup got better. My appreciation of the importance of quality ingredients and simple preparations started with that vegetable soup. It's this lifelong journey of discovery and enjoyment in the kitchen that I want to share with you in *Essential Emeril*.

Growing up in Fall River, Massachusetts, I was a percussionist in a Portuguese band and most every weekend, particularly during the summer, we would travel to festivals throughout New England and as far north as Toronto to play. A big part of any Portuguese festival is the food—*caldo verde*, sno-cones, meat on a stick cooked over an open fire, the Portuguese doughnuts called *malassadas*—and thinking back on those days conjures up the memory of delicious tastes and aromas, intertwined with the

crowds of festival-goers who were there to enjoy the food, music, and other events. From the very beginning, I've connected food with happy people and good music.

My first job in the food world, at age ten, was working in a local Portuguese bakery, washing pots and pans. I was totally intrigued by baking and pastries, and it was my good fortune that the old Portuguese bakers took a liking to me and over time they taught me the basics—brownies, lemon tarts, sweet bread. At a certain point, I stopped washing pots and started working alongside them. I even got interested in cake decorating. That was something the bakers didn't do—the bakery would have special people come in to decorate the cakes. I signed up for a cake decorating course at the local community college even though I was younger than the minimum age requirement by quite a few years. I lied about my age on my application, thankfully got in anyway, and got an education on proper icing techniques. I also learned how to handle a pastry bag to create rosettes and all sorts of other embellishments with frosting and whipped cream.

When I got to be high school age, I decided to apply to a vocational high school that had culinary arts, and spent my high school years learning about cooking and working in different restaurants: Chinese, seafood, a pizzeria—no matter what it was, there was something to learn, from stir-frying to stretching pizza dough by hand (forget a rolling pin!). You'll find recipes in this collection whose creation was sparked by those flavor memories and kitchen experiences.

Everything I did, I enjoyed, and one day I woke up and thought, I really love this. That's when I decided to attend the culinary program at Johnson & Wales University instead of going to the New England Conservatory of Music, which had offered me a full scholarship for percussion.

After I graduated from Johnson & Wales, I was hired by Dunfey Hotels as an executive chef for their restaurant Seasons. The general manager of Dunfey, Philip Georges, was an incredible mentor, and I moved with him to various Dunfey properties in Philadelphia; Washington, D.C.; Maine; New York City; Boston (where I first met and cooked for Julia Child; see page 120); and Cape Cod.

While I was working in Cape Cod, I came to the attention of the Brennan family, who were vacationing

"There is so much to learn about cooking—so many different cuisines, cultures, and ingredients. If you can understand a culture, then you understand the food. If you can understand the food, you understand the people."

there. They must have enjoyed their food, because a few months later, I was invited to apply for the position of executive chef at Commander's Palace in New Orleans, most recently vacated by Paul Prudhomme, who had left to open his own restaurant, K-Paul's.

It was a long interview process and an interesting one. Miss Ella and I would have phone dates, and she asked me questions that got me thinking even more deeply about my cooking. She would ask me:

What have you been cooking over the past week?

Were the dishes successful?

How did you come up with those ideas?

Were you thinking about wines to pair when you developed those dishes?

When I went down to Commander's for the final interview, I never left. I knew I had big shoes to fill, and I took that challenge very seriously. I immersed myself in the city of New Orleans, and I spent my days off out in the country, meeting farmers and fishermen, learning about local ingredients, and finding local sources for everything we needed at the restaurant. Everything was cooked fresh—nothing canned, nothing frozen.

To this day, I am grateful to Ella and Dick Brennan for the opportunity they gave me. They made me feel like a member of their family, and they gave me room to grow as a chef. They were amazing mentors, people, and restaurateurs who molded me into what I am today.

From Dick I learned to taste. Dick would say, even if you've made a dish a thousand times, taste it before service and you'll save yourself a lot of heartache, as you'll have time to make adjustments if something's not working right. Dick is all about teaching and loves to use sports lingo that reflects that—he is always talking about teamwork and "preparing for the game."

Miss Ella's genius is customer service—hospitality is everything. I also learned from her the importance of keeping current. She reads like crazy and can tell you anything you want to know about what is going on in the food world.

From both of them, I learned the importance of leaving your ego at the door and listening. If you don't listen to your customers, if you refuse to hear feedback and don't keep an eye open to trends and changes, you won't be a successful restaurateur.

With the support and blessings of the Brennans, I went on to open my first restaurant, Emeril's (celebrating its 25th anniversary this year), followed by many more in New Orleans and across the country.

My life revolves totally around food, cooking, and my restaurants. I thrive on the energy of the people around me, whether it's the customers, my staff, fellow chefs, or the food purveyors I meet through my TV shows and who supply my restaurants.

I believe you have to grow every day, and if you don't, you're cheating yourself. There is so much to learn about cooking—so many different cuisines, cultures, and ingredients. If you can understand a culture, then you understand the food. If you can understand the food, you understand the people. And when you can connect those dots … that's when everything works.

It has been the great good fortune of my life to have benefitted from the experience, wisdom, and support of a long line of teachers and mentors who generously gave of themselves, starting with my mom, Hilda, in our kitchen in Fall River. And I have very mindfully tried to pay that forward. When I first opened Emeril's, during the pre-service meals for staff, I would often bring food producers in to talk about different ingredients. Many of my chefs started out washing pots and pans but when they demonstrate an interest in the food, I give them the opportunity to grow. And when I put together my first TV show, *The Essence of Emeril*, my goal was to teach people to cook, taking away the intimidation factor. I wanted to expose viewers to different types of cuisines and teach them how to shop and feel comfortable cooking. Sometimes I would devote an entire show to a single ingredient, like mushrooms, or a technique, like grilling. But no matter the topic, it was always about making cooking fun.

Emeril Live kicked up the fun factor mega notches, but I never stopped teaching. One of the things I found most gratifying was that the show was really popular viewing for families. And it turned out that

I wasn't just entertaining the moms and dads, I was teaching the kids, too. In my travels, I'm always meeting folks who watched the show as a child and now love to cook because of *Emeril Live*.

So, when I was thinking about giving back to the community, I knew I wanted to focus on kids and food. The Emeril Lagasse Foundation has given more than $5.5 million to children's education, participating in such projects as Café Reconcile, which provides at-risk teens and young adults the skills they need to succeed in jobs in the hospitality industry; Edible Schoolyard New Orleans, modeled on Alice Waters's project in Berkeley, California, which teaches children how to prepare meals using produce harvested from their own garden; and St. Michael's Special School, which provides vocational training so students can learn the life skills they need for independent living.

In thinking about the 100 or so recipes that made me the chef I am today, I have been looking back, thinking about my journey and all the people and experiences that have contributed to my lifelong and still ongoing education as a chef and restaurateur. You'll find some of those memories in this book. By necessity, there are trips and meals and people who have touched me and changed me in significant ways that are not included in these pages—but they are still in my heart and soul.

I am very proud of this book—it's my ultimate collection, curated over a lifetime of cooking. The flavors are going to knock your socks off, from Corn Bisque with Shrimp, Tomato, and Avocado Salad (page 86) to Slow and Low Pork Candy Ribs (page

108), from Creamy Double-Truffle Scrambled Eggs (page 234) to Mile-High Icebox Chocolate–Peanut Butter Pie (page 267). These are recipes you can rely on, and they will make your family and friends very happy. In many recipes, you'll find my Essentials, tips on how to make the dish or change it up, and notes on ingredients. It's my hope that with every recipe you make from *Essential Emeril*, you'll learn from it as well as enjoy it.

Finally, whatever level you're cooking on, keep it real. Use quality ingredients, read your recipe all the way through (maybe even twice) before you start, and be in it. What I mean by that is, be in the process. Cooking isn't just about what ends up on the plate. It's the journey, having a plan, being prepared, noticing the smells, being mindful of what's going on in the pan. And it's not just about what you see, but what you hear: the hiss when a steak hits a hot cast iron skillet or the gentle burble of a stew slowly simmering on the stove. And always tasting, tasting, tasting.

Essential Emeril is a generous slice of the amazing journey I've had up till now in this glorious world of food. My hope is that these recipes, lessons, and stories might accompany you on yours.

Emeril J. Lagasse

Even with a foolproof recipe in hand, cooking can be a challenge if you don't have the right tools and the right ingredients. Whether you cook occasionally or are at the stove most every night, having a well-equipped kitchen will make the experience that much more enjoyable.

my must-haves

cookware

Pots and pans are available in a multitude of materials, including stainless steel, aluminum, carbon steel, copper, and enameled and regular cast iron. Each has different heating properties. My recommendation is to do your own research and, if you can, go to a store to get some firsthand experience with the pans. You want to see for yourself how the pans feel, especially those that will require lots of lifting. Also, there is no need for all your cookware to be made from the same material or come from the same manufacturer. Different materials and brands may suit you for different uses.

A good-quality pan, if properly cared for, can last a lifetime. Below is a list of the pots and pans that get the most use in my home kitchen. Identify the pieces you think you will use most often, and purchase the best quality you can afford. Then you can add to your collection piece by piece.

- **½-QUART SAUCEPAN:** For heating up small amounts of liquid or sauce; the size limits the surface area, reducing the rate of evaporation.
- **2-QUART SAUCEPOT WITH LID:** For making sauces.
- **6- TO 8-QUART STOCKPOT WITH LID:** For making stock or soups and cooking pasta.
- **6-QUART DUTCH OVEN WITH LID:** With its heavy bottom, this is perfect for making stews and braises on the stovetop and in the oven. It can also be used for frying.
- **9-INCH NONSTICK SAUTÉ PAN:** For making eggs of any type or crêpes.
- **10- AND/OR 12-INCH SAUTÉ PANS:** For sautéing vegetables; searing meat, seafood, and poultry; and making pasta sauces. Choose the size that makes sense for your family.
- **10-INCH HIGH-SIDED SAUTÉ PAN:** For cooking greens and braising meat and chicken.
- **14-INCH SAUTÉ PAN:** For pan searing, stir-frying, sautéing large amounts, and preparing pasta sauces.
- **CAST IRON SKILLET:** Get a size that makes sense for your family. Cast iron holds heat well, with no hot spots. It can go from stovetop to oven (you can even use it on your outdoor grill), and it will last for generations. A cast iron skillet is great for griddling, pan-frying, and cooking burgers and steaks.
- **WOK:** I make stir-fries and fried rice for my family most every week, so my wok sees a lot of action. Its shape makes it easy to toss the ingredients without flipping them over the side and onto the stove. However, if you make stir-fries only occasionally, a 14-inch skillet will work fine.

ovenware

In addition to cast iron skillets, Dutch ovens, and other ovenproof cookware (always check to see whether the handle is ovenproof), here is my short list for baking and roasting.

- **8-INCH SQUARE AND 9 X 13-INCH BAKING DISHES:** Ceramic and glass/Pyrex dishes should not go under the broiler, because they can crack under high heat.
- **2 (8- OR 9-INCH) CAKE PANS**
- **9-INCH PIE PAN:** Aluminum or Pyrex works well.
- **MUFFIN TIN:** Use for muffins and cupcakes or line with puff pastry to make hors d'oeuvres.
- **9-INCH SPRINGFORM PAN**
- **ROASTING PAN WITH A FITTED RACK:** Get a size that best suits what you like to roast.
- **2 RIMMED BAKING SHEETS:** Baking sheets (including jelly-roll pans and half sheet pans) have a multitude of uses (baking cookies, toasting nuts, catching drips from pies, and much more), so you might want to have several on hand, in different sizes.

electric appliances

A very short list for me. In addition to the items below, if you're a waffle lover, I'd say a waffle maker is a must-have.

- **BLENDER:** For pureeing sauces or soups. Be super careful when processing hot liquids, as they will expand. Don't overfill the blender, and place a folded kitchen towel over the top. Keep your hand firmly on the lid while you process to prevent the liquid from exploding out.

- **FOOD PROCESSOR AND/OR MINI CHOP:** When chopping 1 cup or less, a mini chop is more convenient and efficient than a full-size food processor.

- **STAND MIXER:** If you bake a lot, consider investing in a stand mixer. This heavy-duty appliance makes mixing up a batter or bread dough a snap. An electric hand mixer will work fine for most batters, but its use with anything but the softest of doughs will likely burn out the motor. If you intend to use your stand mixer, be sure it comes with a dough hook attachment.

- **ELECTRIC FRYER:** If you deep-fry, even occasionally, consider buying an electric fryer—it makes the process incredibly easy.

knives

Knives are so key to success in the kitchen that chefs work with their own personal set of knives and will travel with them to culinary events. The number of specialty knives available is mind-boggling, but you can do most kitchen tasks with just a few. When buying a knife, choose one that feels comfortable in your hand. As with cookware, buy the best quality you can afford.

- **PARING KNIFE:** For peeling, trimming, and chopping fruits and vegetables

- **SERRATED PARING KNIFE:** For slicing tomatoes, sectioning citrus fruits, and cutting sandwiches

- **8- AND/OR 10-INCH CHEF'S KNIFE:** Both sizes are good for chopping, slicing, and mincing—the smaller blade allows for greater control, a plus for those just beginning to hone their knife skills.

- **SERRATED BREAD KNIFE:** Purchase the size that suits you. In addition to bread, sandwiches, and cake, the serrated knife is my preferred knife for slicing tomatoes.

cutting, grating, and peeling implements

- **KNIFE SHARPENER:** One of the most common causes of knife accidents in the kitchen is using one that is not sharp. To compensate for the lack of edge, the cook presses down harder on the knife, and the knife slips, cutting a finger or hand. Invest in a knife steel or other manual sharpener, and sharpen your knives frequently; if you do, they will hold an edge longer. Once a year or so, take your knives to a professional knife sharpener to put a nice clean edge on them.

- **JAPANESE MANDOLINE:** Nothing beats this tool for making paper-thin slices. Inset with a double-sided cutting blade that can be adjusted for thickness, the mandoline allows you to swipe the ingredient (potato, radish, fennel bulb) back and forth over the blade, making slices of uniform thickness. Take care not to let your fingers get too close to the blade.

- **POULTRY SHEARS:** It's so much cheaper to buy a whole chicken and cut it into serving pieces yourself than to buy it already cut apart. With poultry shears, this is just about as easy as cutting through construction paper with scissors. Once you get a pair, you'll wonder why you didn't buy them sooner.

- **VEGETABLE PEELER:** This works for peeling most any kind of vegetable; you can also use it to shave chocolate and Parmigiano-Reggiano into curls.

- **MICROPLANE:** This wonderful tool makes grating citrus zest a snap. You can also use it to grate nutmeg, fresh ginger, garlic, and hard cheeses such as Parmigiano and Pecorino. Microplanes are available with different-size grating holes.

cutting boards

Wood or plastic? Whichever you prefer. Studies have shown there is no real difference in terms of bacteria persisting on the surface of either. I recommend that you get several of them and devote one solely to the cutting of raw meats, poultry, and seafood.

Be sure to wash your cutting boards in hot, sudsy water and rinse them off well after use. Allow them to air dry, or dry them off completely with a clean dishtowel. When a cutting board starts to show significant wear, it's time to replace it. Those cut lines from your knife become places in which bacteria can lodge.

other tools and utensils

Let's finish outfitting your kitchen.

- Set of **NESTED MIXING BOWLS** in graduated sizes
- Set of **DRY MEASURING CUPS,** from 1/4 cup to 1 cup
- 1-, 2-, and 4-cup **LIQUID MEASURING CUPS**
- Set of **MEASURING SPOONS**
- **CITRUS JUICER/REAMER**
- **FINE-MESH STRAINERS,** large and small
- **COLANDER**
- **COOLING RACKS**
- Set of 6-ounce **RAMEKINS**
- **ROLLING PIN**
- Several **WOODEN SPOONS**

- Several **WHISKS**
- **METAL SPATULAS**
- A **FISH SPATULA** really does a better job than a regular one at turning a fish fillet without breaking it into pieces.
- Heat-resistant **RUBBER OR SILICONE SPATULAS**
- **MEAT MALLET** for pounding cutlets
- **LADLES** in different sizes
- **WINE OPENER/BOTTLE OPENER**
- **CAN OPENER**
- **TONGS**
- **ICE CREAM SCOOP**
- 2- and 4-inch **RING CUTTERS**

stocking the pantry

Equipping the kitchen also includes building a pantry (dry storage, as well as the refrigerator and freezer) that will allow you to put dishes together on the fly or follow a recipe without having to buy ten ingredients in one shot.

my dry pantry

Here is my list of essential items. To best preserve their flavor, dried herbs and spices should be stored in a cool, dry, dark place. Even when stored correctly, herbs and spices lose their punch after a couple of months, so buy them in the smallest containers possible unless it's something you use regularly.

- Dried **THYME**
- Dried **OREGANO**
- Crushed **RED PEPPER**
- **CAYENNE PEPPER**
- **BAY LEAVES**
- **PAPRIKA**—sweet and/or hot and smoked paprika (also labeled "pimentón")
- **CHILI POWDER**
- Ground **CUMIN**
- **SAFFRON:** Be sure to buy threads, not preground saffron.
- **EMERIL'S ORIGINAL ESSENCE** or other Creole seasoning
- **CELERY SALT**
- Ground **CINNAMON**
- **NUTMEG:** Buy whole nutmeg and grate it fresh (there are special nutmeg graters that will also hold the nutmeg when it's not being used). There is no comparison between the flavor of freshly grated and preground nutmeg.
- **KOSHER SALT:** This is what I use when seasoning meats before browning and also when adding the final seasoning to taste, as its coarser texture gives you more control.
- **TABLE AND FINE SEA SALT:** In my recipes, when I call for just plain "salt," I mean table salt or fine sea salt.
- **BLACK PEPPERCORNS:** Always grind pepper fresh. Pepper sold already ground or cracked lacks punch.
- **VANILLA EXTRACT**
- **HONEY**
- **SOY SAUCE**

- **HOT SAUCE:** I keep a number of kinds on hand for different dishes, including Crystal Louisiana hot sauce, Sriracha, and *sambal oelek* (chili garlic sauce).
- **WORCESTERSHIRE SAUCE**
- **LOW-SODIUM CHICKEN, BEEF, AND VEGETABLE BROTHS:** I prefer to use homemade stock, but store-bought broths and stocks will work fine in all my recipes.
- **EXTRA-VIRGIN OLIVE OIL** and **CANOLA** or **VEGETABLE OIL**
- A selection of **VINEGARS:** You'll always find red and white wine, balsamic, cider, distilled white, unseasoned rice, and sherry vinegars in my pantry.
- I like to keep some **LIQUOR** store purchases on hand for cooking/baking: red and white wine, dry sherry, port, Marsala, brandy, and Grand Marnier.
- A selection of **DRIED AND/OR CANNED BEANS:** red, black, and white beans, and chickpeas
- A selection of **DRY PASTAS:** a long pasta like linguine, along with smaller shapes such as penne, and Asian noodles, like rice sticks
- **LONG-GRAIN** and **ARBORIO RICE**
- **QUINOA AND/OR COUSCOUS:** Both cook up quick and can be enjoyed in hot and cold dishes.
- Canned **CHOPPED TOMATOES**
- **TOMATO PASTE,** in cans or in a tube
- **PLAIN DRY BREADCRUMBS,** including panko
- **ALL-PURPOSE FLOUR**
- Granulated **WHITE SUGAR**
- **BROWN SUGAR** (dark and light)
- **CORNMEAL**
- **BAKING POWDER**
- **BAKING SODA**
- **CORNSTARCH**
- **NONSTICK COOKING SPRAY**
- **ONIONS**
- **FRESH GARLIC:** Only fresh garlic, never, ever jarred chopped or whole cloves of garlic—it takes just a minute to chop or slice fresh cloves, and the flavor is far superior.

my refrigerator pantry

Open up my fridge and you will always find:

- **MILK**
- **BUTTER**
- **EGGS:** For the recipes in this book, I use large, and I always prefer farm-fresh organic eggs—nothing beats their flavor.
- A hunk of **PARMIGIANO-REGGIANO** cheese
- A block of **CHEDDAR** cheese
- **YEAST** (pay attention to the expiration date on the packet)
- **MAYONNAISE**
- **LEMONS** and **LIMES**
- A selection of **MUSTARDS:** I like Creole, Dijon, and whole-grain.
- Nonpareil **CAPERS**
- Oil-packed **ANCHOVIES;** anchovy paste is another option.
- Toasted **SESAME OIL**
- **BARBECUE SAUCE**
- **HOISIN SAUCE**
- Asian **FISH SAUCE**
- **OLIVES**
- **BACON**

my freezer pantry

In addition to the ingredients listed below, I keep an arsenal of frozen single portions of soups, stews, and chilis that can be defrosted and enjoyed for lunch, as well as sauces, homemade stock, and cooked beans.

- **GREEN PEAS**
- **EDAMAME**
- **SMOKED SAUSAGE** (chorizo, andouille, kielbasa, and others)
- 1-pound packages of **GULF SHRIMP**
- Different cuts of **MEAT, FISH,** and **CHICKEN** portioned out for a single meal, for quick defrosting
- Box of frozen **PUFF PASTRY:** This is great to have on hand to make quick hors d'oeuvres.
- **IQF BERRIES:** These are berries that have been individually quick frozen, with no syrup added. This makes it easy for you to pour out just the amount you need.
- **NUTS:** To keep nuts from going rancid, it's best to store them in the freezer. I always have walnuts and pecans on hand.

APPETIZERS

When I think of food, I think of music and I think of folks having a good time. Sounds like a party! And if you're going to have a party, it is essential to kick it off right by offering a selection of flavor-packed apps (and cocktails to go with—see page 62 for some favorites).

What you will find in these pages are recipes for foolproof finger foods and first courses that will have your guests talking for weeks to come. One of the things I like about appetizers is that they are meant to just take the edge off your hunger before dinner, so you can get crazy, serving them up in little mouthfuls or super-thin slices, like Gruyère Gougères with Two Mousses (page 26) and House-Smoked Salmon Cheesecake with Parmesan-Panko Crust and Chive Crème Fraîche (page 56).

Planning is important so that you can enjoy your own party, and many of these recipes can be completed in part or entirely the day before. Along with each recipe, you'll find tips for what can be done in advance.

gruyère gougères
with two mousses

Why two mousses? They are both so incredibly good, I couldn't choose one over the other. These crispy, cheesy little stuffed bites are super delicious and versatile. You can substitute other cheeses for the Gruyère (though I like its sharpness in this rich dough) or add a tablespoon or two, but no more, of chopped fresh herbs. You can also serve the gougères on their own with no filling as an appetizer or as part of a cheese board. Any leftover mousse can be served on its own, spread on crackers or toast points. For the chicken liver mousse, make sure your livers are fresh. They should have absolutely no odor.

1 cup whole milk

¼ cup (½ stick) unsalted butter

¼ teaspoon salt

⅛ teaspoon freshly ground black pepper

1 cup all-purpose flour

4 large eggs, at room temperature

4 ounces Gruyère cheese, grated (1 cup)

Marsala-Infused Mortadella Mousse and/or Cognac-Spiked Chicken Liver Mousse (page 28)

1. Preheat the oven to 400°F. Line a baking sheet with parchment paper.

2. In a large, heavy-bottomed saucepan, combine the milk, butter, salt, and pepper over medium-high heat. Bring to a boil, then remove from the heat, add the flour all at once, and stir briskly with a wooden spoon for about 1 minute to incorporate. Return to the heat and continue stirring until the batter thickens, comes together in a ball, and pulls away from the side of the pan, about 1 minute.

3. Turn off the heat. Add the eggs, one at a time, beating until each egg is completely incorporated before adding the next one. Stir in the cheese until it is incorporated.

4. Drop the dough by teaspoonfuls (or transfer it to a pastry bag fitted with a plain tip and pipe mounds approximately 1 inch in diameter) onto the prepared baking sheet, leaving about 1 inch of space between each. Bake for 10 minutes, then reduce the oven temperature to 325°F and bake until golden brown, 20 to 25 minutes. Allow to cool on the baking sheet for 5 minutes, then transfer to wire racks to cool completely.

5. Once cooled, cut the tops off the gougères using a sharp serrated knife and, if necessary, use your fingers to pull out any soft dough from the center. Just before serving them, use a piping bag or small spoon to fill the centers of the gougères with the filling of your choice, then place the tops back on, as if setting a little hat on top.

YIELD: ABOUT 54 SMALL GOUGÈRES

(continued)

Because pâte à choux, or cream puff dough, is so stiff, if you have a stand mixer, transfer the dough to it after Step 2, then proceed with Step 3, using the mixer to beat in the eggs one at a time.

•

For advance preparation for a party, you can make the dough the day before and refrigerate it overnight.

marsala-infused mortadella mousse

I'm a big fan of mortadella. It has a texture similar to that of bologna and a mild flavor with just a hint of pistachio. Don't skip the Marsala—it delivers tremendous richness to the mousse.

1 (8-ounce) slice mortadella, cut into cubes

6 tablespoons ricotta cheese

1/2 teaspoon freshly ground black pepper

1/2 cup finely grated Parmigiano-Reggiano cheese

2 tablespoons Marsala

1 1/2 tablespoons unsalted butter, at room temperature

1. Combine the mortadella, ricotta, and pepper in a food processor and process until mostly smooth. Add the Parmigiano and Marsala and process into a very smooth puree. Add the butter and process briefly to fully incorporate. Taste and adjust the seasoning if necessary, although the saltiness of the mortadella usually does not require any additional salt.

2. Chill for 1 hour before using. It will keep in an airtight container in the refrigerator for up to 2 days.

YIELD: ABOUT 2 CUPS, ENOUGH TO FILL
ABOUT 96 GOUGÈRES

cognac-spiked chicken liver mousse

This is going to make much more than you'll need to fill the gougères. You could cut the recipe in half but chicken livers are sold in one-pound containers, so unless you have another use in mind for the remainder, why not make a full batch of the mousse and enjoy the leftovers spread on slices of crusty French bread?

1/4 cup rendered bacon fat

6 tablespoons (3/4 stick) cold unsalted butter

1/2 cup minced shallots

1 teaspoon minced garlic

1 pound fresh chicken livers, trimmed of any tough membranes, rinsed, and patted dry

1 teaspoon fresh thyme leaves

1/4 cup Cognac

2 tablespoons heavy cream

3/4 teaspoon salt

1/4 teaspoon freshly ground black pepper

2/3 cup finely grated Parmigiano-Reggiano cheese

1. Heat a large skillet over medium-high heat. When hot, add the bacon fat and 2 tablespoons of the butter. When the butter is melted and begins to sizzle, add the shallots and garlic and cook, stirring, for 1 minute. Add the chicken livers and thyme and cook, turning the livers as needed, until they are golden around the edges and just pink in the center, about 5 minutes. Add the Cognac and cook until most of it evaporates.

2. With tongs, transfer the livers to a food processor and add any drippings from the pan along with the cream, salt, and pepper; process until smooth. Add the Parmigiano and the remaining 4 tablespoons butter and process until everything is uniformly incorporated and you have a smooth puree. Taste for seasoning.

3. Transfer the mousse to a bowl, cover with plastic wrap, and chill until firm, 1 to 2 hours. This will keep in an airtight container in the refrigerator up to 1 week.

YIELD: ABOUT 3 CUPS, ENOUGH TO FILL
ABOUT 144 GOUGÈRES

making pâte à choux and filling the gougères

Gougères are made from pâte à choux, an egg-based dough that is cooked on the stovetop, then baked up until light and airy. It is the perfect receptacle for all sorts of fillings, in this case your choice of savory mousse to offer as finger food. Omit the cheese and pepper, and you have the pastry used to make cream puffs and éclairs. It's not hard to make, but you do have to focus your attention 100% on the pan when you're adding the eggs and cooking the dough—no distractions or interruptions.

1. Over medium heat, stir the batter until it comes together in a ball, pulling away from the side of the pan, about one minute. Turn off the heat, and add the first egg. Stir until it is completely mixed into the batter.

2. Do not add the next egg until the previous one is completely incorporated.

3. Mix the batter thoroughly to this consistency before adding the cheese.

4. After baking, cool the gougères completely. Cut the tops off, and remove any doughy bits from the centers, if necessary.

5. Using a teaspoon, add a dollop of filling and replace the top of the gougère.

egg salad timbales
with florida caviar

Egg salad as an appetizer? Yes, when it's presented beautifully like this, topped with American caviar and given a drizzle of brilliant green herb oil.

FRESH HERB OIL:

2 bunches fresh chives, snipped into 2-inch lengths (about 2 cups loosely packed)

¼ cup loosely packed fresh flat-leaf parsley leaves

¾ cup canola, grapeseed, or other neutral-flavored vegetable oil

⅛ teaspoon salt

TIMBALES:

8 large eggs, hard-boiled and peeled

¼ cup finely diced celery

¼ cup finely diced red onion

⅓ cup mayonnaise, homemade or store-bought

4 teaspoons Dijon mustard

Salt and freshly ground black pepper

6 teaspoons (1½ ounces) Florida sturgeon caviar or other American fish roe, or more to taste

Toasted bread points or crackers, for serving

1. Fill a small bowl with ice water.

2. Bring a small pot of water to a boil and add the chives and parsley all at once. Stir to make sure that the leaves are completely submerged and cook for 10 seconds. Using a slotted spoon or a small strainer, immediately transfer the herbs to the ice water until cooled. Drain and transfer to paper towels. Squeeze the towels gently to absorb as much of the water as possible, then transfer the herbs to a blender. Add the oil and salt and blend on high speed until completely smooth. Transfer the herb oil to an airtight container and refrigerate until ready to use, or up to 1 week.

3. Finely chop the eggs and add them to a medium bowl along with the celery, onion, mayonnaise, and mustard. Season to taste with salt and pepper (take care not to oversalt the salad, since the caviar will be salty). Fill a demitasse cup with hot water and set aside.

4. To assemble, empty the demitasse cup and then fill it with egg salad, pressing with the back of a small spoon to compact the salad. Invert the cup onto a small serving plate and tap lightly until the salad releases onto the plate. Repeat with the remaining salad (you will need to rinse the cup with hot water between each plating). Top each serving with 1 teaspoon of the caviar (or more to taste) and then drizzle 1 tablespoon of the herb oil around each salad. Serve immediately with toast points.

YIELD: 6 FIRST-COURSE SERVINGS

the perfect boiled egg

For a hard-boiled egg that is just cooked through to the center, follow these instructions exactly: Place the eggs (directly from the refrigerator) in a saucepan and add enough cool water to cover them by 1 inch. Bring to a boil over high heat, then reduce the heat to medium and cook the eggs at a steady boil for exactly 10 minutes. Immediately drain the eggs, then plunge them into a bowl of ice water. When the eggs are cool enough to handle, tap and roll them on the kitchen counter, then peel under cool running water (beginning at the wider bottom end).

Blanching the fresh herbs before pureeing them with the oil sets their bright green color.

•

It's best not to use super-fresh eggs when you're hard-boiling them, as they are more difficult to peel.

•

Filling the demitasse cup with hot water before packing in the egg salad will help it slide out when you invert the cup over the plate.

potatoes alexa

I served these to Billy Joel when he was at Emeril's New Orleans with his daughter Alexa. I had heard his song "Downeaster Alexa," and when they both gave the dish the thumbs up, I told them that I was going to name it Potatoes Alexa. I've never put it on the menu; instead I'll send it out as an amuse-bouche or as part of a tasting menu for special guests of the restaurant. The combination of the Portobello-Truffle Emulsion and the new potatoes is unbelievable. There won't be any of these left over, trust me—the truffle emulsion would be good on shoe leather. You can serve the potatoes as a plated first course or pass them as hors d'oeuvres; top each one with a dollop of the emulsion and garnish with a sprinkling of chives.

Portobello-Truffle Emulsion (page 34)

12 medium new potatoes, about 2 inches around

Kosher salt

2 teaspoons unsalted butter

3 tablespoons half-and-half

2 tablespoons white truffle oil (see Truffle Products, page 190)

¼ cup plus 2 tablespoons grated Parmigiano-Reggiano cheese

Freshly ground black pepper

2 tablespoons chopped fresh chives, for serving

1. Prepare the Portobello-Truffle Emulsion and reserve at room temperature until ready to serve the potatoes.

2. Place the potatoes in a saucepan with enough water to cover by 1 inch and bring to a boil. Generously salt the water and adjust the heat so the potatoes cook at a steady, gentle boil until they are firm-tender when pierced with the tip of a knife, about 15 minutes. Drain and set aside until cool enough to handle.

3. Preheat the oven to 400°F and line a large baking sheet with parchment paper. Lightly grease the parchment.

4. Cut the potatoes in half. Using a spoon or melon baller, hollow out the cut side of the potatoes, leaving a ¼-inch-thick shell (see page 34). Place the potato flesh in a small bowl and mash until mostly smooth.

5. In a small saucepan over medium heat, melt the butter with the half-and-half. Pour the warm mixture over the mashed potatoes and stir or mash to blend. Stir in the truffle oil and ¼ cup of the cheese and season to taste with salt and pepper.

6. Season the insides of the potato shells lightly with salt and pepper, then spoon ¼ teaspoon of the Portobello-Truffle Emulsion into the bottom of each one. Divide the potato mixture evenly among the shells, setting the filled potatoes on the prepared baking sheet, then sprinkle the tops with the remaining 2 tablespoons cheese. Bake until the potatoes are lightly golden on top and heated through, about 20 minutes.

7. Spoon about 2 tablespoons of the Portobello-Truffle Emulsion onto each serving plate and use the back of a spoon to spread it into a thin, smooth layer. Place three potato halves on each plate and garnish with the chives. Serve immediately.

YIELD: 8 FIRST-COURSE SERVINGS OR
24 INDIVIDUAL HORS D'OEUVRES

(continued)

Always wait until water comes to a boil before adding salt to it; otherwise the salt can pit the bottom of the pot.

If you're concerned about the possibility of salmonella, use a pasteurized egg to make the emulsion. See page 49 for a photo tutorial on making an emulsion.

portobello-truffle emulsion

I came up with this in the early days at Emeril's Restaurant and I've used it in many different dishes over the years. It is delicious on baked potatoes, with seared scallops, and is an integral part of Potatoes Alexa (see page 32). It's easy to make and will keep in an airtight container in the refrigerator for up to one week.

1 portobello mushroom (about 4 ounces), stem removed

2 tablespoons olive oil

Salt and freshly ground black pepper

1 large egg

½ teaspoon fresh lemon juice

1 teaspoon minced shallot

½ teaspoon minced garlic

¾ cup vegetable oil

¼ cup plus 2 tablespoons white truffle oil (see Truffle Products, page 190)

1. Preheat the oven to 400°F.

2. Rub the mushroom with the olive oil, then season it lightly with salt and pepper. Place the mushroom gill side down on a small baking sheet and roast until it softens and the top is slightly wrinkled, about 15 minutes. Remove from the oven and let cool slightly. Chop the mushroom into small dice.

3. Put the egg and lemon juice in a blender and process until frothy. Add the shallot and garlic and process briefly, then add the mushroom and puree until very smooth. With the blender running, add the vegetable and truffle oils in a very slow, steady stream through the lid until a thick emulsion is formed. Season to taste with salt and pepper. If using within an hour, keep at room temperature; otherwise, refrigerate.

YIELD: 1¾ CUPS

hollowing out the potato shells

For this preparation, it is important that you don't overcook the potatoes; otherwise they will come apart as you try to hollow them. They should be cooked until just firm-tender, then allowed to cool until you can hold them comfortably. Cut the potatoes in half.

1. Use a paring knife to score the cut side of the cooked potato to loosen it. Take care not to pierce the skin.

2. Hold the potato firmly but without squeezing it and, with a spoon or melon baller, gently and carefully scoop out the potato flesh.

3. You should leave a shell that is ¼ inch thick.

1   2   3

charlie trotter

I met Charlie when I took one of my apprentices, Bernard Carmouche, up to Charlie Trotter's in Chicago as a graduation present. Charlie and I quickly became very good friends. He would come to visit me down in New Orleans, and I would go to see him in Chicago. We shared a passion for wine, and we travelled together often, chasing the world's great restaurants and wineries in this country, France, and Italy.

One of my favorite memories is a food and wine trip Charlie and I took to France, where we ate our way through a long list of Michelin three star–rated restaurants. Halfway through the trip, we decided that when we got back to Chicago the following week, we would cook a distillation dinner for some of Charlie's top customers and his staff. It was phenomenal. We alternated courses, each of us coming up with dishes based on our taste memories of each of the restaurants we had visited.

Charlie was a culinary dreamer, not only dreaming about food but always dreaming about how he could make his restaurant better. His attention to detail was amazing—his food, his wine, the china on the table, the cleanliness of his kitchen—he strove for perfection and the highest quality.

Charlie was also a great leader and teacher.

He was all about hospitality and he was always, always trying to do more than what his customer expected. He forged an unbelievable connection with his customers and with the city of Chicago. The foodie world came to Charlie.

Charlie's death at age 54 was a tremendous shock. At such an early age, for him to leave this world and to leave the culinary legacy he had built was a huge loss, and a personal one to me. His restaurant was a really special place for a lot of people. It was one of my temples and every time I went to Charlie Trotter's, which was often, I always learned something. Charlie would never stop. Without a doubt, Chicago is the internationally renowned food town it is today because of Charlie Trotter.

a vegetable terrine for charlie

My dear friend Charlie Trotter and I did a lot of charity dinners together and he always made terrines for these events because they are easy to transport and quick to plate. Charlie made guinea hen terrines, pigeon terrines, crawfish terrines, lobster terrines—he was the terrine king. So it only made sense in developing a tribute recipe for Charlie that it be a terrine, incorporating flavors that remind me of him. Charlie loved goat cheese, he loved vegetables of all kinds, he loved the combination of tomato and basil.

This is a fairly easy terrine to make at home and it yields spectacular results in flavor and presentation.

TERRINE:

Wild Mushroom Duxelles (page 39)

3 leeks (white and light green parts only)

2 tablespoons unsalted butter

Salt and freshly ground black pepper

2 large zucchini

3 large summer squash

4 tablespoons extra-virgin olive oil

11 ounces fresh goat cheese, at room temperature

4 ounces cream cheese, at room temperature

Aspic of Herb Vinaigrette (page 39)

TOMATO-BASIL SALAD:

3 cups cherry tomatoes, halved

3 tablespoons extra-virgin olive oil

3 tablespoons Champagne vinegar

3 tablespoons fresh basil chiffonade (see Essentials, at right)

1 teaspoon salt

1/2 teaspoon freshly ground black pepper

1. Prepare the Wild Mushroom Duxelles and set aside until ready to use.

2. Cut away the root portion of the leeks. With a sharp paring knife, cut halfway through each leek lengthwise; you don't want to cut all the way through any of the layers. Place the leeks in a bowl of cold water and agitate them to remove any sand and dirt. Bring a large pot of salted water to a boil and set a large bowl of ice water on the counter. Cook the leeks in the boiling water until the leaves are tender, 5 to 6 minutes. Transfer the leeks to the ice water to cool. When cool enough to handle, remove the large outer layers, separating them from the center portion. Lay the outer layers on a baking sheet or a plate. Coarsely chop the center portion of the leeks. In a small saucepan over medium heat, melt the butter. When it sizzles, add the chopped leeks, 1/2 teaspoon salt, and 1/4 teaspoon pepper. Cook the leeks, stirring as needed, until softened, 3 to 4 minutes. Set aside until ready to use.

3. Preheat the oven to 350°F. Line two baking sheets with parchment paper.

4. Slice the zucchini and summer squash lengthwise about 1/4 inch thick using a mandoline, if you have one. Arrange the slices on the prepared baking sheets in a single layer and drizzle 2 tablespoons of the oil over them. Season with 1 1/2 teaspoons salt and 1/2 teaspoon pepper. Bake until the squash is just tender, about 20 minutes. Remove from the oven and let the squash cool.

5. In a medium bowl, combine the cheeses and the remaining 2 tablespoons of the oil, 1/4 teaspoon salt, and 1/4 teaspoon pepper. With an electric mixer on low speed, beat until the mixture is creamy and completely combined.

(continued)

The key to success here is not rushing the process, allowing enough time for the terrine to set up in the refrigerator. Use a very sharp knife to cut the terrine into slices.

•

To make chiffonade, pile several leaves on top of one another, roll them into a long cylinder, then cut across into thin ribbons.

6. Prepare a terrine mold approximately 3 inches wide by 11 inches long and 3 inches deep by lining it with plastic wrap, leaving an overhang on all sides of about 3 inches. Measure a piece of cardboard the same size as the top of the terrine and cut it to fit so that it will lay flat on top. Wrap the cardboard in aluminum foil and then again with plastic wrap.

7. Arrange the leek strips in the mold horizontally, so the strips cover the bottom of the terrine and go up both sides, then place other strips so that the long sides of the terrine are covered. Trim the leeks even with the top of the terrine.

8. Layer half of the summer squash in a single layer vertically over the leeks. Spoon half of the whipped cheese over the squash and use a rubber spatula to spread it into an even layer. Place one-third of the zucchini over the cheese. Spoon half of the chopped leeks over the zucchini, then half of the Wild Mushroom Duxelles, then the remaining chopped leeks. Top the leeks with a second layer of zucchini. Spread the remaining whipped cheese over the zucchini and top that with the remaining summer squash. Spoon the remaining duxelles over the squash and top with a final layer of zucchini.

9. Fold the plastic wrap over the zucchini and place the cardboard on top. Place a weight, either heavy cans or a brick, on top of the terrine to weight it down, then refrigerate the

terrine. Remove the weight from the top of the terrine after 2 to 3 hours. Refrigerate the terrine overnight and up to 2 days.

10. Early on the day you plan to serve the terrine, prepare the aspic. Remove the cardboard top and the flaps of plastic wrap from the top of the terrine. While the aspic is still slightly warm and easy to pour, pour it in an even layer over the top of the squash. Return the terrine to the refrigerator for at least 2 hours and up to 8 hours.

11. In a medium bowl, combine the ingredients for the Tomato-Basil Salad and mix well. Set aside at room temperature until ready to use and up to 1 hour.

12. Remove the terrine from the refrigerator. Use the plastic wrap flaps to gently lift the terrine out of the mold. Carefully place the terrine on a cutting board and gently unwrap it from the plastic wrap so that the aspic is on the bottom. Using a sharp knife, cut the terrine into 8 slices. Place each slice on a small serving plate and divide the tomato salad among the plates. Serve immediately.

YIELD: 8 FIRST-COURSE SERVINGS

lining the terrine with leeks

The leeks function as a bright green edible vessel for your terrine. First, boil the trimmed leeks until tender, then shock them in cold water; this will set the color. The larger outer leaves are the ones you will use to line the terrine.

1. The leeks need to completely line the inside of the terrine, with no gaps. First line the bottom and short sides of the terrine. Make sure that the leaves overlap.

2. Finish by arranging the leeks so they cover the long sides of the terrine. Once this is completed, trim the leeks even with the top edges of the terrine.

wild mushroom duxelles

The French word "duxelles" refers to what this is, minced or chopped mushrooms sautéed until they have a pastelike consistency. The mixture is often used as a stuffing or pastry filling; here it is used for two of the layers of the terrine.

3 tablespoons olive oil

1 pound mixed wild mushrooms, such as chanterelles, porcini, shiitakes, and/or morels, cleaned, stemmed, and chopped

1/4 cup minced shallots

1 tablespoon minced garlic

2/3 cup Marsala

1/2 teaspoon kosher salt

1/4 teaspoon freshly ground black pepper

1. In a large sauté pan, heat the oil over medium-high heat. When hot, add the mushrooms and cook, stirring occasionally, until they are golden brown, 4 to 5 minutes. Add the shallots and garlic and cook, stirring, until the shallots have softened, another 2 minutes. Add the Marsala, salt, and pepper and cook until all of the liquid has evaporated, about 3 minutes.

2. Remove the pan from the heat and let cool completely. The duxelles can be made up to 2 days in advance; let them cool completely, then store in an airtight container in the refrigerator until ready to use.

YIELD: 1 1/2 CUPS

aspic of herb vinaigrette

Aspic is a jelly, in this case made from gelatin, but it can be prepared using stock. The word also refers to any dish in which ingredients are mixed with gelatin, poured into a mold, then allowed to set or congeal in the refrigerator. The dish is then unmolded and served.

Salt

3/4 cup packed mixed fresh soft herb leaves (1 1/2 ounces), such as tarragon, chervil, chives, and parsley, or basil, cilantro, and mint

1/2 cup extra-virgin olive oil

1/8 teaspoon freshly ground black pepper

1 tablespoon unflavored powdered gelatin (about 1 1/2 packets)

1/4 cup Champagne vinegar

1. Bring a medium pot of water to a boil and add a pinch of salt. Place a large bowl of ice water on the counter.

2. Add the herbs to the pot of water and blanch just until their color changes to a dark green, 10 to 15 seconds. Transfer to the ice bath. Once the herbs are cool, add them to a blender (no need to pat them dry) along with the oil, 1/4 teaspoon salt, and the pepper, and puree until smooth.

3. In a small bowl or measuring cup, sprinkle the gelatin over the vinegar and let the gelatin bloom for 2 to 3 minutes. Heat the gelatin and vinegar in the microwave just until the gelatin begins to dissolve, about 10 seconds, and stir well. Add the herb puree to the vinegar and stir until homogenized. The aspic will begin to set up, so be prepared to use it right away.

YIELD: 1 CUP

mortadella and chile pizza

Mortadella is a mild ground-pork sausage (similar in texture to bologna) that is flavored with a hint of pistachio. When it's used as a topping for pizza, it crisps up just a bit and is an unexpectedly delicious flavor partner for the sharp and creamy Taleggio and hot chiles. And when it comes to shaping the pizza dough, put the rolling pin away—I'll show you how to do it by hand.

Unbleached all-purpose flour, for dusting

4 (8-ounce) rounds Pizza Dough (recipe follows)

Cornmeal, for sprinkling

8 tablespoons extra-virgin olive oil, or as needed

8 ounces thinly sliced mortadella (about 16 slices)

8 ounces Taleggio cheese, grated (2 cups)

3 red serrano or other chile peppers, thinly sliced (about 1/4 cup)

3/4 cup finely grated Parmigiano-Reggiano cheese, plus more for serving, if desired

1. Position the rack in the bottom third of the oven and line with bricks, pizza tiles, or a baking stone. Preheat the oven to 500°F for at least 1 hour before baking the pizzas.

2. Lightly flour a work surface and stretch a round of dough out to a 9-inch circle by gently tapping and turning it, leaving a lip on the edge. Once the center is large enough to fit the palm of your hand, continue to shape the dough by pressing, turning, and pulling it gently with your palm (see opposite).

3. Lightly sprinkle a pizza paddle or rimless cookie sheet with cornmeal and transfer one of the dough rounds to the paddle. Brush the dough with 2 tablespoons of the oil and arrange 4 slices of the mortadella on the pizza. Top with one-fourth of the Taleggio (make sure to sprinkle it in an even layer— don't pile it in the center), one-fourth of the chiles, and about 2 tablespoons of the Parmigiano.

4. Slide the dough onto the hot bricks, tiles, or stone and bake until the crust is golden and the cheese is bubbly, about 10 minutes. Remove from the oven, cut into slices, garnish with additional Parmigiano, if desired, and serve immediately. Repeat with the remaining ingredients.

YIELD: 4 (9-INCH) PIZZAS, 8 TO 10 APPETIZER SERVINGS

pizza dough

1 3/4 cups warm water (110° to 115°F)

1 (1/4-ounce) envelope active dry yeast

1 tablespoon honey

2 tablespoons plus 1 teaspoon extra-virgin olive oil

4 cups unbleached all-purpose flour, plus more for dusting

1 1/2 teaspoons salt

In a large bowl, combine the water, yeast, honey, and 2 tablespoons of the oil and let stand until it begins to bubble, about 5 minutes. (If it doesn't bubble or foam after 10 minutes, it means the yeast is no longer active and you'll need to start again with a fresh packet.)

2. Combine 3 cups of the flour with the salt, then add it to the yeast mixture, stirring with a wooden spoon, until it is all incorporated. Continue adding the remaining 1 cup flour, ¼ cup at a time, working the dough after each addition, kneading it with your hands, until it has all been incorporated. The dough will be slightly sticky. Transfer the dough to a lightly floured work surface and knead several more times, until the dough comes together and is smooth.

3. Add the remaining 1 teaspoon oil to a clean large bowl. Place the dough in the bowl and turn to coat with the oil on all sides. Cover the bowl with plastic wrap or a kitchen towel and set in a warm, draft-free place until the dough nearly doubles in size, about 2 hours.

4. Remove the dough from the bowl and knead it briefly on a lightly floured surface. Divide the dough into four pieces, shape each into a ball, cover with plastic wrap or a kitchen towel, and allow them to rest 15 minutes. Use as directed.

YIELD: 4 (8-OUNCE) ROUNDS

flour matters

Be sure to use unbleached all-purpose flour for the dough; it has a higher protein content than bleached, which will result in a better crumb for the crust.

The dough can be made a day ahead. After its first rise, cover and refrigerate it. The next day, take it out of the refrigerator and leave at room temperature for 1 to 2 hours, then shape and use as desired. You can also freeze it. After the first rise, portion it into 4 balls, then wrap them individually and freeze; they will keep for up to one month.

shaping pizza dough

Make sure to let the dough rest before shaping it, and if you're using dough you've refrigerated, let it come to room temperature. This allows the strands of gluten to relax. Otherwise, you will be fighting the dough as you try to stretch it.

1. With the fingers of both hands, tap the center of the ball of dough, turning the dough as you do so; this will stretch the dough outward. You want to leave the outermost edge slightly thicker than the rest of the crust, forming a raised lip all around the pizza.

2. When you have stretched the dough so that it is large enough that you can fit your palm on it, continue to shape the dough by pressing down on it as you push it out with your palm and turning it so you have an evenly shaped circle.

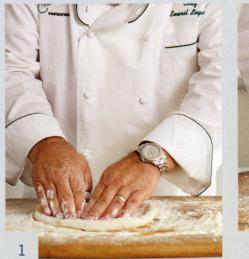

1

2

vietnamese pork and shrimp
spring rolls

These rolls are sublimely delicious, each bite a simultaneous experience of sweet, salt, savory, spice, and crunch.

1 (1-pound) pork tenderloin, trimmed of fat and silverskin

1 shallot, minced

2 cloves garlic, minced

2 tablespoons Vietnamese fish sauce (*nuoc cham*)

1 tablespoon sugar

1/2 teaspoon freshly ground black pepper

2 teaspoons toasted sesame oil

8 cups water

1 lemon, halved

1 tablespoon fine sea salt

1 teaspoon cayenne pepper

1 teaspoon concentrated crab boil

1 pound large shrimp

1 (3.75-ounce) package fine rice vermicelli (*bun*)

12 spring roll wrappers

1 medium cucumber, peeled, seeded, and cut into matchsticks

2 cups very thinly sliced romaine lettuce, plus 4 whole leaves

24 leaves fresh Vietnamese or regular mint

24 leaves fresh cilantro

24 leaves fresh Thai or regular basil

1 medium carrot, peeled and cut into matchsticks

2 tablespoons hoisin sauce

Vietnamese Peanut Sauce (*Nuoc Leo*), for serving (page 44)

1. Place the pork tenderloin in a bowl with the shallot, garlic, fish sauce, sugar, black pepper, and sesame oil and turn to coat. Cover with plastic wrap and marinate, turning occasionally, at least 1 hour and up to overnight in the refrigerator.

2. Preheat a grill to high. Grill the tenderloin, turning occasionally, until just cooked through (slightly pink) and an instant-read thermometer inserted in the thickest part registers 145°F, 8 to 10 minutes. Transfer to a plate and cool; then cut the pork into 1/8-inch-thick slices; set aside, covered and refrigerated, until you are ready to assemble spring rolls.

3. Pour the water into a medium saucepan, squeeze the lemon halves into the water, and add the rinds along with the salt, cayenne, and crab boil. Bring to a boil. Add the shrimp to the water and cook for 2 minutes, stirring occasionally. Drain the shrimp and run under cold water until cool. Peel the shrimp and slice in half horizontally.

4. Cook the rice vermicelli according to the package directions and drain in a colander. Run under cold water until cool and set aside to drain.

5. To assemble the rolls, have the ingredients at arm's reach. Fill a large shallow bowl with lukewarm water. Take a spring roll wrapper and submerge it in the water to soften. Transfer it to a clean work surface. Lay 4 shrimp halves horizontally across the center of the wrapper; top with a few tablespoons of vermicelli. Top with a handful of cucumber, 2 tablespoons of shredded romaine, 4 mint leaves, 2 cilantro leaves, and 4 basil leaves. Add carrot sticks and top with 2 slices of pork. Drizzle 1/2 teaspoon of hoisin on the wrapper above the filling. To fold the rolls, follow Steps 3 and 4 on page 44 for "Making Spring Rolls." Cut the rolls in half on an angle and set them, cut side up, on the lettuce. Serve at room temperature or slightly chilled, with the sauce on the side.

YIELD: 12 SPRING ROLLS, 6 APPETIZER SERVINGS

(continued)

essentials

You want to enjoy these rolls not long after you make them, as the rice paper dries out quickly.

•

Lining the plate with lettuce will keep the spring rolls from sticking.

vietnamese peanut sauce (nuoc leo)

The rich, salty-sweet taste of this dipping sauce plays beautifully against the bright, fresh flavors of the rolls.

1 tablespoon peanut oil

3 cloves garlic, minced

1 tablespoon minced shallot

1 teaspoon *sambal oelek* (chili garlic sauce)

1 teaspoon tomato paste

1/3 cup chicken broth or water

1/4 cup hoisin sauce

2 tablespoons creamy peanut butter

1/2 teaspoon sugar

1/4 cup finely chopped roasted peanuts, for garnish

1 fresh red Thai chile pepper (optional), seeded and thinly sliced, for serving

Sriracha sauce, for serving (optional)

1. Heat the oil in a small saucepan. Add the garlic, shallot, *sambal oelek*, and tomato paste and cook, stirring, until the garlic and shallot are golden brown, about 30 seconds. Add the broth, hoisin, peanut butter, and sugar and whisk to combine. Bring to a boil, reduce the heat to low, and simmer until the sauce has thickened, about 3 minutes. Remove from the heat and let cool slightly before serving. It will keep in an airtight container in the refrigerator for several days.

2. Garnish the sauce with the peanuts and, if you like, the chile pepper and a drizzle of Sriracha sauce.

YIELD: 1 1/4 CUPS

making spring rolls

No matter what you use in the filling, the method for folding the rolls is the same. Before you start, have all your ingredients prepped and arranged in your work area.

1. The rice paper wrapper needs to be softened before you can use it. Working with one wrapper at a time, place it on the surface of a large shallow bowl of warm water and push down on it with the palm of your hand until it is completely submerged. It will take only a few seconds for the wrapper to soften. Remove it from the water; it will be translucent. Let the excess water drip off for a few seconds. Take care when doing this so the wrapper doesn't rip or fold up onto itself—because of all the starch the wrapper contains, it's very sticky.

2. Place the wrapper on a clean work surface and layer on the filling ingredients across the bottom third of the wrapper, leaving about an inch free along the bottom and side edges.

3. With a small spoon, drizzle a line of hoisin sauce above the filling. Start to fold the spring roll by taking the bottom of the wrapper and gently folding it over the bottom of the filling.

4. Roll the wrapper until the filling is covered, then fold the two sides in toward the center, over the filling. Continue to roll the wrapper all the way up.

praline-cayenne bacon

Wonderfully gooey and indulgent, this classic combination of sweet and salt makes it the perfect partner for cocktails, like the Aperol Spritz (page 64). You can also cut it into pieces and use it as a garnish for salads.

Nonstick cooking spray

$^1/_2$ cup (1 stick) lightly salted butter, cubed

1 cup firmly packed light brown sugar

$^3/_4$ teaspoon cayenne pepper

1 pound thick-cut bacon

1. Preheat the oven to 400°F. Line a large rimmed baking sheet with aluminum foil and place a wire rack on top of the baking sheet. Spray the rack thoroughly with nonstick spray.

2. In a small bowl, combine the butter, brown sugar, and cayenne, using a fork to mash it all together until thoroughly blended and smooth.

3. Arrange the bacon slices on top of the wire rack in a single layer so the slices don't overlap. Divide the butter-sugar mixture evenly among the slices of bacon (about 2 tablespoons per slice). With slightly damp hands, spread the mixture evenly over the slices, trying to cover as much of the bacon as possible with an even coating. Bake on the center rack of the oven until the bacon is crisp around the edges and the sugar mixture is caramelized and bubbly, 35 to 40 minutes.

4. Remove the pan from the oven and let the bacon cool slightly, then transfer the strips to a serving plate. Set aside until completely cool, about 20 minutes. (The bacon will continue to harden as it cools.) To serve, cut it into smaller lengths, if desired, and place on a serving plate in a single layer for guests to help themselves. This is best enjoyed the day it is made.

YIELD: 4 TO 6 APPETIZER SERVINGS

crab and corn fritters
with fresh corn mayo

Growing up, there was a park on the water outside of Providence, Rhode Island, called Rocky Point, and they used to serve the best clam fritters. When I ate beignets for the first time in New Orleans, I immediately thought of my childhood clam cakes and wondered how I could give beignets a savory turn. This recipe provides a foundation batter that you can vary as you choose; I've given you two variations in the box on page 48 to get you started. I particularly like making these with eggplant because it almost melts right into the batter.

1 tablespoon unsalted butter

Corn kernels cut from 3 ears (see Essentials, at left)

2 cups all-purpose flour

1 tablespoon baking powder

2½ teaspoons sugar

1½ teaspoons salt

¼ teaspoon cayenne pepper

1 cup whole milk

3 large eggs

1 tablespoon hot sauce

1 teaspoon Worcestershire sauce

1 pound fresh jumbo lump crabmeat, picked over for shells and cartilage (see Essentials, at left)

Vegetable oil, for frying

Coarse sea salt or kosher salt, for serving (optional)

Fresh Corn Mayo, for serving (page 48)

1. Melt the butter in a small saucepan over medium heat. Add the corn and cook, stirring as needed, for about 2 minutes. Remove from the heat.

2. In a medium bowl, sift the flour, baking powder, sugar, salt, and cayenne together.

3. In a small bowl, whisk the milk, eggs, hot sauce, and Worcestershire together to combine. Make a well in the dry ingredients and pour the wet into it. Combine gently with a whisk, then, with a rubber spatula, gently fold in the corn and crabmeat, taking care to not break up the lumps of crab.

4. Add enough oil to come halfway up the side of a deep-sided cast iron skillet or Dutch oven or to the fill line of an electric fryer and preheat to 325°F.

5. Working in batches of 6 to 8 and using a 2-tablespoon scoop (like a melon baller or ice cream scoop), carefully drop the fritter batter into the oil. You don't want the fritters browning too fast, so don't allow the temperature of the oil to go higher than 325°F or to drop below 300°F; adjust the heat under the pot as needed. Cover the pot with a splatter screen or the vented top if using an electric fryer to protect yourself, as individual corn kernels will pop and fly if they make contact with the hot oil. As the fritters float to the top, roll them over in the hot oil to brown them evenly. When they are golden on all sides, which will take 5 to 6 minutes per batch, use tongs, a slotted spoon, or a spider to transfer them to paper towels to drain. Season with salt immediately, if desired, so the salt sticks to the fritters. Repeat until you use up all the batter.

6. Serve hot with the Fresh Corn Mayo.

YIELD: ABOUT 3 DOZEN

(continued)

I use jumbo lump crabmeat so there will be big meaty chunks of crab throughout the fritters but regular lump crabmeat works fine.

•

To cook the corn, sauté it with a little butter and salt and pepper for a few minutes, or fire-roast ears of corn on the grill, then cut off the kernels.

fresh corn mayo

Can you make this with store-bought mayonnaise? Yes, but the flavor won't begin to approach that of from-scratch mayonnaise. It's worth learning how to make mayonnaise, even if you only serve it occasionally. Buy the freshest eggs possible and if you're worried about salmonella, use pasteurized eggs.

1 large egg yolk

1 1/2 teaspoons fresh lemon juice

1 1/2 teaspoons Worcestershire sauce

1 1/2 teaspoons hot sauce

1/2 teaspoon minced garlic

1 cup vegetable oil

1/2 teaspoon salt

1/4 teaspoon cayenne pepper

2 tablespoons chopped fresh flat-leaf parsley

1 1/2 cups fresh corn kernels, cooked (see Essentials, page 46)

1. In a small bowl, combine the egg yolk, lemon juice, Worcestershire, hot sauce, and garlic and whisk vigorously to mix. Drizzling it in very, very slowly, add the oil while you whisk vigorously. Continue to add the oil in a very thin, steady stream, whisking continuously, until the mixture thickens and coalesces into an emulsion. If you have an emulsion but still have oil left, continue to add and whisk; the emulsion will get thicker and stiffer as you do.

2. Once you've got an emulsion and all of the oil has been added, stir in the remaining ingredients. Refrigerate in an airtight container until needed and up to 3 days. Serve alongside the Crab and Corn Fritters (page 46).

YIELD: 2 CUPS

fritters your way

Use this batter to make different kinds of savory fritters. Follow Steps 1–3 on page 46, but instead of adding corn and crabmeat, add 1 pound shrimp, peeled, deveined, and cut into small pieces, and 1/2 pound zucchini, cut into small dice, sprinkled with Emeril's Creole Seasoning (page 108) or other Creole seasoning. OR add 1 large globe eggplant, cut into small dice, sprinkled with salt and Creole seasoning, and sautéed in olive oil or oven-roasted until tender with 1/2-inch pieces roasted red peppers to taste, and, if you like, minced fresh basil.

making an emulsion

What is an emulsion? Remember your mom saying, oil and water don't mix? Well, in an emulsion (which also includes things like hollandaise sauce and beurre blanc), oil and water are made to mix, with the help of another ingredient known as an emulsifier—in the case of mayonnaise, it's an egg yolk.

1. Measure with precision: If you add too much liquid for the amount of oil being used, no matter how long you whisk, you will never achieve an emulsion.

2. Add the oil as slowly as possible, almost drop by drop in a steady stream if you can manage it, especially at the beginning. If you're new to making mayonnaise or any emulsion, if you can get a friend or family member to add the oil while you whisk, that would be ideal—probably the hardest part of this process is adding the oil while you whisk at the same time.

3. Whisk vigorously and continuously. Remember, it is not natural for oil and water to mix—you need to make them go together by whisking the tar out of them.

4. You have an emulsion when, almost like magic, your mixture becomes thick and smooth.

1

2

3

4

my easy barbecue shrimp

"Barbecue shrimp" originated at Pascal's Manale Restaurant & Bar in New Orleans in the 1950s and became hugely popular. When I was getting ready to open Emeril's, I developed my own white tablecloth version, with a kicked-up flavor base that simmered for hours. It's still a signature dish at Emeril's. Here I simplify my interpretation for the home cook, served with jalapeño biscuits.

24 large head-on shrimp (about 2 pounds), peeled and deveined, tails left on, shells and heads reserved

1 tablespoon cracked black peppercorns

2 teaspoons Emeril's Creole Seasoning (page 108) or other Creole seasoning

1 1/2 teaspoons chopped fresh rosemary

3 tablespoons olive oil

1 cup dry white wine

3 cups water

3/4 cup Worcestershire sauce, preferably homemade (page 153)

Juice from 2 lemons (about 1/4 cup)

1/2 cup chopped onion

1 tablespoon minced garlic

1 tablespoon hot sauce

1/4 cup (1/2 stick) unsalted butter, cut into 8 pieces

Jalapeño Biscuits (recipe follows), for serving

1. In a medium bowl, toss the shrimp with half of the cracked pepper, 1 teaspoon of the Creole seasoning, and the rosemary until evenly coated. Cover and refrigerate until ready to use.

2. Heat 1 tablespoon of the oil in a 12-inch skillet over high heat. Add the shrimp shells and heads, the remaining 1/2 tablespoon pepper and 1 teaspoon Creole seasoning, and cook, stirring a few times, for 3 minutes. Add wine, water, Worcestershire, lemon juice, onion, garlic, and hot sauce. Bring to a boil, reduce the heat to a simmer, and let gently bubble for 45 minutes. Strain through a coarse strainer; you should have about 1 cup of barbecue base.

3. Heat a 14-inch skillet over high heat. Add the remaining 2 tablespoons oil, then the shrimp and cook for 2 minutes, searing on both sides. Pour in the barbecue base, reduce the heat to medium, and simmer until the shrimp are cooked through, about 1 minute. Remove from the heat; whisk in the butter, one piece at a time, not adding another until the previous piece is fully incorporated in the sauce.

4. Transfer the shrimp to a serving platter or small individual plates. Spoon the sauce over the shrimp and serve immediately with the Jalapeño Biscuits.

YIELD: 4 FIRST-COURSE SERVINGS

jalapeño biscuits

1 cup all-purpose flour

1 teaspoon baking powder

1/8 teaspoon baking soda

1/4 teaspoon salt

1/4 cup cold unsalted butter, cut into small pieces

2 tablespoons chopped seeded jalapeño pepper

1/4 cup buttermilk, or as needed

1. Preheat the oven to 375°F. Line a baking sheet with parchment paper.

2. Sift the dry ingredients into a small bowl. Work the butter into the flour with a fork until the mixture is crumbly. Stir in the jalapeño. Mix in the buttermilk a little at a time, adding just enough so that it comes together into a smooth ball of dough. Do not overwork the dough.

3. On a lightly floured work surface, roll the dough into a 7-inch round, 1/2 inch thick. Using a 1-inch cookie cutter, press out 12 rounds. Reroll scraps to make additional biscuits. Transfer the rounds to the baking sheet. Bake until the tops are golden and the bottoms browned, about 15 minutes. Serve warm.

YIELD: 24 MINI BISCUITS

Get head-on shrimp if you can, as the fat that's in the head adds incredible flavor to the barbecue shrimp base.

•

For tender biscuits, once the liquid is added, mix just until it comes together (I always mix by hand) and then handle the dough as little as possible when rolling it and cutting out the biscuits.

shrimp and mozzarella phyllo wraps
with smoked tomato butter dipping sauce

This is a great little hors d'oeuvre that can be prepped a day ahead and popped in the oven when your guests arrive. You can change up the filling ingredients to suit your own tastes. For these, you can use scallops or rock shrimp instead of Gulf shrimp. I really like the butteriness of the mozzarella, but you could substitute Jack, Cheddar, or another good melting cheese.

1 pound medium Gulf shrimp, peeled, deveined, and cut in half lengthwise

1 tablespoon Emeril's Creole Seasoning (page 108) or other Creole seasoning

2 tablespoons olive oil

1/2 cup minced onion

1/4 cup minced celery

1/2 tablespoon minced garlic

1/2 cup heavy cream

2 teaspoons Worcestershire sauce

2 teaspoons hot sauce (I like Crystal for this)

1/4 cup panko breadcrumbs

4 ounces mozzarella cheese, coarsely grated (about 1 cup)

2 tablespoons finely grated Parmigiano-Reggiano cheese

8 sheets phyllo dough, thawed

1/2 cup (1 stick) unsalted butter, melted

2 tablespoons plus 2 teaspoons plain dry breadcrumbs

Smoked Tomato Butter Dipping Sauce (recipe follows)

1. Season the shrimp with the Creole seasoning, tossing to coat evenly. In a large heavy skillet, heat the oil over medium heat. Add the onion, celery, and garlic and cook, stirring a few times, until translucent, about 3 minutes. Increase the heat to high, add the shrimp, and cook, stirring as needed, until they are opaque, about 3 minutes. Stir in the cream, Worcestershire, and hot sauce, reduce the heat to medium, and simmer for 2 minutes. Add the panko, stir to combine, and cook for 1 minute to thicken. Remove from the heat and let cool completely. Fold in the mozzarella and Parmigiano.

2. Preheat the oven to 425°F. Line a rimmed baking sheet with parchment paper. Place a sheet of phyllo on a clean work surface with a long side closest to you. Cover the remaining sheets with a damp kitchen towel to keep them moist. Brush the right half of the phyllo sheet with melted butter, then sprinkle with 1 teaspoon of the breadcrumbs and fold the left side over

the right. Brush the top edge of the folded phyllo sheet with butter. Place about 1/3 cup of the shrimp filling along the bottom edge of the phyllo sheet and shape into a 1-inch-wide by 4-inch-long log. Fold 1 inch of the phyllo over each side of the filling. Starting at the bottom, fold the phyllo over the filling and roll up to form a tight cylinder. Brush the top of the phyllo roll with melted butter and place on the prepared baking sheet. Repeat with remaining phyllo, melted butter, breadcrumbs, and filling. Place the baking sheet in the refrigerator for at least 10 minutes prior to cooking.

3. Bake the wraps until golden brown, 12 to 15 minutes. Serve them warm with the dipping sauce.

YIELD: 8 WRAPS, 6 TO 8 APPETIZER SERVINGS

smoked tomato
butter dipping sauce

This sauce is excellent, a nice twist on the usual marinara served with fried seafood. You can easily double this recipe for a large party. Instead of using the smoker setup I describe below for smoking the tomatoes, you can use any stovetop smoker.

1 pound Roma tomatoes, cored and halved

½ cup olive oil

Salt and freshly ground black pepper

¼ cup wood chips (I like alder, hickory, or apple for this)

9 tablespoons cold unsalted butter, cut into tablespoons

1 medium onion, finely chopped

1 rib celery, finely chopped

1 tablespoon tomato paste

1 cup Rich Chicken Stock (page 68) or store-bought low-sodium chicken broth

¼ teaspoon salt

Few drops of balsamic vinegar, or to taste

Hot sauce of your choice

1. In a medium bowl, toss the tomatoes with the oil and season with salt and pepper to taste.

2. Set a large pot with a steamer insert on the stove. Remove the insert and set aside. Line the inside bottom of the pot with aluminum foil. On another piece of foil, about the width of the pot, add the wood chips. Place another sheet of foil on top (don't crimp the sheets together) and transfer to the pot. Add the steamer insert.

3. Add the tomatoes to the steamer, cut side down. Cover the pot with the lid. Wrap two bricks or other heavy objects with foil and set on top of the pot. (You want to prevent the smoke from escaping from the pot.) Turn the heat to high and cook for 10 minutes to get the smoke going. Reduce the heat to low and continue to cook 10 minutes longer. Turn off the heat and allow the tomatoes to smoke an additional 5 minutes. Remove the tomatoes from the steamer and set aside.

4. In a medium saucepan over medium heat, melt 1 tablespoon of the butter. Add the onion and celery and cook until translucent, stirring a few times, about 3 minutes. Add the smoked tomatoes and any accumulated juices, tomato paste, and stock and bring to a boil. Reduce the heat to low and simmer for 20 minutes.

5. Transfer the mixture to a blender and carefully puree until smooth. Strain through a coarse strainer (discard the solids), return the sauce to the pot, and simmer over medium-low heat until thickened, about 5 minutes longer. Whisk in the remaining 8 tablespoons cold butter, 1 tablespoon at a time, not adding a new piece until the previous one is fully incorporated. Add the salt, vinegar, and hot sauce to taste. Remove from the heat and serve immediately or cover to keep warm until needed. This can be made up to 1 week ahead and refrigerated in an airtight container, but the sauce will need to be reheated very gently— it will separate if brought to a boil.

YIELD: ABOUT 2 CUPS

working with phyllo

To ensure good results, you need to treat phyllo right; because the sheets are so thin, they dry out quickly when exposed to air. When you unroll phyllo, place a slightly damp kitchen towel on top of the sheets you're not working with to keep them supple.

emeril's hawaiian-style poke

Poke (say *poke-aay*) is a traditional Hawaiian appetizer that is a tuna tartare deliciously amped up with pan-Pacific flavors. I was introduced to poke by my good friend Sam Choy, who has thrown the spotlight on the dish with his annual Keauhou Poke Contest, the ultimate poke showdown, as chefs and home cooks from all over Hawaii compete for the bragging rights of having the best poke in the islands. This is seriously good stuff. If you can't find it locally, look for the seaweed online.

2 tablespoons crunchy peanut butter

2 tablespoons unsweetened coconut milk

1 tablespoon soy sauce, plus more to taste

2 teaspoons Vietnamese chili garlic sauce (*tuong ot toi*), plus more to taste

2 teaspoons fresh lime juice

1/2 teaspoon toasted sesame oil, plus more to taste

1/2 teaspoon minced or grated peeled fresh ginger (the finer, the better)

1 pound sushi-grade ahi tuna, trimmed of any sinew or bloodline and cut into 1/3- to 1/2-inch dice (about 3 cups diced)

3/4 cup ogo or arame seaweed, rinsed and chopped

1/4 cup minced Maui or other sweet onion

2 tablespoons finely chopped toasted macadamia nuts

2 tablespoons roughly chopped fresh cilantro

1/2 teaspoon grated lime zest

Hawaiian sea salt (I use pink but any fine, flaky sea salt works)

Canola oil, for frying

24 wonton wrappers, for serving

1. In a food processor, combine the peanut butter, coconut milk, soy sauce, chili garlic sauce, 1 teaspoon of the lime juice, the sesame oil, and ginger and process on high speed until smooth.

2. Place the tuna in a large bowl, add the seaweed, onion, macadamia nuts, cilantro, lime zest, and remaining 1 teaspoon lime juice and toss well.

3. Pour the peanut butter mixture over the tuna and mix well. Season to taste with more soy sauce, chili garlic sauce, sesame oil, and Hawaiian salt. Cover and refrigerate until chilled, 1 1/2 to 2 hours.

4. While the poke is chilling, fry the wontons. Heat 1 inch of oil in a high-sided medium skillet or Dutch oven to 350°F. Working in batches, add the wrappers to the hot oil and fry until golden brown, 2 to 3 minutes. Stir to keep them from sticking together and to promote even browning. Using tongs, remove the wrappers from the pan and drain on a paper towel–lined plate. Season lightly with Hawaiian salt.

5. Serve the poke in a bowl with the crispy wontons for dipping.

YIELD: 4 TO 6 APPETIZER SERVINGS

toasting macadamias

You can sometimes buy macadamia nuts already toasted. If not, spread them on a baking sheet and toast in a preheated 350°F oven until golden, 7 to 9 minutes. Remove them from the sheet immediately so they don't continue to toast.

In Hawaii, ahi tuna refers to bigeye tuna and yellowfin tuna. When buying tuna, look for line caught (this is ecologically preferable to fish caught using dredging, bottom trawling, or gill nets, which is often the case with bluefin tuna). The flesh should range from a dark pink to almost red and feel firm. When serving raw, tuna should always be chilled.

house-smoked salmon cheesecake
with parmesan-panko crust and chive crème fraîche

The original inspiration for this came from Lora Brody, a fellow native of Massachusetts and terrific pastry chef. I loved her concept of a savory cheesecake and I've had one on the menu at Emeril's since day one. This is insanely rich, which makes it a great choice for a buffet—we say it serves 12 to 16 but that's being very conservative. I've garnished it with salmon roe, but you can kick that up as many notches as you want to, using whatever kind of caviar you prefer and can afford. Don't soak the wood chips—the salmon smokes for such a short time that you want maximum smoke as quickly as possible.

5 cups cold water

5 tablespoons plus
1 teaspoon salt

1 (1-pound) skinless wild salmon fillet, pin bones removed

¼ cup wood chips (I like to use alder, hickory, or apple for this)

1 cup panko breadcrumbs

1 cup finely grated Parmigiano-Reggiano cheese (4 ounces)

¼ cup (½ stick) unsalted butter, melted

1 large egg white, lightly beaten

1 tablespoon olive oil

1 cup chopped onion

½ cup chopped yellow bell pepper

½ cup chopped red bell pepper

8 cups fresh spinach, washed well and trimmed of heavy stems

2 (8-ounce) packages cream cheese, at room temperature

1 (15-ounce) container ricotta cheese, at room temperature

1 tablespoon finely grated lemon zest

2 tablespoons fresh lemon juice

4 large eggs, at room temperature

Chive Crème Fraîche (see opposite), for serving

About 2 ounces salmon roe, for serving

1. Combine the water and 5 tablespoons salt and stir until the salt is dissolved. Transfer to a nonreactive baking dish large enough to hold the salmon. Add the salmon to the brine, cover with plastic wrap, and refrigerate for 20 minutes.

2. Remove the salmon from the brine, discarding the brine. Rinse the salmon and pat dry. Place it on a wire rack set over a rimmed baking sheet and refrigerate at least 2 hours and up to overnight, allowing the salmon to form a pellicle (this is a tacky surface that will help the smoke adhere to the salmon).

3. Set a large pot with a steamer insert on the stove. Remove the insert and set aside. Line the inside bottom of the pot with aluminum foil. On another piece of foil about the width of the pot, arrange the wood chips. Place another sheet of foil on top (don't crimp the sheets together) and transfer to the pot. Add the steamer insert.

4. Cut the salmon into several pieces so that they will fit in one layer on the steamer rack. Add to the steamer. Cover the pot with the lid. Wrap two bricks or other heavy objects with foil and set on top of the pot. You want to prevent the smoke from escaping. Turn the heat to high and cook for 10 minutes to get the smoke going. Reduce the heat to low and cook for 10 minutes longer. Turn off the heat and allow the salmon to smoke an additional 5 minutes. Remove the salmon from the steamer. Once it is cool enough to handle, flake into pieces and set aside.

5. Preheat the oven to 350°F.

6. In a small bowl, combine the panko, cheese, melted butter, egg white, and ½ teaspoon of the salt. Transfer to a 10-inch springform pan and flatten the mixture over the bottom in an even layer. Set the pan on a rimmed baking sheet and bake until lightly browned, about 10 minutes. Set aside to cool, then wrap the bottom of the pan with foil. Set the springform in a roasting pan.

7. Heat the oil in a small skillet over medium heat. Add the onion, bell peppers, and ¼ teaspoon of the salt and cook until softened, about 10 minutes, stirring. Transfer to a small bowl. Add the spinach to the pan and cook, stirring, until wilted, about 5 minutes. Season with the remaining ¼ teaspoon of the salt. Transfer the spinach to a strainer to drain, squeezing out as much liquid as you can from it, then chop and set aside.

8. Add the cream cheese to the bowl of a stand mixer fitted with the paddle attachment and mix on low speed until creamy (or use a handheld electric mixer). Add the ricotta, sautéed vegetables and spinach, and lemon zest and juice, and continue to mix until well combined. Add the eggs, one at a time, beating well after each addition. Stir in the flaked salmon until just mixed.

9. Pour the filling over the crust, using a rubber spatula to smooth the top, and place the springform and roasting pan in the oven. Add hot tap water to the pan to come up about 1 inch on the side of the springform and bake until the cheesecake is firm, about 1 hour and 15 minutes. Transfer the cake to a wire rack to cool for several hours at room temperature before serving, or cover and refrigerate for up to 1 week. (I do not recommend freezing this.)

10. Remove the cheesecake from the refrigerator about 1 hour before serving. To serve, cut the cheesecake in thin wedges with a warm knife. Top each slice with a generous dollop (about 2 tablespoons) of the Chive Crème Fraîche and a garnish of salmon roe.

YIELD: 12 TO 16 SERVINGS

chive crème fraîche

2 (8-ounce) containers crème fraîche

¼ cup chopped fresh chives

2 teaspoons grated lemon zest

2 tablespoons fresh lemon juice

¾ teaspoon salt

In a small bowl, combine all the ingredients. Cover and refrigerate until ready to use.

YIELD: 2 CUPS

changing it up

If you don't want to smoke your own salmon, replace the water, 5 tablespoons salt, and fresh salmon with 1 pound hot-smoked salmon (not lox) and proceed. You can also prepare this with trout, lobster, or crabmeat (don't smoke the lobster or crab).

bahamian-style ceviche

I developed this dish to re-create a wonderful experience I had with my son, EJ, when we were on vacation in the Bahamas. We left the resort to do some exploring on foot and came across what must have been a co-operative or communal kitchen. Just then, a guy came along on a bike with two huge fish wrapped in paper in his basket. We watched as one of the men in the kitchen took the fish and began to clean, filet, and cut them into small pieces. As he was doing that, another man chopped up peppers, onions, tomatoes, herbs, and avocado. When they were done, they tossed the fish and the vegetables together, doused the mix with lots of fresh lime juice, and served it up to everyone, including EJ and me. Bright, vibrant, fresh flavors—that's what ceviche is all about.

1 pound very fresh firm white fish (I like to use mangrove and red snapper, which are fished out of the Gulf of Mexico)

$1/2$ cup chopped ripe tomato

$1/4$ cup fresh lime juice

2 tablespoons fresh orange juice

2 tablespoons fresh lemon juice

2 tablespoons olive oil

2 tablespoons chopped fresh cilantro

$1^1/2$ tablespoons finely diced seeded serrano pepper

$1^1/2$ tablespoons finely diced seeded jalapeño pepper

1 tablespoon finely diced red bell pepper

1 tablespoon finely diced red onion

1 teaspoon coarse sea salt

$1/4$ teaspoon cayenne pepper

1 ripe avocado, peeled, pitted, and cut into $1/4$-inch dice

Thin tortilla chips, for serving (I love Milagros brand; they're super thin and crispy—perfect for this)

Lime wedges, for serving

2. Remove the ceviche from the refrigerator. Add the avocado and mix well. Serve on small plates with the tortillas and lime wedges.

YIELD: 4 TO 6 FIRST-COURSE SERVINGS

1. Using a very sharp knife, cut the fish into $1/4$-inch dice and place in a glass bowl. Add the remaining ingredients, except the avocado, tortillas, and lime wedges, and toss well. Place a piece of plastic wrap directly on top of the mixture (this will keep the fish from drying out) and refrigerate until the fish is "cooked" through, which, depending on the seafood you use, will take between 30 minutes and $1^1/2$ hours. Once the ceviche has been in the fridge for 30 minutes, start checking on it. And once it is "cooked" (see opposite), serve it as soon as possible and certainly within 3 hours.

preparing ceviche

In ceviche, the acid action of citrus juice denatures the fish proteins in much the same way exposure to heat would. Any kind of citrus or other fruit juice with an acid edge can be used—sour orange, yuzu, passion fruit, lime, lemon, pineapple, or papaya. Be aware that pineapple and papaya juices contain enzymes that are powerful natural tenderizers; if you use either of them, it's particularly important to enjoy your ceviche just as soon as it's ready.

1. The key to success is to use only the freshest seafood. All types of fish as well as scallops, shrimp, or squid are candidates for ceviche. But use only one kind, as the density of each is slightly different (even among different types of white-fleshed fish), and you want the seafood to "cook" through at the same time.

2. You also want the seafood to "cook" as quickly as possible (so the outside of a piece isn't noticeably softer than the inside), so cut it into very small pieces before adding it to the citrus mixture.

3. Texture is everything in ceviche, so serve it just as soon as the fish is "cooked," which is when it is opaque all the way through, as shown here, with no translucency. You can check by cutting a piece in half. The longer you let the fish sit, the softer it will become (after a while, it will be downright mushy), as the action of the citric acid continues.

hot & crispy fried grouper
fingers with homemade tartar sauce

The Gulf of Mexico is prime fishing grounds for grouper, which is an amazingly sweet-tasting fish. Whenever I am lucky enough to land one, this is what my family wants me to make. It's such a simple preparation but it lets the delicate flavor of the fish shine through. You can substitute other white-fleshed fish for the grouper, like hake, drum, or snapper.

1¼ to 1½ pounds skinless fresh grouper or other firm white-fleshed fish fillets, trimmed of any bloodline

1 tablespoon plus 1½ teaspoons Emeril's Creole Seasoning (page 108) or other Creole seasoning, plus more for sprinkling

2 cups buttermilk

2 tablespoons hot sauce (I like Crystal for this)

Vegetable or canola oil, for frying

1 cup all-purpose flour

½ cup yellow cornmeal

¼ cup corn flour (masa)

Homemade Tartar Sauce (recipe follows), for serving

1. Cut the fish into 5- to 6-inch-long pieces about 1 inch thick. You should have approximately 26 to 28 "fingers." Place the fish strips in a bowl and season with 1½ teaspoons of the Creole seasoning. Add the buttermilk and hot sauce and stir to combine. Refrigerate for about 30 minutes.

2. Add enough oil to a large Dutch oven to fill it halfway, and no more. Preheat the oil to 365°F over high heat.

3. In a shallow bowl or in a zip-top plastic bag, combine the flour, cornmeal, corn flour, and the remaining 1 tablespoon Creole seasoning. Stir or shake to combine.

4. Working in batches, remove 6 to 8 pieces of the fish from the buttermilk marinade and dredge in the flour mixture until completely coated. Tap off any excess. One at a time, gently slip the fish into the hot oil. Fry until the fish is crispy and golden brown and floats on the surface of the oil, usually 2 to 3 minutes.

5. Using a slotted spoon or a spider, transfer the fried fish to paper towels or a wire rack to drain, then sprinkle with Creole seasoning and serve with the tartar sauce for dipping while hot.

YIELD: 8 APPETIZER SERVINGS

homemade tartar sauce

Sure, you can buy prepared tartar sauce, but this is so easy to put together and the taste will knock your socks off. Feel free to put your own personal spin on it—add sweet corn, or chopped celery, or a dash of ketchup, whatever rocks your boat. Don't skip the tarragon, though—it adds something special.

1 cup mayonnaise

2 green onions, finely chopped

1 clove garlic, minced

1 shallot, minced (2 tablespoons)

2 tablespoons chopped cornichons or dill pickle

1 tablespoon nonpareil capers, drained and finely chopped

1 tablespoon chopped fresh flat-leaf parsley

1 teaspoon chopped fresh tarragon or pinch of dried tarragon, crumbled between your fingers

1 teaspoon Dijon mustard

⅛ teaspoon cayenne pepper

Salt, to taste

In a small bowl, whisk all the ingredients together. Refrigerate until ready to serve and up to several days in an airtight container.

YIELD: ABOUT 1½ CUPS

For my dredge, I like to use a combination of flour, cornmeal, and masa. The flour and masa give the fish pieces a nice fine coating (the masa contributing an extra kick of corn flavor) and the cornmeal fries up crispy when it hits the hot oil.

Clockwise from top: Classic Margarita with Grand Marnier, Cucumber Saketini, Tchoup Chop's Mai Tai Roa Ae, and Aperol Spritz

classic
margarita
with grand marnier

I love Grand Marnier and I love tequila. This margarita is just one step away from a shot of tequila with a wedge of lime and salt, kicked up with a dose of Grand Marnier. I prefer mine shaken until chilled, then strained and enjoyed straight up, but if you like, you can serve this over ice for a drink that will mellow as you sip along. Enjoy with Pork Shoulder Tacos (see page 112).

1½ ounces (3 tablespoons) best-quality reposado tequila

1 ounce (2 tablespoons) strained fresh lime juice

1 ounce (2 tablespoons) Grand Marnier

Ice cubes

1 lime wedge

Kosher salt, for rimming the glass (optional)

1. Combine the tequila, lime juice, and Grand Marnier in a cocktail shaker over ice.

2. Take the lime wedge and run it around the rim of a single old-fashioned glass or other glass of your choice. Place enough salt in a shallow saucer and dip the moistened glass rim in the salt to coat, if you want a salt-rimmed glass.

3. Shake the cocktail shaker vigorously to chill the drink, then strain it into the rimmed glass. Garnish with the lime wedge and enjoy.

YIELD: 1 SERVING

aperol
spritz

Aperol is an Italian aperitif made from bitter orange, rhubarb, and gentian. Combined with club soda and Prosecco (or an unoaked Chardonnay), it makes for a lightly bitter quaff that is very popular in Europe. It's a favorite summertime refresher of Martha Stewart and one I enjoyed sipping while visiting with her at her home in Bedford, New York. This pairs perfectly with Mortadella and Chile Pizza (page 40) and Praline-Cayenne Bacon (page 45).

Ice cubes

2 ounces (¼ cup) chilled Aperol

1 ounce (2 tablespoons) chilled club soda

4 ounces (½ cup) chilled Prosecco

1 thin lime slice

Fill a white wine glass three-quarters of the way with ice. Pour in the Aperol, then the soda. Top with the Prosecco. Float the lime slice on top.

YIELD: 1 SERVING

cucumber
saketini

This cocktail pairs nicely with Bahamian-Style Ceviche (page 58), thanks to the addition of grapefruit and lime, which gives it citrusy undertones. The brand of gin you use makes a difference—Hendrick's has a pronounced herbal flavor that is perfect in combination with the cucumber and cilantro.

1 (1-inch) piece cucumber, peeled, seeded, and thinly sliced

5 fresh mint leaves

2 cups crushed ice

2 ounces (1/4 cup) sake

2 ounces (1/4 cup) Hendrick's gin

1 ounce (2 tablespoons) strained fresh lime juice

2 teaspoons Cilantro Syrup, or to taste (recipe follows)

Grapefruit soda, as needed

1. Place the cucumber and 3 of the mint leaves in the bottom of a cocktail shaker and press vigorously with a muddler until the cucumber has released its liquid and the mint becomes fragrant. Add 1 cup of the ice, the sake, gin, lime juice, and Cilantro Syrup to the shaker and shake well.

2. Fill a highball glass with the remaining 1 cup ice and strain the cocktail into the glass. Top it off with grapefruit soda and garnish with the remaining 2 mint leaves.

YIELD: 1 SERVING

cilantro syrup

1 cup coarsely chopped fresh cilantro, both leaves and stems

1/2 cup sugar

1/4 cup water

Grated zest from 1 lime

Combine all the ingredients in a 1-quart saucepan and bring to a boil, stirring occasionally to dissolve the sugar. Once the mixture comes to a boil, remove the pan from the heat and let cool completely. Strain the cooled syrup through a fine-mesh strainer. It will keep in an airtight container in the refrigerator for up to 3 weeks.

YIELD: 1/2 CUP

tchoup chop's
mai tai roa ae

There is a resurgence in the popularity of tiki drinks, and for good reason—they're fun and tasty! This is the Mai Tai we serve at my restaurant Tchoup Chop in Orlando, Florida, and we can't make 'em fast enough for our customers. The flavors pair well with Asian foods like my Vietnamese Pork and Shrimp Spring Rolls (page 43).

1 1/4 ounces (2 1/2 tablespoons) Myers's dark rum

1 ounce (2 tablespoons) Wray & Nephew White Overproof Rum or Rhum Barbancourt Three Star

1/2 ounce (1 tablespoon) Gaetano Orange Curaçao or Grand Marnier

1/2 ounce (1 tablespoon) Monin Almond (Orgeat) Syrup

1/2 ounce (1 tablespoon) Simple Syrup (recipe follows)

1 ounce (2 tablespoons) strained fresh lime juice

Ice cubes

1 maraschino cherry, for garnish

1 lime wedge, for garnish

1 sprig fresh mint, for garnish

1. In a cocktail shaker, combine the rums, curaçao, almond and simple syrups, and lime juice over ice and shake until well chilled.

2. Strain over fresh ice into a double old-fashioned glass and garnish with the cherry, lime wedge, and mint sprig.

YIELD: 1 SERVING

simple syrup

2/3 cup sugar

2/3 cup water

1. In a small saucepan, combine the sugar and water and bring to a boil over high heat. Cook, stirring a few times, until the sugar is completely dissolved.

2. Remove from the heat and set aside to cool, then store in the refrigerator in an airtight container for up to 1 month.

YIELD: 1 CUP

SOUPS

The first thing my mother taught me to cook was vegetable soup. To me, soup is an essential food, sustaining the body and the soul. When you're hungry, or blue, or feeling under the weather, a bowl of soup (or chowder or gumbo) can sate and comfort. Also, these recipes, in general, are forgiving and adaptable. Make chicken soup with homemade broth and it's sublime in its simplicity, the rich, delicate flavor of the chicken hitting you on multiple levels. Make it with canned broth and it's still a bowl full of goodness.

In this chapter, you'll find recipes inspired by my favorite flavors and preparations, from my version of Vietnamese pho made with roasted duck to a new spin on a soup I grew up with, Portuguese kale soup. And along the way you will learn techniques, like making a roux. These are soups I feed my family, friends, and customers—and I hope they bring your diners the same deep pleasure they do mine.

chicken noodle
soup from homemade stock

This is a very basic and satisfying recipe that I make at home for my family. Because of the deep flavor of the stock, you don't need to add a lot of ingredients. I consider this recipe a canvas that I can add to and change up as I like. Sautéing the vegetables in a little butter adds richness.

Rich Chicken Stock (recipe follows), with reserved chicken meat

2 tablespoons unsalted butter

4 ounces white mushrooms, sliced

1 cup finely diced onion

1 cup thinly sliced carrot

1 cup finely diced celery

2¼ teaspoons salt, plus more to taste

½ teaspoon freshly ground black pepper, plus more to taste

¼ pound dried vermicelli noodles, broken into pieces

2 tablespoons chopped fresh flat-leaf parsley

1. Make the Rich Chicken Stock and reserve the shredded chicken meat and stock.

2. Melt the butter in a large stockpot over medium-high heat. Add the mushrooms and cook, stirring a few times, until golden, 3 to 4 minutes. Add the onion, carrot, and celery and cook, stirring as needed, until the vegetables are softened, 3 to 4 minutes. Add the stock and bring to a boil over high heat, then reduce the heat to a simmer and cook for 30 minutes.

3. Add the reserved chicken, salt, pepper, and vermicelli to the pot and simmer until the noodles are cooked through, 10 to 12 minutes. Remove from the heat and stir in the parsley. Taste and adjust the seasoning if necessary. Serve hot.

YIELD: ABOUT 5½ QUARTS, 10 TO 12 SERVINGS

rich chicken stock

This recipe gives you the deep, layered flavor of stock without the hours of simmering.

1 (4- to 5-pound) chicken

2 quarts store-bought chicken stock or low-sodium chicken broth

2 quarts water

2 medium onions, quartered

2 carrots, roughly chopped

2 ribs celery, roughly chopped

4 cloves garlic, smashed

4 sprigs fresh thyme

5 or 6 fresh parsley stems

2 bay leaves

½ teaspoon salt

¼ teaspoon freshly ground black pepper

1. Rinse the chicken well under cool running water and remove the neck, gizzard, heart, and liver from the cavity if present. Place the chicken in a large stockpot or Dutch oven along with any parts (except the liver; it can give the stock a bitter taste), and cover with the stock and water. Add the remaining ingredients. Bring to a boil, partially cover, and reduce the heat to a simmer. Cook for 1 hour; at that point, the chicken should easily pull away from the bones.

2. Using tongs, remove the chicken from the stock and set aside until cool enough to handle. Strain the cooking liquid through a fine-mesh strainer lined with cheesecloth, discarding the vegetables. Pull the chicken meat off the bones, discarding the bones, skin, and any fat. Shred and reserve the meat, and refrigerate until needed. Cool the stock, then store in an airtight container in the refrigerator for up to 4 days or the freezer for 6 months.

YIELD: ABOUT 4 QUARTS STOCK

If you like pasta in your chicken soup and want to add more or use a thicker pasta, you might be better off cooking the pasta separately, then adding it to the soup. When you add uncooked pasta to a soup, it absorbs liquid from the soup; add enough pasta to your soup and it might soak up all the broth.

•

A nice addition to this soup is a little homemade or store-bought pesto stirred into each serving.

christmas
root vegetable
soup with crispy carrot strips

If I don't make soup to kick off the meal at Thanksgiving and Christmas, I've got some very disappointed folks on my hands. If you prefer, finish each serving with a drizzle of truffle oil instead of the crème fraîche. This soup tastes even better the next day.

1 (1½-pound) butternut squash, peeled and cut in ½-inch-thick half moons

1 (1-pound) celery root, ends trimmed, peeled, cut in half and across into ½-inch-thick half moons

1 large onion, cut into ½-inch wedges

10 ounces parsnips (2 large), peeled and cut into ½-inch-thick rounds

8 ounces carrots (2 medium), peeled and cut into ½-inch-thick rounds

1 (8-ounce) sweet potato, peeled and cut into ½-inch-thick rounds

1 (8-ounce) pear, peeled, cored, and diced

1 (1-ounce) piece fresh ginger (about 1 inch long), peeled and sliced ¼ inch thick

4 cloves garlic, peeled

¼ cup olive oil

1 tablespoon salt

1 teaspoon freshly ground black pepper

½ teaspoon ground cardamom

⅛ teaspoon ground cloves

⅛ teaspoon ground allspice

⅛ teaspoon ground ginger

3 quarts Rich Chicken Stock (page 68) or vegetable stock or store-bought low-sodium broth

⅓ cup crème fraîche, sour cream, or plain yogurt

Crispy Carrot Strips (recipe follows), for garnish

1. Preheat the oven to 400°F. Line two baking sheets with aluminum foil or parchment paper.

2. In a large bowl, combine the vegetables, pear, ginger, garlic, oil, salt, pepper, and spices, and stir to mix well. Arrange the mixture on the prepared baking sheets in an even layer. Cover with foil and roast until tender, 40 to 45 minutes.

3. Transfer the roasted mixture to a large stockpot. Add the stock and bring to a boil over medium-high heat. Reduce the heat to a simmer and cook, partially covered, for 30 to 35 minutes.

4. Remove the pot from the heat and let cool slightly. Working in batches, carefully transfer the soup to a blender and puree until very smooth. Transfer the pureed soup to another pot. When it has all been pureed, taste and adjust the seasonings, if necessary. Gently reheat before serving.

5. To serve, ladle the soup into bowls and top with crème fraîche and a sprinkling of carrot strips.

YIELD: 6 TO 8 SERVINGS

crispy carrot strips

6 medium carrots, peeled

2 tablespoons olive oil

1 teaspoon fine sea salt

¼ teaspoon ground ginger

¼ teaspoon ground black pepper

1. Preheat the oven to 200°F. Line a baking sheet with parchment paper.

2. Using a vegetable peeler, peel the carrots into long strips. In a bowl, toss the strips with the remaining ingredients until well combined. Transfer to the prepared baking sheet and bake until the carrots are completely dry and crisp, about 3 hours. Store in an airtight container at room temperature for up to 1 week.

YIELD: 4 CUPS

The carrot strips are really pretty if you can make them with a mix of yellow, red, white, purple, and orange heirloom carrots.

•

To get the carrots crispy, remove all the water from them, which is what you're doing by baking them at a very low heat. Raise the temperature and the chips will burn. If you've got a dehydrator, use that instead.

brandy-fueled french onion soup with gruyère croutons

French onion soup is one of those preparations with a multitude of versions—many cooks base it on beef broth as I do here, but you'll also find it made with chicken or veal stock. Red wine shows up, as do Calvados, vermouth, and other spirits—my preference is a shot of brandy. What every version shares is a huge pile of sliced onions reduced very slowly to a delicious golden-brown tangle. I use Spanish onions but Shep Gordon, a very dear friend and my first agent, made this for me with Maui onions when I visited him in Hawaii. These mild onions add another layer of natural sweetness in addition to caramelizing the onions; if you can't find Maui onions, substitute another sweet variety, like Vidalia or Walla Walla.

1 French baguette	1½ teaspoons salt
6 tablespoons (¾ stick) unsalted butter	1 teaspoon freshly ground white pepper
10 large Spanish onions, halved lengthwise and thinly sliced into half moons (about 4 quarts)	½ cup brandy
	8 cups homemade beef stock or store-bought low-sodium beef broth
5 to 6 sprigs fresh thyme, tied in a bundle	12 ounces Gruyère cheese, grated (about 4 cups)

1. Preheat the oven to 300°F. Cut six 1- to 1½-inch-thick slices of the baguette wide enough to span the width of six individual ovenproof soup crocks (they must be able to withstand 500°F). (Or cut it so when you put two pieces side by side, they cover the soup and support the cheese.) Set the slices in a single layer on a baking sheet and toast in the oven just until they dry out (don't let them color), 30 to 45 minutes. Remove from the oven.

2. Melt the butter in a 6-quart Dutch oven over medium-high heat. Add the onions, thyme, salt, and pepper and cook, stirring the onions frequently with a wooden spoon, scraping the browned bits up off the bottom and into the onions, for about 45 minutes. Continue to stir until the onions are golden brown and caramelized throughout, about another 10 minutes.

3. Add the brandy to the pot. Continue to cook and stir, scraping the bottom and sides, for about 1 minute. Add the stock and bring

to a boil; reduce the heat to a simmer and let gently bubble for 30 minutes. Turn off the heat and discard the thyme. If you want to make the soup ahead of time, you may stop at this point and cool, cover, and refrigerate. Reheat on the stove before proceeding.

4. Position the rack in the lower third of the oven; preheat to 500°F. Set the soup crocks on a rimmed baking sheet; fill each to within 1 inch of the rim. Top each crock with a baguette slice or two, and sprinkle with a generous amount of cheese, about ½ cup. Put in the oven for 12 to 15 minutes, checking often, until the cheese is golden brown and bubbly. Garnish with fresh thyme, if desired, and serve immediately, being sure to remind guests that the bowls are very hot.

YIELD: 6 SERVINGS

caramelizing the onions

The flavor of French onion soup is largely derived from deeply browning the onions. It will take almost an hour; you need to pay attention once the onions start to brown and the process can't be rushed. If you don't brown the onions enough, the soup will lack depth. Let them scorch and you'll have to throw them out and start again.

1. Ten onions may seem like a crazy amount, but they start to cook down pretty fast.

2. At the beginning, stir the onions as needed with a wooden spoon.

3. After about 45 minutes, browned bits will begin to accumulate in the pot and the onions will be a light brown. You now need to stir the onions frequently, scraping those bits up off the bottom and into the onions, to prevent burning.

4. Continue to stir in this way until the onions are golden brown and caramelized throughout, as shown here, about another 10 minutes.

1

2

3

4

new-style caldo verde

This recipe is an excellent example of how simple ingredients can be transformed into comfort food that will satisfy and sustain. My mother, Hilda, made this traditional Portuguese soup most every week when I was growing up. When I became chef at Commander's Palace, I made it for my staff, using andouille sausage instead of the traditional chorizo. When I opened Emeril's, I put it on the menu.

While I prefer Portuguese chouriço, I use the more common Spanish chorizo here. Try them both and use what you like best.

2 tablespoons olive oil

1 pound hot cured Spanish chorizo, cut into ¼-inch-thick rounds

1 cup chopped yellow onion

½ teaspoon salt

¼ teaspoon freshly ground black pepper

2 tablespoons minced garlic

3 cups diced (½-inch) peeled russet potatoes

3½ quarts (14 cups) Rich Chicken Stock (page 68) or store-bought low-sodium chicken broth

2 bunches red- or green-leaf kale, washed well and stemmed (¾ to 1 pound)

¼ cup packed fresh flat-leaf parsley leaves

3 bay leaves

2 sprigs fresh thyme

Crushed red pepper, to taste

¼ cup fresh mint chiffonade
(see Essentials, page 37)

1. In a large pot, heat the oil over medium-high heat. When hot, add the chorizo and onion and season with the salt and pepper. Cook, stirring a few times, until the onion begins to soften, 3 to 5 minutes. Add the garlic, potatoes, and 3 quarts (12 cups) of the stock. Bring to a simmer and cook for 5 minutes.

2. Meanwhile, roughly chop the kale. Put 3 cups in a blender and the remainder in the soup pot. Add the remaining 2 cups stock and the parsley to the blender and blend into a smooth, juice-like puree. Set aside.

3. Add the bay leaves, thyme, and crushed red pepper to the soup, and continue to simmer until the potatoes are tender, about 15 minutes longer, then stir in the kale puree and cook for another 10 minutes.

4. Remove from the heat and stir in the mint chiffonade. Serve the soup in large bowls with crusty bread.

YIELD: 4 QUARTS, 8 TO 10 SERVINGS

chorizo & chouriço

Chorizo, from Spain, and chouriço, from Portugal, are both dry pork sausages laced with paprika. My mom is second-generation Portuguese, so I grew up with chouriço. Every butcher in town made their own—I remember my mom buying it from Michael's, Gaspar's, and Furtado's. Chouriço is smoked, has a more pronounced garlic flavor, and doesn't contain quite as much paprika as chorizo. Spanish chorizo (which can be smoked or not) is a bit firmer than chouriço and is made using pimentón, or smoked sweet or hot paprika. Both types are available in degrees of hotness. (There is also Mexican chorizo, which is a fresh sausage.)

I came across a woman at the market in Porto, Portugal, once who sold very finely shredded kale that she used to make caldo verde—this small change yielded a beautiful bright green color and fresh flavor. I wanted to achieve that same effect in my own way, so here I chop the kale, puree part of it with the parsley and a little broth, and add that in at the very end of the cooking.

double chile-spiked tortilla soup

In my travels throughout the United States, I have eaten many bowls of tortilla soup, from Texas to California. I wanted to come up with a recipe that synthesized everything I like best about it—the brightly flavored broth, courtesy of the inclusion of chiles, cilantro, garlic, and a shot of fresh lime juice; the tender, lightly spiced chicken; and the tortillas, both thickening the soup and providing a welcome crunch. A lot of folks use chicken breast, but I went with all thighs for a richer chicken flavor.

1 pound boneless, skinless chicken thighs, cut into 1/2-inch pieces

1 tablespoon ground cumin

1 tablespoon ground coriander

1 tablespoon chili powder

2 tablespoons vegetable oil, plus more for frying tortillas

10 (6-inch) corn tortillas, 4 left whole, 6 cut into 1/4-inch-wide strips

2 cups chopped onions

1 cup finely chopped seeded poblano peppers (about 2)

2 large jalapeño peppers, chopped (leave the seeds in)

1/2 cup chopped fresh cilantro (stems included)

2 tablespoons chopped garlic

1 1/2 teaspoons salt

1 tablespoon tomato paste

8 cups Rich Chicken Stock (page 68) or store-bought low-sodium chicken broth

1 tablespoon fresh lime juice

1/2 cup chopped fresh cilantro leaves, for garnish

1. In a medium bowl, toss the chicken with the cumin, coriander, and chili powder until evenly coated. Set aside.

2. Heat 1 inch of vegetable oil in a 10-inch skillet over medium heat until hot but not smoking. Frying one at a time, add the whole tortillas to the hot oil and fry until golden, about 2 minutes per side. Using tongs, transfer to paper towels to drain. Add the tortilla strips in batches to the oil and fry, stirring as needed, until golden. Using tongs or a slotted spoon, transfer the fried strips to paper towels to drain until ready to use.

3. Heat the 2 tablespoons oil in a 4-quart or larger soup pot over medium-high heat. Add the onions, peppers, cilantro, garlic, and salt and cook, stirring as needed, until the onions are soft and golden, about 10 minutes. Stir in the tomato paste and cook for 1 minute. Add the chicken and cook until browned, about 5 minutes. Add the stock, increase the heat to high, and bring

to a boil. Break up the fried whole tortillas and add to the pot. Reduce the heat to a simmer and cook, uncovered, for 45 minutes. Remove from the heat and stir in the lime juice.

4. Ladle the soup into bowls. Garnish with the chopped cilantro leaves and fried tortilla strips.

YIELD: 6 SERVINGS

flavor vs. fire

The milder poblano is included for flavor while the jalapeños contribute chile fire. Leaving their seeds in amps up the heat even more.

frying tortilla strips

It's easy to fry your own tortilla strips and the flavor is so much fresher than the chips you buy. Cut them wider and enjoy them with salsa, or slice them thin and use them like I do here, as a garnish for the tortilla soup.

1. Slice the tortillas into ¼-inch-wide strips.

2. Add the strips to the hot oil in batches; you want to give them plenty of room to fry up quick and golden. Stir so they brown evenly.

3. With tongs or a slotted spoon, remove the strips to drain on paper towels.

roasted duck pho

South Louisiana is home to a large Vietnamese population, many of whom work in the shrimp fleets, and Vietnamese food has become enormously popular in New Orleans, with restaurants and pho shops popping up all over. My favorite place to order from is Pho Tau Bay—I love their entire menu but pho is always in my order. Pho (pronounced *fuh*) is considered the national dish of Vietnam and is an aromatic soup based on a deeply spiced stock that is served in large bowls with rice noodles, herbs, and thinly sliced meat or meat balls—pork, chicken, beef. The great fun of pho is customizing your bowl with your choice of herbs, bean sprouts, chiles, and hot sauce.

I love pho so much that I wanted to do my own spin on it, and I chose to make it with duck. This dish is an investment in time, but if you're looking for something to make for a special dinner, this is amazing. You can break the tasks up, making the stock the day before.

1 (5- to 6-pound) duck

3 pounds duck or chicken wings

2 medium onions

12 cloves

8 cloves garlic, unpeeled

1 medium carrot, cut in half

1 rib celery, cut in half

1 jalapeño pepper, cut in half

1 (2-inch) piece fresh ginger, cut in half

10 quarts water

6 star anise

3 cinnamon sticks

2 dried shiitake mushrooms

1 dried red chile, preferably Thai red bird chile

½ cup Vietnamese fish sauce (*nuoc cham*)

1 teaspoon Chinese five-spice powder

¾ teaspoon kosher salt

¼ teaspoon freshly ground black pepper

12 ounces rice stick noodles

FOR SERVING:

Lime wedges

Sprigs from 1 bunch fresh cilantro

Sprigs from 1 bunch fresh mint

Sprigs from 1 bunch fresh basil, preferably Thai basil

Bean sprouts

Sliced jalapeño peppers

Thinly sliced onion

Sriracha sauce

Hoisin sauce

1. Preheat the oven to 400°F.

2. Place the duck, breast side up, on a cutting board. Using poultry shears, cut under and through the wing joint to remove the wing. Repeat the process with the other wing and set both aside. Use both hands to pull back on a leg to separate it from the joint. Use the shears to cut the leg away from the body. Repeat with the other leg. Trim any excess fat from the legs and set the legs and fat aside. Make a slit on either side of the breastbone and carefully run the point of a knife along the rib cage, being careful not to leave any of the meat on the bone. Cut through the fat on the back side to remove the breast from the carcass. Repeat with the other side. Refrigerate the duck breasts and legs until ready to use. Remove as much of the fat and skin as possible from the carcass and set aside. Transfer the carcass and wings to two rimmed baking sheets.

3. Peel the onions and cut them in half lengthwise. Press 3 cloves into each onion half. Divide the onions, garlic, carrot, celery, jalapeño, and ginger between the baking sheets. Roast the duck and aromatics until golden brown, 45 to 50 minutes.

4. Transfer the carcass, wings, and aromatics to a large stockpot. Add the water, star anise, cinnamon sticks, mushrooms, and dried chile, and bring to a boil over high heat. Reduce the heat to a simmer and let bubble gently, uncovered, for 3 to 4 hours, skimming off and discarding any foam and fat that rises to the surface. The broth should be flavorful at this point but not super-concentrated.

5. Strain the duck broth through a fine-mesh strainer and discard the solids. Transfer the broth to a clean stockpot and bring to a boil. Turn the heat down to a simmer and let gently bubble until the broth has reduced to 4 quarts. It should be very flavorful and aromatic. Stir in the fish sauce and remove the broth from the heat. You can make the broth a day ahead, let cool completely, and refrigerate. (It will keep in the freezer up to 6 months.) Bring it back to a simmer before serving. While the strained broth is cooking, preheat the oven to 400°F.

6. Cut the reserved duck skin and fat into small pieces and place in a small saucepan over medium-low heat to render the fat. Once the skin is completely brown and crispy, strain off the fat and reserve for another use. Season the crisped skin (the cracklings) with ½ teaspoon of the five-spice powder and ¼ teaspoon of the salt. Set the cracklings aside until ready to use.

7. Season the duck breasts and legs with the remaining ½ teaspoon five-spice powder and ½ teaspoon salt, and the black pepper. Place the duck breasts and legs, skin side down, in a large ovenproof sauté pan over medium heat. Cook for 3 to 4 minutes to render the fat and crisp the skin. Turn them over and transfer the pan to the oven. Roast until the skin on the duck breasts is crisp, the meat feels firm to the touch, and the juices run clear, 5 to 7 minutes; transfer the breasts to a platter. Continue to roast the legs for another 8 to 10 minutes, until the skin is crisp, the meat begins to pull away from bone, and the juices run clear; transfer the legs to the platter. Let the duck rest until cool enough to handle. Cut the breast across the grain into thin slices. Cut the meat from the legs and roughly chop it.

8. Cook the rice stick noodles according to the package directions.

9. When ready to serve, arrange the lime wedges, herbs, bean sprouts, jalapeños, sliced onion, and cracklings on a serving platter. Divide the noodles and meat among the serving bowls. Ladle the hot broth over all and serve immediately. Each person can garnish the soup to taste with the ingredients on the serving platter as well as the Sriracha and hoisin sauces.

YIELD: 6 SERVINGS

the power of broth

If you're going to make pho, you have to make it from homemade broth. There is simply no way to get the same depth of flavor starting with store-bought stock or broth. And make sure you include all the spices in the amounts I've indicated—they work in delicate balance with one another.

alden's egg drop soup

When my wife, Alden, is looking for a pick-me-up, I whip this simple, protein-packed soup together for her. I don't serve tofu often at home, but this soup is a real family favorite. You can add as much or as little of it as you like. This is the way we like it.

½ cup diced (½-inch) carrot

½ cup chopped onion

½ cup thinly sliced peeled celery

1 teaspoon minced garlic

2 tablespoons toasted sesame oil

6 cups Rich Chicken Stock (page 68) or store-bought low-sodium chicken broth

4 ounces shiitake mushrooms, stems removed and caps thinly sliced

8 ounces medium-firm tofu, cut into ¼-inch dice

3 large eggs

¼ cup thinly sliced green onions

½ teaspoon salt, or to taste

¼ teaspoon freshly ground white pepper

1 teaspoon soy sauce, or more to taste

1. In a medium saucepan over medium-high heat, sauté the carrot, onion, celery, and garlic in 1 tablespoon of the sesame oil until softened, about 4 minutes. Add the stock and bring to a boil, then reduce the heat to a simmer and cook for 10 minutes.

2. Add the mushrooms and tofu to the stock and simmer for another 10 minutes.

3. In a small bowl, whisk the eggs with the remaining 1 tablespoon sesame oil. Stir the eggs into the simmering stock, add the green onions, salt, and pepper, and cook until the eggs are set, 1 to 2 minutes. Stir in the soy sauce, taste, adjust the seasonings, if necessary, and serve.

YIELD: 4 TO 6 SERVINGS

essentials

I like this with shiitakes, but you can use any kind of fresh mushroom you prefer.

•

Whisking some of the sesame oil with the eggs before pouring the eggs into the stock yields a more intense final flavor.

•

To keep the eggs from clumping when they're added to the soup, whisk them well and stir the soup as you add them to the pot in a stream.

chicken and andouille gumbo

Chicken and andouille is my favorite of the classic gumbo combinations, the chicken tender and filling and the sausage adding a rich spike of heat. Make it a day or two in advance for the best flavor and reheat it slowly so that the chicken meat does not fall apart. It freezes exceptionally well and is a great choice for parties or tailgating. Don't skip the white rice—gumbo isn't gumbo if it isn't served over a mound of rice—or the hot sauce at the table.

In Louisiana, everyone has his or her own preference when it comes to gumbo thickness. This one is about middle of the road, which is the way I prefer it—not too brothy and not too thick. It is easy to adjust the thickness by using less broth for a thicker gumbo and/or adding more for a thinner consistency.

Rich Chicken Stock (page 68), with reserved chicken meat

1 cup vegetable oil

1 cup all-purpose flour

3 medium onions, chopped

2 ribs celery, finely chopped

3 tablespoons minced garlic

1 green bell pepper, seeded and finely chopped

½ teaspoon cayenne pepper, plus more to taste

1½ pounds andouille sausage, cut into ⅓-inch-thick rounds

1½ teaspoons salt, plus more to taste

¾ teaspoon freshly ground black pepper

1 bay leaf

1 bunch green onions, thinly sliced

⅓ cup chopped fresh flat-leaf parsley

Cooked white rice, for serving

Louisiana hot sauce, for serving

Filé powder, for serving (optional)

1. Make the Rich Chicken Stock and reserve the shredded chicken meat and broth as the recipe instructs. If using it the same day, let the broth cool before starting the gumbo.

2. With the oil and flour, make a roux the color of milk chocolate following the directions opposite.

3. Immediately add the onions, celery, garlic, bell pepper, cayenne, and sausage, and cook, stirring, until the vegetables are softened, 5 to 7 minutes. If the broth has cooled by this time, add it to the roux mixture along with the salt, black pepper, and bay leaf, and bring to a gentle simmer. Continue to simmer, skimming any foam or excess oil that comes to the top, until the sauce is flavorful and thickened to the desired consistency, and any trace of floury taste is gone, about 2 hours.

4. Add the chicken, green onions, and parsley to the gumbo and continue to simmer about 30 minutes longer. Don't stir too much or the chicken will fall apart into shreds. Adjust the thickness, if necessary, by adding water or more broth. Adjust the seasoning with salt and cayenne as needed.

5. Serve the gumbo in shallow bowls over hot white rice. Have the hot sauce and filé at the table for guests to use to their liking.

YIELD: 4½ QUARTS, 8 TO 10 SERVINGS

making a roux

Roux is a mixture of flour and oil cooked on the stovetop to different stages. The darker the roux, the deeper and more complex its flavor becomes, taking on more pronounced toasty overtones the longer it is cooked. Roux is also used as a thickener. When making roux, you must stir, stir, stir, reaching into every corner of the pot, or else you will end up with some burnt bits, which will ruin its flavor.

1. Roux starts with flour and oil, usually in a 1:1 ratio. Combine them in a heavy-bottomed pot, like a cast iron or enameled cast iron skillet or Dutch oven. Stir constantly over medium-high heat with a wooden spoon.

2. The roux is now starting to color ever so slightly, and is what is called a blonde roux. Blonde roux is used in preparations where you want the benefit of roux's thickening properties but you don't want it to affect the taste of the dish, like in a white sauce. If your recipe calls for a darker roux, turn the heat down now to medium or medium-low.

3. The roux has now cooked to the color of peanut butter. If your recipe calls for it to be cooked darker than this, be even more vigilant about stirring and paying attention to what is going on in the pot. If at any point you feel the roux is browning too fast, turn the heat down further.

4. The roux is now the color of a copper penny. You can stop here or you can continue to cook it until it is the color of milk chocolate, as called for in this gumbo. The best way to keep a roux from getting any darker is to have the vegetables and sausage prepped for the next step and to add them as soon as the desired color of roux is achieved; this will immediately drop the temperature of the roux.

shrimp and okra gumbo

Make this rouxless gumbo, another favorite that's quicker and simpler than using a roux, that relies on the okra to provide the thickening.

2 pounds small okra

1/4 cup vegetable oil

1 (14.5-ounce) can diced tomatoes, undrained

1 cup chopped onion

1/2 cup chopped celery

1/2 cup chopped green bell pepper

1/4 cup chopped green onions

2 teaspoons salt

3/4 teaspoon cayenne pepper

2 bay leaves

2 quarts Shrimp Stock (recipe follows)

2 pounds medium shrimp, peeled and deveined

Cooked white rice, for serving

Hot sauce, for serving (optional)

1. Wash the okra in cool water. Cut off the stem caps and cut the pods into 1/4-inch-thick rounds. Heat the oil in a large pot over medium-high heat. When hot, add the okra and cook, stirring constantly, until most of the slime disappears, 10 to 12 minutes.

2. Add the tomatoes, onion, celery, bell pepper, and green onions to the pot and cook, stirring often, until the okra and other vegetables are soft and the slime has completely disappeared, another 18 to 20 minutes.

3. Add the salt, cayenne, bay leaves, and stock. Stir and bring to a boil. Reduce the heat to medium and simmer, uncovered, for 15 minutes. Add the shrimp and cook, stirring occasionally, for 30 minutes (see Essentials, at left).

4. Remove the bay leaves and serve the gumbo ladled into deep bowls over hot white rice. Serve with hot sauce, if desired.

YIELD: 6 SERVINGS

shrimp stock

Shrimp stock is such an easy way to add an extra layer of flavor to a seafood dish. Get in the habit of saving the shells when you have shrimp; store them in the freezer in a zip-top plastic bag, adding to it until you have enough to make stock.

2 tablespoons vegetable or olive oil

6 cups shrimp shells (from 2 pounds medium head-on shrimp)

3 quarts water

1 small onion, cut in half

1 carrot, peeled and cut into quarters

1 rib celery, cut into quarters

1 clove garlic, smashed

2 bay leaves

1 teaspoon black peppercorns

1 sprig fresh thyme

1 sprig fresh parsley

1. In a large stockpot, heat the oil over medium-high heat. When hot, add the shrimp shells and cook, stirring, until they begin to turn pink, 5 to 7 minutes. Add the remaining ingredients and bring to a boil. Immediately reduce the heat to medium, and simmer for 45 minutes, skimming off any scum that rises to the top.

2. Remove from the heat and strain through a fine-mesh strainer, discarding the solids. Use immediately, or let cool and store in airtight containers. It will keep in the refrigerator for 3 to 4 days and in the freezer for up to 6 months.

YIELD: 2 QUARTS

Why do you simmer the shrimp in the gumbo for 30 minutes when they take less than 10 minutes to cook? Because with that extra time, you develop a whole lot more shrimp flavor throughout the gumbo.

corn bisque

with shrimp, tomato, and avocado salad

It was my good fortune that when I left Commander's Palace to open Emeril's, Lou Lynch came with me as my pastry chef. In addition to the desserts, Mr. Lou also made a lot of the soups, and he and I, when we first opened the restaurant, would make either shrimp and corn or crab and corn bisque every Friday.

Sweet corn bisque is one of summer's most satisfying soups. Farmers' markets throughout the South sell different varieties of sweet corn during the season, such as Aztec and Bonanza in early summer and Silver Queen and Silver King later on. Corn is generally harvested all at the same time during short spurts, which is why there are so many varieties grown, to lengthen the season. To intensify the corn flavor in this bisque, after cutting the kernels off, we make a stock with the corncobs, much as you would with lobster shells for lobster bisque.

Summer in Louisiana also provides vine-ripened Creole tomatoes and Gulf shrimp, the inspiration for the "salad" (or call it a generous garnish) that goes right into the bowl over the soup. You could easily substitute jumbo lump blue crab for the shrimp—both are out of sight.

4 cups fresh corn kernels cut from the cobs, cobs reserved (about 4 ears)

1 quart cold water

3 tablespoons olive oil

½ cup minced yellow onion

2 tablespoons minced shallot

2 tablespoons minced celery

1 tablespoon minced garlic

3 tablespoons all-purpose flour

2 bay leaves

2 sprigs fresh thyme

1 quart half-and-half

1 teaspoon liquid crab boil

1 teaspoon coarse sea salt

½ teaspoon Worcestershire sauce

Shrimp, Tomato, and Avocado Salad (see opposite)

1. Place the reserved corncobs in a medium saucepan and cover with the water. Bring to a boil, then reduce the heat to a simmer and let it gently bubble until the corncob stock has reduced to 2 cups. Strain through a fine-mesh strainer and discard the cobs. The stock can be used immediately or cooled and stored in an airtight container in the refrigerator for 2 days or in the freezer for 3 months.

2. Heat the oil in a large saucepan over medium heat. Add the corn kernels, onion, shallot, celery, and garlic, and cook until the vegetables are tender, 2 to 3 minutes, stirring as needed. Add the flour and continue to cook, stirring to pick up any brown bits stuck to the bottom of the pan, for 3 to 5 minutes. Add the corncob stock, bay leaves, and thyme, and bring to a boil. Reduce the heat to a simmer and cook for another 5 minutes. Whisk in the half-and-half, crab boil, salt, and Worcestershire, and cook until the soup begins to thicken, about 10 minutes longer.

3. Remove the pan from the heat and cool slightly. Carefully transfer half of the bisque to a blender and puree until smooth. Transfer the puree back to the pot. Taste and adjust the seasonings if necessary.

4. Ladle the soup into the bowls, then divide the Shrimp, Tomato, and Avocado Salad among them. Serve immediately.

YIELD: 4 TO 6 SERVINGS

corn tips

It is best to cook corn as soon as you can because the sugars begin to turn to starch right after it is harvested. If you have to store corn, refrigerate it in its husk.

When cutting the kernels off the cobs, to keep them from bouncing all over the place, I put a clean kitchen towel on top of my cutting board.

shrimp, tomato, and avocado salad

This can be prepared up to a day ahead, though the flavor is best the day it is made. Add the avocado right before serving.

8 ounces jumbo shrimp, peeled and deveined	1 tablespoon finely diced jalapeño pepper
2 teaspoons Emeril's Creole Seasoning (page 108) or other Creole seasoning	1 tablespoon chopped fresh cilantro
1 tablespoon olive oil	1 tablespoon fresh lime juice
1 cup chopped ripe tomatoes	$1/2$ teaspoon minced garlic
$1/2$ cup fresh corn kernels cut from the cob	$1/2$ teaspoon sea salt
2 tablespoons finely diced red bell pepper	$1/8$ teaspoon ground coriander
	$1/8$ teaspoon ground cumin
	1 ripe avocado, peeled, pitted, and cut into small dice

1. In a small bowl, toss the shrimp with the Creole seasoning.

2. Heat the oil in medium sauté pan over medium-high heat. Add the shrimp, and cook just until opaque all the way through, about 1 minute per side. Transfer the shrimp to a clean cutting board. Set aside until cool enough to handle.

3. In a medium bowl, combine the tomatoes, corn, bell pepper, jalapeño, cilantro, lime juice, garlic, salt, coriander, and cumin, and mix well.

4. Chop the shrimp into bite-size pieces, and add them to the tomato mixture. Fold in the avocado, being careful not to break up the dice.

5. Serve the salad cool or at room temperature with the bisque.

YIELD: 3 CUPS

oysters rockefeller
soup with herbsaint cream

Oysters Rockefeller was born in the French Quarter, created by Jules Alciatore, the owner of Antoine's Restaurant, in 1899, and it's still on the menu there, more than 115 years later. It is a much-loved flavor combination (the balance of the oysters' saltiness with the richness of the sauce) and almost every chef who has spent any time in New Orleans has created a dish that plays on it. Chris Wilson, my culinary director, turned it into this decadent first-course soup. It is offered on our holiday menus at Emeril's, NOLA, and Delmonico's and will be a memorable addition to your own table. Because of its beautiful color, it's a perfect fit for that time of year—plus Gulf oysters are at their briny peak in December and January.

½ cup plus 3 tablespoons Herbsaint (or Pernod or Ricard)

½ cup sour cream

1 tablespoon buttermilk

Salt and freshly ground black pepper

1 pint shucked raw oysters, with their liquor (see Essentials, at left)

5 ounces (about 5 strips) applewood-smoked bacon, chopped

2 cups chopped onions

½ cup chopped celery

½ cup chopped fennel bulb

3 tablespoons minced garlic

10 ounces baby spinach

1¾ cups heavy cream

Small sprigs fresh fennel fronds and torn fresh flat-leaf parsley, for garnish

1. Make the Herbsaint Cream: Pour ½ cup Herbsaint in a small sauté pan over medium-high heat, and bring to a boil. Using a long match and keeping drooping sleeves out of the way, carefully ignite the liqueur and cook until the flames subside on their own and you have about 1½ tablespoons remaining in the pan. Set aside to cool. In a small bowl, whisk the sour cream with the buttermilk, then stir in the reduced Herbsaint to make a smooth cream for drizzling. Season with salt and pepper to taste, and set aside (or refrigerate in an airtight container if you won't be using it the same day).

2. Drain the oysters, pouring their liquor into a measuring cup; if you have 1½ cups, proceed with the recipe. If not, add enough water to the liquor to make 1½ cups, then pour the liquid into a medium bowl, add the oysters, and let sit at room temperature for 1 hour to let the oysters flavor the water.

3. In a medium, heavy-bottomed saucepan over medium heat, cook the bacon, stirring as needed. Once most of the fat has rendered from the bacon, add the onions, celery, fennel, and garlic and cook, stirring a few times, until the vegetables are tender and translucent, about 3 minutes more. Add the oysters with their liquor and bring to a boil.

4. Remove the pan from the heat and let cool briefly. Working in small batches, transfer the soup, spinach, and remaining 3 tablespoons Herbsaint to a blender (for each batch of soup, add a handful of spinach and some of the Herbsaint), and puree until completely smooth, then return to the saucepan. Stir in the cream, and season with salt and pepper to taste. Bring the soup to a very gentle simmer over low heat; don't cook it too much or you'll lose the bright green color of the spinach. This soup can be refrigerated up to 2 days and frozen up to 2 months.

5. To serve, ladle the soup into shallow soup bowls and serve drizzled with the Herbsaint Cream and garnished with the herbs.

YIELD: 6 TO 8 SERVINGS

my way grouper chowder

My hometown is just a stone's throw away from Rhode Island, so I grew up eating both New England– and Rhode Island–style clam chowders. New England style is dairy based, while Rhode Island style has a clear broth, with no milk or cream added. Salt pork is optional in New England chowder, depending on the recipe, but is always there in Rhode Island chowder. In coming up with this recipe, I wanted the salt pork base, as it adds rich flavor and a meatiness that I love in combination with seafood. In a nod to all the time I spend fishing in the Gulf of Mexico, I chose to make this with grouper, but any firm white fish will work. The addition of a final splash of cream is up to you.

2½ pounds grouper, monkfish, tilefish, redfish, or other firm white fish fillets, cut into 1-inch pieces

1 tablespoon Emeril's Creole Seasoning (page 108) or other Creole seasoning

1 tablespoon olive oil

8 ounces salt pork, cut into ¼-inch dice

3 cups chopped yellow onions

1½ cups chopped celery

1½ cups chopped red bell peppers

2 tablespoons minced garlic

1 tablespoon salt, plus more for seasoning

½ teaspoon cayenne pepper

3 pounds russet potatoes (about 3 large), peeled and cut into ½-inch dice

2½ quarts Fish Stock (recipe follows)

3 tablespoons chopped fresh flat-leaf parsley

Freshly ground black pepper, to taste

½ cup heavy cream (optional)

1. Season the grouper with the Creole seasoning, cover, and refrigerate until ready to use.

2. Heat the oil and salt pork in a large pot or cast iron Dutch oven over medium heat. Cook the salt pork, stirring as needed, until crisped and its fat is rendered, 8 to 10 minutes. Add the onions, celery, and bell peppers and cook, stirring often, until the vegetables soften, about 5 minutes. Add the garlic, salt, and cayenne and cook 1 minute. Add the potatoes and stock, bring to a boil, reduce the heat to low, and simmer, uncovered, until the potatoes are fork-tender, 15 to 20 minutes.

3. Add the grouper and simmer until cooked through, about 5 minutes. Stir in the parsley. Season to taste with salt and black pepper as needed. Stir in the cream, if desired, and serve.

YIELD: 3 QUARTS, 6 TO 8 SERVINGS

fish stock

1 tablespoon olive oil

Bones and head (gills removed) from a 5- to 5½-pound grouper or other firm white fish, rinsed

2 onions, sliced

2 carrots, chopped

2 ribs celery, chopped

1 head garlic, halved

1 cup dry white wine

3 quarts cold water

2 lemons, halved

8 bay leaves

1 cup coarsely chopped fresh flat-leaf parsley, including stems

1 sprig fresh thyme or 1 teaspoon dried

¾ teaspoon black peppercorns

Heat the oil in a large stockpot over medium heat. Add the bones, onions, carrots, celery, and garlic and cook, stirring, for about 5 minutes. Add the wine and water. Squeeze the lemon juice into the pot and add the rinds, bay leaves, parsley, thyme, and peppercorns. Increase the heat to medium-high; when it begins to boil, reduce the heat to low and simmer for 45 minutes. Remove from the heat and let cool for a bit. Strain through a fine-mesh strainer into another container. Use the stock immediately, or let it cool and refrigerate up to 1 week or freeze for 3 months.

YIELD: 2½ QUARTS

The best way to make this is to buy a whole grouper at the fish counter; you'll need one that weighs 5 to 5½ pounds. Have the fishmonger clean and filet it for you and tell him you want to take the head (ask him to remove the gills) and bones to make stock.

•

To keep the potatoes from browning, as you cut them, place them in a container of water; drain before adding to the pot.

MEAT
& POULTRY

"Pork fat rules!" was one of my mottoes on *Emeril Live* and still is. I love the full, rich flavor of a pork shoulder studded with garlic, rubbed down with a chipotle-fueled spice mix, and then braised for hours, bathing in its own delicious, slowly melting fat. It comes apart in tasty shreds with the touch of a fork in my Pork Shoulder Tacos with Oven-Roasted Salsa (page 112). Pork ribs count as one of my food groups. Beef, lamb, and poultry are favorites, too, and the recipes in this chapter showcase what I love best about each of these proteins and cuts—from roasted rack of lamb with a crunchy rosemary-mustard crust (page 114) to buttermilk fried chicken spiked with hot sauce and served with a spicy-sweet pepper jelly (page 126).

I even show you how to prepare your own duck confit from scratch (make it once and I guarantee it will always be in your refrigerator—it's that easy). Along the way, I'll teach you about searing, braising, pan-frying, and much more.

veal parmesan
with fresh tomato sauce

One of my favorite Italian restaurants in New York City is Il Vagabondo on East 62nd Street. It opened nearly 50 years ago as a bar where locals could play bocce on the indoor court, which is still there. My wife and I have enjoyed delicious meals there, including the best veal Parmesan I've ever had. Frying the veal in olive oil and butter yields a rich, crunchy coating.

6 tablespoons (¾ stick) unsalted butter

6 tablespoons olive oil

2 ounces thinly sliced pancetta or 2 strips bacon, chopped

½ cup finely chopped yellow onion

1 tablespoon minced garlic

½ cup dry vermouth

2 to 2½ pounds vine-ripened tomatoes, preferably heirloom, roughly chopped

1 tablespoon chopped fresh basil

1 teaspoon chopped fresh flat-leaf parsley

1 teaspoon chopped fresh oregano

1 teaspoon crushed red pepper

1 cup all-purpose flour

1 cup plain dry breadcrumbs, preferably homemade

2 tablespoons Emeril's Creole Seasoning (page 108) or other Creole seasoning

1 large egg

½ cup milk

8 thin veal cutlets (about 2½ ounces each)

1 teaspoon salt

½ teaspoon freshly ground black pepper

½ cup finely grated Parmigiano-Reggiano cheese

8 ounces mozzarella cheese, thinly sliced

1. Heat 1 tablespoon of the butter with 1 tablespoon of the oil in a medium saucepan over medium heat. When the butter sizzles, add the pancetta and cook, stirring as needed, until crisp. Transfer to a paper towel–lined plate. Add the onion and cook, stirring, until it is softened, about 6 minutes. Add the garlic and cook until fragrant, about 30 seconds. Add the vermouth, increase the heat to high, and cook for 2 minutes, scraping up any browned bits from the bottom of the pan. Add the tomatoes, herbs, and red pepper. Bring to a boil. Reduce the heat to medium-low, stir in the pancetta, and simmer until the sauce thickens slightly, stirring occasionally, about 20 minutes. Keep warm until ready to use. Preheat the broiler.

2. Place the flour and breadcrumbs each in a shallow bowl and season each with 1 tablespoon Creole seasoning. Beat together the egg and milk in a shallow bowl. Follow the steps for preparing the cutlets (opposite).

3. Heat the remaining 5 tablespoons each butter and oil in a large, heavy-bottomed skillet over medium-high heat until sizzling. Add the veal and cook until golden, about 2 minutes per side (you may need to do this in two batches). Transfer veal to ovenproof platter, and sprinkle cutlets with salt and pepper.

4. Spoon the tomato sauce over each cutlet, then top with a sprinkling of Parmigiano and a slice of mozzarella. Place the platter under the broiler until the cheese is slightly melted and starting to brown, 2 to 3 minutes. Serve immediately.

YIELD: 4 SERVINGS, 2 CUTLETS PER PERSON

pan-frying cutlets

The method I use here for coating the cutlets—dredging in flour, dipping in egg wash, then dredging in breadcrumbs—seals in the moisture and yields a crunchy crust. You can also use it with fish fillets (skip the pounding step) and chicken or pork cutlets.

1. To cook evenly, cutlets should be pounded between two sheets of plastic wrap to a thickness of about ⅛ inch.

2. Working with one cutlet at a time, first dredge it in the flour, coating it completely on both sides and tapping off any excess.

3. Dip both sides in the egg wash, coating the cutlet completely.

4. Dredge both sides in the breadcrumbs. Repeat the process for the rest of the cutlets.

5. Pan-fry the cutlets until golden on both sides and just cooked through.

1

2

3

4

5

barolo-braised short ribs
with mascarpone polenta

I've loved Billy Joel's music all my life, and got to meet him when he came in for dinner at Commander's Palace. We've since become good friends. When I have the opportunity to cook for him and his friends Steve Cohen, Max Loubiere, and Brian Ruggles, I like to make Italian food, which he loves. For this meal, I braised short ribs low and slow in a bottle of Barolo, the king of Italian red wines, and served them with mascarpone polenta.

½ cup all-purpose flour

4½ to 5 pounds beef short ribs

Kosher salt and freshly ground black pepper

2 tablespoons olive oil

3 cups chopped onions

1 cup chopped celery

10 cloves garlic, peeled

1 pound carrots, peeled and cut into 2-inch lengths

1 sprig fresh oregano

1 (750-ml.) bottle light, fruity Barolo wine

Mascarpone Polenta, for serving (recipe follows)

1. Preheat the oven to 300°F. Put the flour in a small bowl. Season the ribs all over with the 1 tablespoon salt and 2 teaspoons pepper, then dredge them completely in the flour, tapping off any excess. Set aside.

2. Heat the oil in a large, heavy-bottomed Dutch oven over medium heat until very hot. Brown the ribs, in batches, until they are nice and crusty on all sides. This will take about 30 minutes in total for all the ribs. As the ribs are browned, transfer them to a platter.

3. Discard all but 1 tablespoon of oil from the Dutch oven and add the onions, celery, garlic, carrots, and oregano. Cook for 2 minutes, stirring as needed, and season to taste with salt and pepper. Return the short ribs to the pot, add the wine, bring to a boil, cover, and transfer to the oven. Cook until the short ribs are very tender, about 2½ hours.

4. Transfer the short ribs and carrots to a platter, and tent with aluminum foil. Skim and discard the fat from the liquid in the pot. Bring the cooking liquid to a simmer over medium-high heat and reduce for 5 minutes, until bubbles break the entire surface. Strain the liquid through a large-hole strainer, pressing the onions, garlic, and celery with a spoon against the strainer. Discard the solids. Return the strained sauce to the Dutch oven along with the short ribs and carrots, cover, and keep warm. Serve the short ribs and carrots over the polenta, drizzled with the sauce.

YIELD: 4 TO 6 SERVINGS

mascarpone polenta

3 cups whole milk

3 cups water

2 tablespoons unsalted butter

2 teaspoons salt

1½ cups polenta or yellow cornmeal

1 (8-ounce) container mascarpone

1. In a 2-quart heavy-bottomed saucepan, combine the milk, water, butter, and salt. Bring to a boil over medium heat. Don't let it boil over.

2. Add the polenta, whisking constantly until the mixture comes back to a boil. Reduce the heat to a simmer and cook, stirring often, until the polenta is creamy and tender, about 45 minutes.

3. Remove from the heat and stir in the mascarpone. Cover and keep warm until ready to serve.

YIELD: 4 TO 6 SERVINGS

Barolo can be very expensive; I would not use a pricey one to make this (I'd much rather drink it!). Look for what is called a "modern style" Barolo, which is less expensive than the big Barolos built for long-term cellaring. I've also made this using a Barbera; a full-bodied Zinfandel would work, as well.

down home chili
cheeseburger

There are still a couple of old-school spots in New Orleans, such as Frostop, Bud's Broiler, and Lee's Hamburgers, where locals can go to get an old-fashioned griddled burger—thin patties cooked on a flattop or griddle along with bacon, onions, and whatever else might be cooking. I like to make these with 80 percent lean ground beef because that bit of extra fat keeps them moist and juicy. They're great with just the onions, but the chili puts them over the top—it's a burger version of a chili dog, with cheese!

It drives me crazy when I see folks flip their burgers, then press down on them with a spatula—leave them alone! All you're doing is squeezing out the juices. Even before your burger hits the grill, try to handle the ground beef as little as possible when you're forming it into patties—if you overwork the meat, you'll end up with a tough burger.

1½ pounds ground chuck, preferably 80% lean

1 tablespoon olive oil

1 cup thinly sliced yellow onion

1 teaspoon Emeril's Creole Seasoning (page 108) or other Creole seasoning

Fine sea salt and freshly ground black pepper

2 teaspoons Worcestershire sauce

8 ounces sharp Cheddar cheese, cut into 8 slices

4 hamburger buns

Down Home Chili (recipe follows)

1. Form the ground beef into 8 patties about ⅓ inch thick. Preheat a griddle or cast iron skillet over medium-high heat until hot. Add the oil to the griddle. Season the onion slices with ¼ teaspoon each of the Creole seasoning, salt, and pepper. Add the onions to the griddle and cook, stirring until lightly golden, about 8 minutes.

2. Lightly season the patties on both sides with the remaining ¾ teaspoon Creole seasoning, ¾ teaspoon salt, ¼ teaspoon pepper, and the Worcestershire. Push the onions off to one side, then place the patties on the hot griddle and cook for 3 to 4 minutes for medium, turning once halfway through. Flip the patties again, add 1 slice of cheese to the top of each, and continue to cook for 1 to 2 minutes, until cheese is melted. Place the hamburger buns, cut sides down, on the griddle, and cook until warmed through and lightly toasted, about 2 minutes.

3. For each burger, place one toasted bun on a serving plate. Place one patty on the bottom half of the bun, spoon chili on top of the patty, and top with a second patty and more chili. Place a portion of onions on the chili, and finish off with the top of the bun. Serve immediately.

YIELD: 4 SERVINGS

down home chili

2 tablespoons vegetable oil

2 cups chopped yellow onions

1 tablespoon minced garlic

2 tablespoons chili powder

2 teaspoons ground cumin

1 teaspoon Emeril's Creole Seasoning (page 108) or other Creole seasoning

1 teaspoon salt

¼ teaspoon freshly ground black pepper

1½ pounds ground beef, preferably 80% lean

1 (14.5-ounce) can peeled whole tomatoes, undrained

2 tablespoons tomato paste

1 teaspoon light brown sugar

2 cups beef stock or low-sodium beef broth

1. In a heavy-bottomed 6-quart pot, heat the oil over medium-high heat. Add the onions, garlic, chili powder, cumin, Creole seasoning, salt, and pepper, and cook, stirring, until the onions are softened, about 4 minutes. Add the beef and cook, stirring, until the meat is brown and cooked through, about 5 minutes, breaking up any clumps. Spoon off and discard the rendered fat.

2. Crush the tomatoes with your hands and add them to the pot along with their juices. Add the tomato paste, brown sugar, and stock; stir well and bring to a boil. Reduce the heat to medium-low and simmer, uncovered, until thickened, 50 to 55 minutes. Keep warm until ready to serve.

YIELD: 6 CUPS

classic steak au poivre
with brandy cream sauce

There is a reason some recipes, like steak au poivre, are classics—they satisfy the taste buds in a way that never goes out of style. A steakhouse and French restaurant staple, steak au poivre is easy to make and the kind of dish your guests won't forget.

½ cup black peppercorns

4 (8- to 10-ounce) New York strip, ribeye, or petite filet steaks, 1 inch thick

¼ cup Dijon mustard

2 teaspoons coarse salt

2 tablespoons olive oil

½ cup minced shallots

2 tablespoons minced garlic

½ cup brandy

2 cups beef stock or low-sodium beef broth

¾ cup heavy cream

3 tablespoons chopped fresh flat-leaf parsley

1. Use the bottom of a small skillet to crack the peppercorns by pressing repeatedly on the skillet in a rocking motion. Rearrange and press on the peppercorns until they are all split open.

2. Lightly brush the steaks with the mustard on one side, and press the mustard side into the peppercorns to coat. Brush the other side of the steaks with the remaining mustard, turn them over, and press into the peppercorns to coat as well. Season both sides with the salt, and set aside on a plate.

3. Heat the oil in a large skillet over medium-high heat until very hot but not so hot that the oil begins to smoke. Add the steaks, reduce the heat to medium, and sear for 4 to 5 minutes on each side to develop a crust, turning them carefully with a metal spatula. Remove the steaks from the pan to a plate.

4. Add the shallots and garlic and cook, stirring, for 30 seconds. Add the brandy, and cook until reduced to about 1 tablespoon; if you like, you can flambé it (see opposite). Add the stock, increase the heat to high, and cook until the liquid has reduced to about ¼ cup. Stir in the cream and any juices that have accumulated on the plate holding the steaks. Let heat through for 1 minute or to the desired consistency; stir in the parsley.

5. Transfer the steaks to a serving platter or individual dinner plates. Pour the sauce over the steaks, and serve immediately.

YIELD: 4 SERVINGS

taking temperature

The best way to ensure a steak is cooked how you like it is to test it with a meat thermometer—I cook mine to 128°F, which after a five-minute rest will increase another 5 degrees or so, yielding a medium-rare steak. There is no crime in using a thermometer when you cook. All of the cooks in my kitchens—including me—carry thermometers.

making a pan sauce

A pan sauce is made from the flavor drippings left in the skillet after you've cooked a cutlet or steak. It's quick and easy and can be done from ingredients you have on hand.

1. Add chopped shallots (plus garlic if you like) to the pan and sauté until softened.

2. Add the brandy or another alcohol like wine or sherry. You can flambé it, which will help it reduce faster and burn off some of the alcohol. To light it, use a long match. If at any time you feel uncomfortable with the flames, put a lid on the skillet.

3. When the alcohol has reduced sufficiently, add stock or broth. Also, pour in any juices from the plate your protein is sitting on. Reduce this to ¼ cup, scraping up any browned bits that might be stuck to the bottom of the pan.

4. Enrich the sauce by adding heavy cream.

5. Pour the sauce over your steak and enjoy!

1

2

3

4

5

roy choi

I first started following Roy when he was crisscrossing Los Angeles selling Korean barbecue tacos out of food trucks. Colleagues from L.A. were calling and saying, this guy is doing crazy things. Then as I was getting ready to fly to Alaska for the *Top Chef* semifinal—where Roy was going to be a guest judge—I got a call from Shep Gordon, a mutual friend who is also Roy's agent. "Roy's written a book and you're in the book. Actually, let me rephrase that—you're a chapter in the book." He went on to say, "I don't want you to be caught off guard, but there's a personal story here—you changed his life—and he may be talking about it when you meet him."

And he left it at that.

So Roy and I met for the first time in Alaska and our assignment was to cook a meal for the three semifinalists that reflected the moment when we knew we wanted to be a chef. I made skillet cornbread because, when I was ten, I worked at a Portuguese bakery in my hometown, Fall River, Massachusetts, washing pots and pans. The bakers took a liking to me and taught me how to make bread, and that was the end of it for me—I knew food was my future. Roy prepared a Korean short rib dish, which I assumed he picked because his mega success began with his short rib tacos.

But when we sat down to eat, I found out that was not the case. Roy told the group this incredible story of

having hit rock bottom in his twenties after numerous addictions and bad choices, lying on the couch and watching me on *Essence of Emeril* and having an almost out-of-body experience, with me coming out of the TV, smacking him in the head, and yelling, "What are you doing? Smell this, taste that. Do something with your life." He picked himself up off the couch and never looked back.

I was stunned. I had tears in my eyes. And what am I cooking on that show? Braised short ribs in red wine.

So, for this book I wanted to return the compliment and riff on Roy's tacos, which are a culinary mashup of the tastes of L.A. Instead of short ribs, I chose that old reliable pot roast cut, beef chuck roast, giving it a good, long soaking in a Korean-inspired marinade before braising it into a shredded pile of goodness.

roy choi–inspired korean-style
pot roast tacos

These tacos are all about the interplay of flavor and texture: beef chuck braised in a sweet-sour-savory-salty barbecue marinade until a fork can shred it, nestled in a warm tortilla with vinegary sesame cucumber slices and a kimchee-fired coleslaw.

1/2 cup peeled, cored, and chopped Asian pear (about 1/2 medium pear)

1/2 cup peeled, cored, and chopped Granny Smith apple (about 1/2 small apple)

1/2 cup chopped yellow onion

4 cloves garlic, minced

2 green onions, cut into 1-inch lengths

3 tablespoons soy sauce

2 tablespoons toasted sesame oil

1 tablespoon light brown sugar

2 teaspoons Korean red chili paste (*gochujang*)

2 teaspoons mirin

1 (3- to 4-pound) beef chuck roast

2 tablespoons vegetable oil

FOR SERVING:

Warm flour tortillas

Hot Sesame Pickled Cucumbers (page 104)

Quick Kimchee Coleslaw (page 104)

Fresh cilantro leaves

Sriracha sauce (optional)

1. In a blender, combine the Asian pear, apple, onion, garlic, green onions, soy sauce, sesame oil, brown sugar, chili paste, and mirin. Process to form a smooth paste, then transfer to a zip-top plastic bag. Add the chuck roast, seal the bag, and move the roast all around until it's completely coated with the marinade. Refrigerate overnight.

2. Remove the bag from the refrigerator and let the roast come to room temperature, which will take 1 to 2 hours. Remove it from the bag, reserving the marinade. There's no need to pat the roast dry.

3. Preheat the oven to 350°F.

4. Heat the vegetable oil in a large, heavy-bottomed Dutch oven over medium-high heat until really hot. Add the beef and sear it until well browned and crusty on all sides, 10 to 12 minutes total. Add the reserved marinade, cover, and place in the oven. Cook until you can pull the roast apart with a fork with no resistance, 2½ to 3 hours.

5. Transfer the beef to a cutting board and pull it into shreds with two forks. Return the shredded beef to the pot and cover to keep warm.

6. Prepare the tacos by placing ¼ cup of the beef on each warm tortilla, and top as desired with the pickled cucumbers, coleslaw, and cilantro. Drizzle with Sriracha, if desired. Fold and feast.

YIELD: 12 TACOS, ABOUT 6 SERVINGS

(continued)

The marinade for the pot roast has unbelievable flavor and works equally well with pork, poultry, and cuts of beef beyond chuck roast (I've used it on filet mignon with fantastic results).

hot sesame pickled cucumbers

If you can't find Korean chili paste, substitute Sriracha or Chinese chili garlic sauce, both of which have a similar heat level.

1/4 cup unseasoned rice vinegar

2 tablespoons granulated sugar

1 tablespoon Korean red chili paste (gochujang)

1 teaspoon salt

1 teaspoon toasted sesame oil

1 teaspoon sesame seeds

6 Persian or small Kirby cucumbers, cut into 1/8-inch-thick rounds

1 clove garlic, thinly sliced

1 green onion, thinly sliced on a diagonal

1. Combine the vinegar, sugar, and chili paste in a small saucepan and bring to a simmer, stirring to dissolve the sugar. Once it has dissolved, remove the pan from the heat. Add the remaining ingredients, and toss until the cucumbers are well coated with the vinegar mixture.

2. Refrigerate the mixture in an airtight container or covered bowl for at least 12 hours before serving. The cucumbers will keep for 2 to 3 days, though they will be less crisp after the first day. Serve chilled or at room temperature.

YIELD: 2 CUPS, ENOUGH FOR 12 TACOS

quick kimchee coleslaw

Barbecue sandwiches are traditionally enjoyed with a vinegary coleslaw on the side or right on the sandwich. For these tacos, I wanted a Korean twist, so I used rice vinegar instead of the usual cider or white vinegar, and added store-bought kimchee to give the slaw an extra kick of heat, sour, and salt.

1/2 small head napa cabbage, cored and shredded

2 medium carrots, peeled and cut into thin shreds with a vegetable peeler

1/4 cup chopped kimchee

2 tablespoons unseasoned rice vinegar

1 teaspoon salt

1 teaspoon granulated sugar

1 teaspoon chopped fresh cilantro

1 teaspoon toasted sesame oil

Chopped roasted peanuts or cashews, for garnish

1. Combine all the ingredients except the peanuts in a large bowl, cover, and refrigerate until ready to use. It can be made several days in advance; the cabbage will soften as it sits but the flavor will still be delicious. If you like crunch in your coleslaw, serve it as soon as possible after making it.

2. Garnish with the roasted peanuts, and serve.

YIELD: 4 CUPS, ENOUGH FOR 12 TACOS

roasted portuguese pork loin
with homemade pimenta moida

This is my taste memory of the pork loin my mom made. A key component (as it was for my mother's) is *pimenta moida*. *Pimenta moida* (pronounced mweeda) is a pepper sauce that originated in the Azores. Portuguese immigrants brought it with them, and it can be found in areas with Portuguese communities, such as Fall River, New Bedford, and Swansea, Massachusetts. Or you can make your own, like my dad used to.

1 (3½- to 4-pound) boneless pork loin, preferably with fat cap still attached

Kosher salt and freshly ground black pepper

3 tablespoons minced garlic

1 cup Homemade Pimenta Moida (recipe follows)

½ cup chopped fresh cilantro

½ cup plus 2 tablespoons extra-virgin olive oil, preferably Portuguese or Spanish

1½ to 2 pounds Yukon Gold potatoes, cut into 1½-inch pieces

1. Using a sharp knife, score the fat on the top of the roast in a crosshatch pattern, cutting just into the meat layer so the marinade can penetrate it. Place the roast in a baking pan and season on all sides with 2 teaspoons salt and 1 teaspoon pepper. Pat the garlic all over the roast, then coat on all sides with the *pimenta moida*, rubbing the seasonings into the slits on the top of the roast. Sprinkle the cilantro all over the roast, then drizzle with ½ cup of the oil, and rub all the seasonings to evenly distribute. Cover with plastic wrap, and refrigerate overnight.

2. Allow the roast to come to room temperature, 1½ to 2 hours. Preheat the oven to 425°F. Transfer the roast to a baking pan large enough to hold it and the potatoes in one layer. Drizzle some of the marinade juices over the top of the roast. Place the potatoes in the first pan and toss with the remaining marinade. Add the potatoes and marinade to the roast, arranging the potatoes around it; sprinkle the potatoes with the remaining ¼ teaspoon salt

and pinch of pepper, and drizzle with the remaining 2 tablespoons oil. Roast the pork until lightly golden and the slits on top of the roast have opened up, 25 to 30 minutes.

3. Reduce the oven temperature to 350°F and cook until an instant-read thermometer inserted into the center of the roast registers 140°F, 35 to 40 minutes longer. Remove from the oven and set aside to rest at least 15 minutes before serving. (If the potatoes are not yet golden around the edges and cooked through, transfer the roast to a plate, then return the potatoes to the oven and roast for 10 to 15 minutes longer while the meat rests.) Carve the roast into thin slices and serve with the potatoes, drizzling any pan drippings over the pork.

YIELD: 6 TO 8 SERVINGS

homemade pimenta moida

1¾ pounds red medium-hot chiles, such as Fresno	½ cup plus 2 tablespoons distilled white vinegar
3½ tablespoons fine sea salt	½ cup water
	Olive oil, for storing (optional)

1. Remove and discard the stems from the chiles, and deseed half. Coarsely chop the chiles. Place in a blender along with the salt, and process until it becomes a semi-smooth mixture—still with some texture. Transfer to a saucepan and bring to a simmer over medium heat. Cook until the peppers soften a bit, 4 to 5 minutes.

2. Remove the pan from the heat and stir in the vinegar and water. Cool to room temperature, then transfer to clean jars with tight-fitting lids. Top with a bit of olive oil, if desired, then refrigerate the pepper sauce until ready to use; it will keep up to several months.

YIELD: ABOUT 3 CUPS

Pimenta moida *can be found online, sold by its Portuguese name or as hot crushed or chopped peppers; I like the Star brand.*

•

Choosing a pork loin with a nice fat cap is important to the success of this dish. The cap really helps keep the meat from drying out and also gives it flavor.

slow and low
pork candy ribs

This recipe is loosely based on Chinese *char sui* BBQ, the ribs rubbed with an East-West mix of Chinese five-spice powder (with the dominant sweet note of star anise) and spicy hot Creole seasoning.

2 tablespoons plus ½ teaspoon Chinese five-spice powder

2 tablespoons Emeril's Creole Seasoning (recipe follows) or other Creole seasoning

1 teaspoon ground ginger

2 (2½-pound) slabs St. Louis or baby back pork ribs

½ cup hoisin sauce

⅓ cup soy sauce

¼ cup shaoxing rice wine (or pale dry sherry)

3 tablespoons light brown sugar

3 tablespoons honey

2 tablespoons Vietnamese chili garlic sauce (*tuong ot toi*)

2 tablespoons fresh lime juice

1½ tablespoons minced garlic

1 tablespoon toasted sesame oil

1 tablespoon minced peeled fresh ginger

1. Preheat the oven to 300°F.

2. In a small bowl, combine 2 tablespoons of the Chinese five-spice powder, the Creole seasoning, and ground ginger.

3. Lay each slab of ribs, meaty side up, on a piece of aluminum foil that is long enough to wrap it up completely. Rub the ribs on both sides with the spice mixture, using it all up. Wrap the ribs well, sealing all the edges of the foil to make an airtight packet. Place the packets in a single layer on a baking sheet, and bake until the meat is so tender you can pull it off the bone, about 3 hours.

4. In a small bowl, combine the remaining ingredients (including the remaining ½ teaspoon five-spice powder) and blend until smooth. (The sauce yields 2 cups.)

5. After 3 hours, remove the ribs from the oven, open the foil packets, and baste the ribs with the sauce. Return the ribs to the oven, uncovered, and cook for 15 minutes longer. Baste the ribs again and return to the oven until they look glossy, about another 15 minutes.

6. Remove the ribs from the oven and let stand for 15 minutes. Using a sharp knife, cut the slabs into individual ribs and serve with the remaining sauce.

YIELD: 6 SERVINGS

emeril's
creole seasoning

This is a close approximation to my Emeril's Original Essence, sold in supermarkets.

5 tablespoons sweet paprika	2 tablespoons cayenne pepper
¼ cup salt	2 tablespoons dried oregano
¼ cup garlic powder	
2 tablespoons freshly ground black pepper	2 tablespoons dried thyme
2 tablespoons onion powder	

In a small bowl, combine all the ingredients thoroughly. Store in an airtight container for up to 6 months.

YIELD: MAKES ABOUT 1⅓ CUPS

I am not a believer in cooking ribs on the grill. It's too easy for them to get overcooked or to apply the sauce too soon and have it burn into a bitter mess. This slow and low oven method guarantees melt-in-your-mouth tenderness and flavor that will blow the top of your head off. What's not to like?

fall river chow mein

One of my favorite food memories growing up was at least once a week going to either Mee Sum or China Royal to get a chow mein sandwich to go. Served on a hamburger bun, complete with crispy chow mein noodles, the sandwich originated in Fall River in the 1930s or '40s; you can find it in neighboring towns in Massachusetts and Rhode Island, but nowhere else. Once I left Massachusetts, I still had to have my fix, so my mom would send me boxes of Hoo-Mee Chow Mein mix, which includes the noodles and the gravy packet, so I could make my own.

I've since turned it into a main course that has become a family favorite, made from scratch using all fresh ingredients, including frying up my own crispy noodles. If you prefer to use store-bought chow mein noodles, you won't get any complaints from me!

Vegetable oil, for frying, plus 3 tablespoons

12 ounces wonton wrappers (doesn't matter which size), cut into $1/8$-inch strips

Salt

$2^1/_2$ cups beef stock or low-sodium beef broth

$1/4$ cup shaoxing rice wine (see Essentials, at right)

2 tablespoons black bean paste

2 tablespoons cornstarch

2 teaspoons soy sauce

1 teaspoon toasted sesame oil

$1/2$ teaspoon plus 2 pinches freshly ground black pepper

1 large onion, cut lengthwise into $1/2$-inch strips

3 ribs celery, trimmed and cut on the diagonal into $1/2$-inch-thick slices

4 ounces shiitake or button mushrooms, stems removed (for shiitake) or trimmed and caps thinly sliced

$1^1/_3$ pounds ground pork or beef

2 teaspoons minced garlic

1. Heat at least 2 inches of vegetable oil in a Dutch oven or other heavy-bottomed pot to 350°F. Working in batches, fry the wonton strips until golden, about 30 seconds, stirring so they cook evenly. With a slotted spoon or a spider, transfer the fried wontons to a paper towel–lined baking sheet to drain, and season lightly with salt. Set aside while you make the gravy.

2. In a medium bowl, combine the stock, wine, black bean paste, cornstarch, soy sauce, sesame oil, and $1/2$ teaspoon of the pepper, and stir to mix well. Set aside.

3. Heat a large skillet or wok over high heat. When hot, add the 3 tablespoons vegetable oil. When the oil shimmers, add the onion, celery, and mushrooms, and season with a pinch of salt and a pinch of black pepper. Cook, tossing occasionally, until the vegetables are crisp-tender, 3 to 4 minutes. Transfer to a bowl and set aside.

4. Add the ground meat to the hot skillet and season with a pinch of salt and a pinch of pepper. Cook, stirring with a spoon to break up any clumps, until the meat is nicely browned, 2 to 3 minutes. Add the garlic and cook, stirring, for 1 minute longer. Stir the stock mixture, then add it all at once to the pan and cook, stirring, until the sauce comes to a boil and thickens enough to coat the back of a spoon, 2 to 3 minutes. Stir in the vegetables and, when they are just heated through, serve the chow mein sauce in large bowls spooned over a mound of the crispy noodles.

YIELD: 6 SERVINGS

If you can't find shaoxing rice wine, substitute a pale dry sherry.

111

pork shoulder tacos
with oven-roasted salsa

The layers of flavor in these tacos are mind-blowing. The pork shoulder gets a deep spice massage and garlic injection before being cooked slow and low for hours. The flavors in the salsa are incredibly complex because of the super-hot roasting the ingredients get. Finally, don't skimp on any of the garnishes for serving. They all play a part in a taco that is out-of-control good.

6 cloves garlic, peeled and cut in half if large

1 (3½- to 4-pound) pork shoulder roast (Boston butt), bone-in preferred

¼ cup Spicy South of the Border Seasoning (see opposite)

3 tablespoons olive oil

1 large onion, quartered

2 cups Rich Chicken Stock (page 68) or store-bought low-sodium chicken broth

½ cup coarsely chopped fresh cilantro (stems and leaves)

Salt

FOR SERVING:

Mexican crema, crème fraîche, or sour cream

Fresh cilantro leaves

Avocado slices

Oven-Roasted Salsa (see opposite)

Julienned radishes

Lime wedges

6-inch corn tortillas, toasted in a hot skillet brushed with a bit of oil

1. Using a sharp paring knife, cut as many slits as you have pieces of garlic all over the pork roast, and insert one piece of garlic into each slit. Sprinkle the seasoning mix all over the meat and then rub it into the meat, making sure it all adheres.

2. Preheat the oven to 325°F.

3. Heat a heavy-bottomed Dutch oven just big enough to fit the roast over medium-high heat until hot. Add the oil, then add the roast and sear until it is nicely browned, about 3 minutes per side. Add the onion, stock, and cilantro, bring to a boil, cover, and place in the oven. Braise, turning the roast once midway through the cooking time, until the pork is pull-apart tender, about 3 hours.

4. Remove the pot from the oven and, using two forks, pull the meat into large chunks in the pot. Let the meat cool in the cooking liquid for at least 15 minutes, then pull it into shreds using your hands or two forks, discarding any bones and fatty pockets. Place the meat in a heatproof bowl and add enough of the cooking liquid to keep it moist. Season to taste with salt, cover, and keep warm until you are ready to serve the tacos.

5. When ready to serve, assemble the garnishes and toast the tortillas. Allow diners to prepare the tacos to their liking.

YIELD: 6 TO 8 SERVINGS

spicy south of the border seasoning

This is a great all-purpose seasoning for taco fillings, soups, refried beans—you name it.

2 tablespoons chipotle chile powder

2 tablespoons hot paprika

1 tablespoon salt

1 tablespoon dried Mexican oregano

1 tablespoon ground coriander

1 tablespoon garlic powder

1 tablespoon onion powder

1 tablespoon finely grated lime zest

2 teaspoons ground cumin

1 teaspoon freshly ground black pepper

1 teaspoon cayenne pepper

1 teaspoon crushed red pepper

Combine all the ingredients thoroughly.

YIELD: ABOUT ¾ CUP

make ahead

If you have the time, braise this pork the day before, let it cool to room temperature in its cooking liquid, then refrigerate. The next day, remove and discard the congealed fat, then reheat the pork in a 325°F oven for 20 to 30 minutes before continuing with the recipe.

oven-roasted salsa

Roasting the vegetables for the salsa at such a high temperature concentrates all the individual flavors and adds a smoky char. This is also great on nachos or just with tortilla chips.

1½ pounds Roma tomatoes, halved

1 large yellow onion, quartered

1 large poblano pepper

1 jalapeño pepper

2 tablespoons olive oil

1 clove garlic, mashed into a paste

¼ cup coarsely chopped fresh cilantro

2 tablespoons fresh lime juice, or more to taste

½ teaspoon salt

1. Preheat the oven to 500°F. Line a large baking sheet with parchment paper.

2. Place the tomatoes, onion quarters, and peppers on the baking sheet and drizzle with the oil. Using your hands, toss and rub the vegetables, making sure they are evenly coated with the oil. Roast on the upper rack of the oven until the skins are blistered and charred in places, 20 to 25 minutes. Turn the vegetables over and continue to cook until blistered and charred in places on the other side, 15 to 20 minutes longer. Remove from the oven and set aside to cool to room temperature.

3. Remove the skins and stems from the peppers and discard. Remove the skins from the tomatoes. Transfer the peppers, tomatoes, onion pieces, and the remaining ingredients to a food processor. Pulse until everything is blended but you still have a slightly chunky texture. Taste and adjust the seasoning if necessary. Set aside at room temperature until ready to serve or refrigerate in an airtight container for up to 1 week (return to room temperature before serving).

YIELD: 2 GENEROUS CUPS

rack of lamb
with apple-mint puree

When I became Chef at Commander's Palace, I was surprised to find no lamb on the menu. I quickly remedied that, adding a rack of lamb that I sourced from a ranch in Colorado. It ended up becoming one of Commander's five most popular dishes.

1 rack of lamb with 8 bones (about 2 pounds), excess fat trimmed

1 tablespoon plus ½ teaspoon Emeril's Creole Seasoning (page 108) or other Creole seasoning

¾ cup plain dry breadcrumbs

2 teaspoons chopped fresh rosemary

¼ cup extra-virgin olive oil

¼ cup Creole or other whole-grain mustard

Apple-Mint Puree, for serving (recipe follows)

4 sprigs fresh mint, for garnish, optional

1. Preheat the oven to 400°F. Line a rimmed baking sheet with parchment paper. Season the lamb rack on all sides with 1 tablespoon of the Creole seasoning; set aside.

2. In a small bowl, combine the breadcrumbs, remaining ½ teaspoon Creole seasoning, the rosemary, and oil, and mix until all the crumbs are moist. Set aside.

3. Heat a 14-inch skillet over medium heat until hot. Place the lamb rack, fat side down, in the pan, and brown well. Give each side a good sear, 18 to 20 minutes in total. Remove the skillet from the heat.

4. When the rack is cool enough to handle, transfer it to the prepared baking sheet. Brush the fat side of the rack generously with the mustard, and top with the breadcrumb mixture, packing it on lightly with your hands to form an even crust. Roast until an instant-read thermometer inserted in the center registers 135°F (medium-rare), 25 to 30 minutes, or to your desired degree of doneness. Remove from

the oven and let rest 15 minutes before carving between the bones.

5. To serve, smear some of the Apple-Mint Puree decoratively on 4 serving plates. Set two chops on the puree so their bones cross one another, and, if desired, garnish with a mint sprig.

YIELD: 4 SERVINGS

apple-mint puree

I've been making a version of this puree for years, which is as close to mint jelly as you'll see me get.

2 medium Pink Lady, Gala, or Fuji apples	2 tablespoons unsalted butter
2 cups apple cider	2 tablespoons chopped fresh mint
¼ cup chopped onion	
3 teaspoons cider vinegar	

1. Peel and core the apples, chop them into 2-inch pieces, and add to a small pot. Add the cider, onion, and 2 teaspoons of the vinegar. Bring to a boil, reduce the heat to a simmer, and cook until the apples are tender and the flavors have come together, about 20 minutes. Remove from the heat.

2. Transfer the apple mixture to a blender and add the butter, mint, and remaining 1 teaspoon vinegar. Blend until you have a smooth puree. Serve warm. This will keep in an airtight container in the refrigerator for several days.

YIELD: 2¾ CUPS

To get a really good sear, pat the lamb dry on both sides with a paper towel before placing it in the hot pan.

•

Finishing the lamb in the oven provides even heat on all sides, allowing the rack to cook evenly and the crust to get crispy and golden without burning.

turkey roulade

I am the roulade king. They take a bit of work to prepare, but they make such a nice presentation at the table and are so easy to carve and serve. Of course, you'll want to offer Sweet Potato Soufflé with Maple Sugar and Pecans (page 201) with this!

1 (3½-pound) boneless turkey breast

1½ tablespoons kosher salt

2 teaspoons freshly ground black pepper

3 cups Sausage Stuffing (recipe follows)

1. Preheat the oven to 350°F.

2. On a large cutting board, place the turkey breast, skin side down, on top of a piece of plastic wrap. Cut the tenders from the breast and save them for another use. Cover the turkey breast with additional plastic wrap, and, using the smooth side of a meat mallet, pound it to an even thickness of a little less than ½ inch (you're going to want to channel every bit of your latent aggression because you need to really strong-arm that mallet to get the breast to that thickness), forming a roughly rectangular piece of meat.

3. Remove the plastic wrap from on top of the turkey, and season both sides of the turkey evenly with the salt and pepper. Spread the stuffing down the length of the turkey in the center, then roll one side up and over the stuffing and continue rolling the entire thing into a long cylinder. Tie the roulade every couple of inches using kitchen twine.

4. Set the roulade on a wire rack set in a roasting pan, and bake until an instant-read thermometer inserted in the center reads 155 °F, 50 to 60 minutes. Remove the pan from the oven and let rest for at least 15 minutes before cutting across into 1-inch-thick slices.

YIELD: 8 SERVINGS

sausage stuffing

This recipe makes more stuffing than you'll need for the roulade. Put the extra in a casserole dish and bake it alongside—if you like, you can bake the entire recipe in a casserole and serve it with another protein.

1 tablespoon extra-virgin olive oil

1 pound mild fresh Italian sausage, casings removed

1½ cups finely diced onion

½ cup finely diced celery

1 tablespoon minced garlic

1 tablespoon chopped fresh sage

½ teaspoon fresh thyme leaves

1 teaspoon salt

½ teaspoon freshly ground black pepper

¼ teaspoon freshly grated nutmeg

1½ cups finely diced cored Pink Lady or Granny Smith apples (leave the peel on)

½ cup roughly chopped chestnuts

1 (11-ounce) bottle hard apple cider, such as Crispin (about 1⅓ cups)

4 cups cubed (½-inch) sourdough bread, toasted in a 350°F oven until crisp

1 large egg, beaten

4 ounces fresh goat cheese, crumbled, at room temperature

1. Heat oil in a medium sauté pan over medium heat. When hot, add the sausage and cook until it begins to brown, 2 to 3 minutes. Add the onion, celery, garlic, sage, thyme, salt, pepper, and nutmeg, and cook, stirring as needed, until the vegetables have softened, 5 minutes. Stir in the apples, chestnuts, and cider, and cook 3 to 4 minutes. Remove the pan from the heat and let cool slightly.

2. Place the bread in a large heat-resistant bowl, pour the onion mixture over it, and toss well. Add the egg and goat cheese, and toss well. Refrigerate until ready to use.

YIELD: 6 TO 8 CUPS

A turkey roulade is a great alternative to the usual roast turkey, particularly if you're not having a huge gathering.

•

Because the turkey breast has no fat to protect it, you've got to roast the roulade on a rack, keeping the breast away from direct contact with the pan.

•

You can leave the chestnuts out or substitute pecans or walnuts.

my brined
roast chicken

Why include a roast chicken in this cookbook? Because I make one for my family every week. I got my first lesson on perfect roast chicken from Julia Child, who believed in trussing the bird and starting it off in a hot oven to jump-start browning, then bringing the temperature down for the remainder of the cooking time. For maximum moistness, I brine my chicken and roast it in a moderate oven for the entire cook time.

2 quarts water

½ cup kosher salt

½ cup sugar

2 sprigs fresh thyme

1 teaspoon black peppercorns

3 heads garlic, halved crosswise

1 (4- to 4½-pound) chicken

2 sprigs fresh thyme

12 ounces carrots, cut crosswise into 1-inch pieces

½ cup chopped celery

2 medium onions, halved and sliced lengthwise into ¼-inch-thick slices

2 tablespoons unsalted butter, softened

Freshly ground black pepper

1. Combine the water, salt, sugar, thyme, peppercorns, and 4 of the garlic halves in a medium saucepan, and bring to a simmer. Remove from the heat and let cool completely.

2. Place the chicken in a bowl large enough to hold it, and add the cooled brine. Cover with plastic wrap, and refrigerate for 4 hours or overnight.

3. Preheat the oven to 350°F.

4. Remove the chicken from the brine and pat dry. Discard the brine. Fill the cavity of the chicken with the remaining garlic halves, thyme, and half of the carrots and celery.

5. Cut a piece of kitchen twine three times the length of the chicken. Position the middle of the string around the end of the legs and tie together with a knot. If present, tie the tail nub of the chicken to the legs to tie the cavity closed. Bring the string around the thigh of the chicken (at the joint), then lift the chicken just enough to cross the string around the back. Bring the twine to the front of the chicken and tie the wings to its sides. Make a knot across the chest of the bird. Cut the twine.

6. Place the remaining carrots and celery and the onions in a baking pan. You can set a roasting rack on top of them and then place the chicken on the rack, or just set the chicken directly on the vegetables. Rub the butter all over the chicken, and sprinkle generously with pepper. Roast the chicken for 1 hour, then baste with the cooking juices in the pan and continue basting periodically until the chicken is nicely browned and an instant-read thermometer inserted in the thigh registers 165°F, another 45 to 60 minutes.

7. Remove the chicken from the oven and let it rest for 20 minutes to allow its juices to redistribute through the meat. Carve into serving pieces and serve with its juice ladled over it.

YIELD: 4 TO 6 SERVINGS

The challenge is keeping the breast meat moist while cooking the thighs and drumsticks all the way through. That's where brining comes in. Giving the chicken a good soak prior to roasting allows the breast meat to absorb extra moisture, ensuring a tender breast and a fully cooked thigh. The sugar in the brine also aids in the browning.

julia child

I first met Julia when I was one of the chefs de cuisine at the restaurant Parker's in the Parker House in Boston. I couldn't have been much older than 20. One day the maître d' came back and told me that Julia Child would be coming for dinner that night. I was super excited. When she came that evening, they called me out to the dining room to meet her, and she asked if I would create a dish for her that wasn't on the menu. It happened that I had periwinkles in the kitchen, something I had grown up with. As a boy, I would gather periwinkles with my parents and then my mother would cook them when we got home. For Julia, I lightly steamed the periwinkles, then took them out of their shells and presented them to her as an appetizer in a beurre blanc sauce I made with Champagne, shallots, and vanilla bean.

Later, I was truly honored when Julia asked me to represent the cooking of New Orleans in her PBS series *Cooking with Master Chefs*. My friends Bill and Anne Grace generously offered up their beautiful home in the Garden District for the shoot, and the first day, I made shrimp étouffée for Julia in their kitchen, with the fresh Gulf shrimp that we are so lucky to have available to us in Louisiana almost year-round.

The second day, we moved outdoors, and I prepared a crawfish boil in the backyard. I'll never forget that day, sitting in the garden at a table piled high with crawfish, showing Julia how to suck the tasty fat from the crawfish head, then to pinch the shell from the tail. She just loved it, and so did I!

Julia was a fabulous lady. She was very intense and serious on the subject of food. It didn't matter whether you were going to make a hamburger or a pâté, she had in her mind the perfect way to do it. Julia was a perfectionist, but at the same time she was a human being. She never called herself a chef; she always referenced herself as Julia, and she paved the way for teaching Americans what a good cook should be.

grill-roasted
lime-chile chicken

I loved what my Southwest chef buddies Stephan Pyles, Mark Miller, and Dean Fearing were doing in their restaurants in the 1990s, and I was inspired to create this dish, which I put on the menu at Emeril's. The dish was a huge success.

1 cup chopped poblano peppers (about 2 chiles)

¾ cup chopped fresh cilantro (stems included)

½ cup chopped onion

1 cup vegetable oil

¼ cup fresh lime juice

1 teaspoon chile powder of your choice

4 cloves garlic, peeled

2 (3- to 4-pound) chickens, halved, with the wishbone, breastbone, backbone, and first and second segments of the wings removed

3 to 4 (6-inch) corn tortillas, cut into ⅛-inch or thinner strips

Emeril's Creole Seasoning (page 108) or other Creole seasoning

Chile-Spiked Stewed Black Beans (page 124)

Pico de Gallo (page 124)

1. Place the poblanos, cilantro, onion, ½ cup of the oil, the lime juice, chile powder, and garlic in a blender, and blend on high until smooth. Transfer ¾ cup of the marinade to a small container, and refrigerate until ready to cook the chicken.

2. Place the chicken halves in large zip-top plastic bags, and divide the remaining marinade between them. Seal the bags and massage the marinade all around until the chicken halves are coated with it. Refrigerate overnight.

3. Preheat a well-oiled grill to medium low. Preheat the oven to 400°F.

4. Remove the chicken from the marinade; discard the marinade. Place the chicken, skin side down, on the grill and cook for 4 to 5 minutes. Carefully, to avoid breaking the skin, turn the chicken 45 degrees and cook for 4 to 5 minutes longer, to create nice grill marks. If you notice hot spots on the grill, alternate the chicken halves between the spots. Turn the chicken skin side up, brush it with the reserved marinade, and cook for another 10 minutes. While the chicken is cooking, you can close the grill, but continue to monitor it so that the grill doesn't begin to flame the chicken. Once the chicken is nicely browned, transfer it to a rimmed baking sheet or large baking dish, brush with the remaining marinade, and roast in the oven until an instant-read thermometer inserted into the thigh registers 165°F, about 20 minutes longer.

5. Heat the remaining ½ cup oil in a 10-inch skillet over medium-high heat. Once the oil is hot, add half the tortilla strips and fry, stirring as needed with a slotted spoon, until golden. Remove from the oil, place on paper towels to drain, and season with a little Creole seasoning. Repeat with the remaining tortilla strips. (You can also fry the tortillas in an electric deep-fryer preheated to 350°F for 2 minutes.)

6. Serve each chicken half in a large shallow bowl over the stewed black beans. Top with the Pico de Gallo and fried tortilla strips.

YIELD: 4 SERVINGS

(continued)

Grilling chicken is tricky for most people and leads them to do nasty things like preboiling it before putting it on the grill. Please don't do that. Starting the chicken on the grill gives you the fire-smoked flavor we all love. Finishing it in the oven makes sure that the pieces are cooked all the way through and allows you to do it without incinerating the outside of the chicken.

chile-spiked stewed black beans

Try these over yellow rice with a side of sliced ripe avocados and tomatoes.

2 tablespoons vegetable oil

2 cups chopped onions

1 cup chopped poblano peppers (about 2 chiles)

1 jalapeño pepper, seeded and chopped

2 tablespoons minced garlic

2 tablespoons ground cumin

1 tablespoon dried oregano

½ cup chopped fresh cilantro (stems included)

1 pound dried black beans, picked over, soaked in water to cover overnight, and drained

11 cups Rich Chicken Stock (page 68) or store-bought low-sodium chicken broth, plus more as needed

1 teaspoon salt

Heat the oil in a large pot over medium heat. When hot, add the onions, poblanos, jalapeño, garlic, cumin, oregano, and cilantro, and cook, stirring as needed, until softened, about 5 minutes. Add the beans and broth, bring to a boil, reduce the heat to a simmer, and cook until the beans are tender, about 3 hours. (The bean cooking liquid should be thickened but the beans still whole.) The beans will keep in an airtight container in the refrigerator for up to 4 days or in the freezer for up to 6 months.

YIELD: ABOUT 2 QUARTS

pico de gallo

This is also delicious served as a fresh salsa for chips.

2 cups chopped seeded plum tomatoes

1 cup chopped tomatillos or plum tomatoes

¼ cup chopped fresh cilantro leaves

3 tablespoons fresh lime juice

4 teaspoons minced garlic

½ teaspoon salt

¼ teaspoon freshly ground black pepper

Combine all the ingredients in a small bowl. Set aside until ready to use, or store in an airtight container in the refrigerator for up to 2 days. Pull it out at least 1 hour before serving so that it can sit at room temperature.

YIELD: ABOUT 3 CUPS

chicken with champagne
and 40 cloves of garlic

The slow cooking of the garlic makes this dish sweet, nutty, and creamy. Some folks like to cut up a whole chicken, but I prefer all thighs—they braise well and the meat stays juicy. I used Champagne because I love the subtle flavor it adds, but any dry white wine could be substituted.

2 tablespoons olive oil

10 to 12 large bone-in chicken thighs (about 5 pounds)

Kosher salt and freshly ground black pepper

40 cloves garlic, peeled (3 whole heads)

¼ cup fresh lemon juice, or to taste

1 cup Champagne or other dry sparkling or white wine

2 cups Rich Chicken Stock (page 68) or store-bought low-sodium chicken broth

6 sprigs fresh thyme

3 tablespoons all-purpose flour

2 tablespoons unsalted butter, at room temperature

3 tablespoons chopped fresh flat-leaf parsley

1. Preheat the oven to 325°F. Heat a large, heavy-bottomed Dutch oven over medium-high heat. When hot, add the oil. Season the chicken on both sides with 2 teaspoons salt and 1 teaspoon pepper. Working in batches so as to not crowd the pot, sear the chicken, skin side down, until golden brown, about 6 minutes per batch. Brown briefly on the second side, then transfer the browned chicken to a plate.

2. Add the garlic to the pot and cook, stirring, until lightly golden, 1 to 2 minutes. Add the lemon juice, Champagne, broth, and thyme, and return the chicken to the pot, nestling the pieces down into the liquid. Make sure some of the garlic is sitting on top of the chicken. Bring the liquid to a boil, cover the pot, and place in the oven. Cook, stirring once midway to ensure even cooking, until the chicken is falling-off-the-bone tender, about 1 hour and 15 minutes.

3. Transfer the chicken and some of the garlic to a platter, and cover to keep warm. Remove and discard the thyme sprigs.

4. In a medium bowl, mash the flour and butter together to form a smooth paste. Slowly whisk ½ cup of the hot juices from the pot into the paste until smooth, then add this mixture to the pot along with 2 tablespoons of the parsley, and whisk to combine. Don't worry if some of the garlic cloves get smashed—they will help to thicken and enrich the sauce. Cover and cook over medium heat until the gravy has thickened, 10 to 20 minutes longer. Season the sauce with ½ teaspoon salt and ¼ teaspoon pepper, or more to taste. Serve the chicken with the gravy spooned over the top and sprinkled with the remaining 1 tablespoon parsley.

YIELD: 6 TO 8 SERVINGS

spicy buttermilk
fried chicken with pepper jelly drizzle

In this twist on fried chicken, the traditional buttermilk soak is jet-fueled with hot sauce, imparting a heat that penetrates down into the moist flesh of the bird. The Pepper Jelly Drizzle adds a delicious sweet-hot pop.

1 quart buttermilk

¼ cup hot sauce (I like Crystal for this)

3 tablespoons minced garlic

2 teaspoons celery salt

Salt and freshly ground black pepper

1 (3½- to 4-pound) chicken, cut into 8 serving pieces

4 cups all-purpose flour

4 large eggs

½ cup milk

Vegetable oil, for frying

Pepper Jelly Drizzle, for serving (recipe follows)

1. In a large bowl, whisk together the buttermilk, hot sauce, garlic, celery salt, 2 teaspoons salt, and 1 tablespoon pepper. Add the chicken, making sure it is evenly coated with the buttermilk mixture. Cover and refrigerate overnight.

2. Remove the chicken from the refrigerator and let come to room temperature, about 1 hour. Remove it from the marinade; discard the marinade.

3. In another large bowl, whisk together the flour, 5 teaspoons salt, and 4 teaspoons pepper. In a medium bowl, whisk the eggs, milk, and 1 teaspoon salt to combine. Working with one piece of chicken at a time, dredge the chicken completely in the flour, shaking to remove any excess, then dip it in the egg wash, allowing any extra to drip off, then give it a final roll in the flour. As you coat each piece, place it on a wire rack.

Allow it to sit on the rack for 20 to 30 minutes—this will help "set" the crust.

4. Heat 1½ to 2 inches of oil in a large cast iron skillet with high sides or Dutch oven to 325°F (don't fill it more than half full with the oil). Working in batches, fry the chicken, turning it occasionally to promote even browning, until golden brown and crispy on all sides and cooked all the way through, 15 to 20 minutes. Wings and breasts will cook more quickly than the drumsticks and thighs. Transfer to a wire rack to drain, and let cool briefly before serving with Pepper Jelly Drizzle.

YIELD: 4 SERVINGS

pepper jelly drizzle

½ cup minced, seeded red bell pepper

1 tablespoon crushed red pepper

¾ cup cider vinegar

3¼ cups sugar

2 jalapeño peppers, thinly sliced

2 Fresno chiles, thinly sliced (or substitute red jalapeño or Thai chiles)

1 clove garlic, minced

Pinch of salt

In a food processor or blender, combine the bell pepper, crushed red pepper, and vinegar, and blend for a few seconds. Transfer to a medium, heavy-bottomed saucepan and stir in the remaining ingredients. Heat over high heat until it comes to a vigorous boil that cannot be stirred down. Remove from the heat and let cool to room temperature undisturbed (stirring will encourage the formation of sugar crystals). Use immediately, or store in an airtight container in the refrigerator for up to 6 months.

YIELD: ABOUT 3 CUPS

Refrigerating the chicken overnight in the buttermilk–hot sauce–garlic marinade ensures that the fried chicken will be moist and full flavored.

To avoid fried chicken that is uncooked in the middle, keep the temperature of the oil close to 325°F, and don't let it get higher than 350°F.

louisiana-style cassoulet

I spent most of a year cooking in restaurants in France. One of the side benefits was that I got to eat a lot of cassoulet. Depending on where I ate it, the method stayed the same, but what went into it changed: the types of beans, the kind of sausage, did it have confit, did it have offal? I realized, because it's a homey dish, cooks put into it what they had on hand. I mention this because folks can get caught up in thinking that a dish has to be made in a particular way to be "authentic."

This is my American interpretation of cassoulet, via South Louisiana, which starts with a deeply toasted roux. Pancetta, pork butt, smoked sausage, and ham all contribute different layers of flavor. For a further change-up, I make it with chicken confit, though you can certainly use duck (see page 134).

1/4 cup (1/2 stick) unsalted butter

1/4 cup all-purpose flour

1 (2-ounce) slice pancetta, diced

1 cup finely diced yellow onion

1/2 cup finely diced celery

1/2 cup finely diced carrot

3 cloves garlic, minced

1/2 teaspoon kosher salt

1/4 teaspoon freshly ground black pepper

1 1/2 pounds boneless pork butt, trimmed of fat if necessary and cut into 1-inch cubes

1 pound smoked sausage, cut into 1 1/2-inch pieces

8 ounces ham, cut into 1-inch cubes

2 1/2 cups Rich Chicken Stock (page 68) or store-bought low-sodium chicken broth

1 bay leaf

1/2 teaspoon chopped fresh thyme

Cannellini Beans (page 130)

Chicken Confit (page 130), leg quarters cut apart into drumsticks and thighs

1 cup plain dry breadcrumbs (coarsely ground homemade crumbs are best)

1/2 cup freshly grated Parmigiano-Reggiano cheese

3 tablespoons chopped fresh flat-leaf parsley

2 tablespoons olive oil

1. Melt the butter in a large Dutch oven over medium heat. Add the flour and stir constantly until you have a roux the color of peanut butter (see page 83). Add the pancetta and cook, stirring, for 2 minutes to render some of the fat and brown the meat. Add the onion, celery, carrot, garlic, salt, and pepper, and cook, stirring, until the vegetables are tender, 3 to 4 minutes. Add the pork butt and cook, stirring, until the meat begins to brown, about 5 minutes. Add the sausage pieces and cook another 2 minutes, turning the sausage several times to brown. Add the ham, stock, bay leaf, and thyme, and stir well to pick up any brown bits that may be stuck to the bottom of the pan. Increase the heat to medium-high, and bring to a boil.

2. Add the beans, and place the chicken pieces on top. Reduce the heat to medium-low, cover the pot, and cook for about 1 hour. The liquid should be gently bubbling; you may need to adjust the heat.

3. Preheat the oven to 450°F. In a small bowl, combine the breadcrumbs, cheese, parsley, and oil, and mix well. Spoon the mixture evenly over the top of the cassoulet, and bake until the crumbs have slightly browned, about 10 minutes.

4. Serve the cassoulet in large shallow bowls, making sure to include all the components.

YIELD: 8 SERVINGS

(continued)

The final sprinkling of breadcrumbs and Parmesan on top of the cassoulet and its crisping in the oven are key to the success of the dish—it offers a textural contrast to the soft richness of the cassoulet.

•

Once the confit is used up, any remaining oil can be stored in an airtight container in the refrigerator and used to fry potatoes.

129

cannelini beans

If you like, you can make the cassoulet with canned beans (just be sure to rinse and drain them well before using), but the flavor of freshly cooked is so much better.

1 tablespoon olive oil

½ cup chopped yellow onion

¼ cup chopped celery

¼ cup chopped carrot

1 pound dried cannellini beans, picked over, soaked overnight in water to cover, and drained

2 quarts water

½ teaspoon salt

¼ teaspoon freshly ground black pepper

2 bay leaves

1. In a medium Dutch oven or heavy-bottomed saucepan, heat the oil over medium heat. Add the onion, celery, and carrot and cook, stirring, until the vegetables are slightly wilted, 3 to 4 minutes. Add the remaining ingredients, and increase the heat to high. Bring to a boil, then reduce the heat to medium-low, partially cover, and cook the beans, stirring occasionally, until they are tender but not falling apart, about 2 hours.

2. Cool the beans in their cooking liquid and set aside until ready to use. The beans can be made ahead of time and stored in an airtight container in the refrigerator for 2 to 3 days or frozen for up to 6 months.

YIELD: 2 QUARTS

chicken confit

I'll be honest, chicken confit is not nearly as rich as duck, but it's still darn good and a less expensive alternative. Any leftovers can be used to make a tasty hash or chicken salad.

2 chicken leg portions with thighs attached, excess fat trimmed and reserved

Kosher salt and freshly ground black pepper

5 cloves garlic, peeled

2 bay leaves

2 sprigs fresh thyme

¾ teaspoon black peppercorns

¼ teaspoon table salt

4 cups vegetable oil

1. Arrange the leg portions on a platter, skin side down. Sprinkle with 1½ teaspoons salt and ¼ teaspoon ground black pepper. Place the garlic cloves, bay leaves, and thyme sprigs on top of one of the leg portions. Place the other leg quarter, flesh to flesh, on top. Put the reserved fat from the chicken in the bottom of a glass or plastic container large enough to hold the chicken. Top with the sandwiched leg quarters. Season with two pinches of salt. Cover and refrigerate for up to 12 hours.

2. Preheat the oven to 300°F.

3. Reserve the garlic, bay leaves, thyme, and chicken fat. Rinse the chicken under cool running water, rubbing off some of the salt and pepper. Pat dry with paper towels.

4. Place the reserved garlic, bay leaves, thyme, and chicken fat in the bottom of a 3½-quart heavy-bottomed Dutch oven. Sprinkle evenly with the peppercorns and table salt. Lay the chicken on top, skin side down. Add the oil. (It should thoroughly cover the chicken.) Place the Dutch oven over medium-high heat and cook until small bubbles appear on the surface of the oil. Transfer the pot to the oven and bake, uncovered, until the meat easily pulls away from the bone, about 2 hours.

5. Remove the chicken from the oven and set it aside, allowing the chicken to cool in the fat for at least 1 hour before using it. The chicken can be stored (covered in the oil) in the refrigerator for up to 1 month.

YIELD: 2 LEG PORTIONS; ABOUT 2 CUPS SHREDDED CHICKEN CONFIT

duck confit
with killer bacon waffles

The inspiration for this comes from Chef Norman van Aken, who has pioneered the use of New World ingredients throughout his career. Norman was the third point of a triangle of friendship that included Charlie Trotter and me. Charlie was working as a busboy when Norman hired him to work in the kitchen of a restaurant where he was executive chef. The three of us were as close as brothers and traveled and cooked together all over the world. Norman is a truly dear and close friend, as is his wife, Janet, who works closely with him.

I love Norman's Down Island French Toast, which I have enjoyed many times at Norman's at the Ritz-Carlton Orlando in Florida. Slices of brioche French toast are layered with foie gras that has been marinated in vanilla and orange zest–spiked Cointreau and pan seared, served drizzled with a citrus caramel sauce based on chicken stock.

For a tribute to Norman, I wanted to do my own twist on it. Duck provides the rich, savory silkiness of the foie gras, and waffles—stoked with bacon—take the place of the French toast. Maple syrup with blueberries and black pepper supplies just the right balance of sweet, smoky, and hot notes to balance and tie together the flavors of all the components. You can serve this as a special brunch, but for me it's dinner-party fare.

Duck Confit (page 134)

Killer Bacon Waffles (page 134)

8 cups cleaned spinach

1 tablespoon extra-virgin olive oil

2 teaspoons balsamic vinegar

Salt and freshly ground black pepper

4 to 6 tablespoons (1/2 to 3/4 stick) unsalted butter, melted, as needed

Blueberry Maple Syrup (page 134), for serving

1. Remove the confitted duck legs from the fat, and pat dry. Set a medium skillet over low heat and add the legs, skin side down. Cook gently until the skin is crispy, about 10 minutes. Turn the duck and cook on the other side until warmed through, about 5 minutes longer.

2. Make the waffles, and keep warm.

3. Add the spinach to a bowl, and toss with the extra-virgin olive oil, vinegar, and salt and pepper to taste. Remove the duck from the skillet, and set aside. Add the dressed spinach to the hot pan, and toss until wilted, about 1 minute; remove the pan from the heat.

4. For each serving, place a waffle on a plate and drizzle with melted butter to taste. Top with the wilted spinach, a duck leg, and a sprinkling of duck cracklings, if you were able to keep from eating them when you made the confit. Serve immediately, with the syrup drizzled around the edge of the plate.

YIELD: 4 SERVINGS

(continued)

duck confit

4 duck legs with thighs attached (about 2 pounds)

Coarse salt

12 large cloves garlic, smashed

1/2 teaspoon black peppercorns

4 large bay leaves

4 sprigs fresh thyme

Duck fat and olive oil as needed (about 3 cups)

1. Remove excess fat from the duck and trim excess skin. Cut that fat and skin into small pieces; place in a small, heavy pot over low heat. Cook, stirring, until most of the fat has rendered and the skin is crispy. Let the fat cool and refrigerate. Sprinkle the cracklings with salt; reserve them to use as garnish later.

2. Lay the duck legs, skin side down, on a platter. Sprinkle the flesh side of each with 1/2 teaspoon salt. Transfer two of the legs, skin side down, to an 8-inch baking dish. Top with the aromatics, gently pressing them into the flesh. Top with the other legs, flesh to flesh. Cover and refrigerate overnight.

3. Rinse the legs in a colander to remove the salt. Pat dry; return them to the dish along with the aromatics. Preheat the oven to 300°F. Melt the rendered duck fat in a saucepan. Pour over the legs; add enough oil to just cover them. Cover with foil, set on a baking sheet, and bake until the duck is very tender but not falling off the bone, 3 to 3 1/2 hours. Let cool and store in the fat. Will keep refrigerated for up to 1 month.

YIELD: 4 SERVINGS

blueberry maple syrup

1/2 cup maple syrup

1 cup fresh blueberries

1/2 teaspoon freshly ground black pepper

In a small, heavy saucepan, combine all the ingredients. Bring to a boil, reduce the heat to a simmer, and let gently bubble for 10 minutes to allow the flavors to develop. Serve warm or at room temperature. It will keep in the refrigerator for up to 1 week.

YIELD: ABOUT 1 CUP

killer bacon waffles

You can enjoy these waffles anytime on their own topped with maple syrup. Make a double batch and freeze the extras in an airtight container. Reheat as many as you need on a baking sheet in a 350°F oven; it will take just a few minutes.

2 tablespoons unsalted butter

6 ounces sliced bacon, chopped

1 cup chopped onion

1 3/4 cups cake flour

2 tablespoons sugar

1 tablespoon baking powder

1/2 teaspoon salt

1 teaspoon freshly ground black pepper

2 1/2 cups whole milk, plus more if needed for thinning

2 large eggs, separated

1. Preheat a waffle iron.

2. Melt the butter in a small skillet over medium heat. Add the bacon and onion and cook, stirring as needed, until the onion is soft and the fat has rendered from the bacon, about 10 minutes. Remove from the heat.

3. Sift the flour, sugar, baking powder, salt, and pepper into a large bowl. In a medium bowl, whisk the milk and egg yolks together.

4. In a small bowl with an electric mixer on high speed, beat the egg whites until stiff peaks form.

5. Add the milk mixture to the dry mixture, and whisk gently to combine. Stir in the bacon and onion, along with the bacon drippings. Add the egg whites, gently folding them in with a whisk. If necessary, thin the batter with additional milk. The batter will appear frothy on top—this is OK.

6. Add 3/4 to 1 cup of the batter to the waffle iron, and cook according to the manufacturer's instructions. Repeat with the remaining batter. Keep the waffles warm in a low oven until ready to serve.

YIELD: 4 TO 6 WAFFLES, DEPENDING ON THE SIZE OF YOUR WAFFLE IRON

creole duck breasts with sweet & sour figs

Duck hunting is a very popular pastime in South Louisiana, and over the years I've had numerous customers who would bring me a duck in the morning, with the request that I prepare a dish with it for them to enjoy at dinner that evening. For me, pairing duck with figs is a natural; in New Orleans, fig trees are planted just about everywhere. Most of them are the Celeste variety, which looks and tastes like the more widely available Black Mission fig.

You can also make this dish using chicken breasts; if you do, there is no need to score the skin, and be sure to cook it all the way through. This is delicious served with Wild Mushroom Bread Pudding (page 214).

2 (8- to 10-ounce) domestic duck breasts

1 teaspoon salt

½ teaspoon freshly ground black pepper

1 cup Champagne vinegar

1 cup granulated sugar

1 pint fresh Black Mission figs (about 12)

1 (12-ounce) bottle Abita Turbo Dog or other stout beer

1 cinnamon stick

3 tablespoons cold unsalted butter, cut into small pieces

1. Preheat the oven to 400°F. With a sharp knife, score the skin of the duck breasts in a crosshatch pattern. Season the duck breasts with the salt and pepper on both sides.

2. Heat an ovenproof medium sauté pan over medium to medium-high heat for 1 minute, then place the breasts, fat side down, in the pan and cook until the fat on the breast renders and the skin is brown and crispy, about 15 minutes; adjust the heat as needed to keep the fat from burning instead of browning. If necessary, carefully spoon out some of the fat from the pan as it is rendered off. Do not discard the fat; set it aside for later use. Gently turn the duck breasts over to the meat side, place the pan in the oven, and roast for 6 to 8 minutes.

3. Meanwhile, in a small saucepan, combine the vinegar and sugar and bring to a brisk boil, stirring until all of the sugar has dissolved. Add the figs, reduce the heat to low, and simmer for 5 minutes. Set aside until ready to use.

4. Transfer the duck breasts to a platter and spoon off any fat that may be in the pan. Place the pan over medium heat, add the beer and cinnamon stick, and simmer until the sauce

reduces by half, 4 to 5 minutes. Add ¼ cup of the syrup used to cook the figs, and simmer for 2 minutes longer. Add the butter to the pan piece by piece, whisking constantly to incorporate each piece before adding another. Once all of the butter is incorporated into the sauce, remove from the heat, add the figs to the pan, and shake the pan to coat the figs with the sauce.

5. Slice the duck breasts and place 4 or 5 slices in a fan arrangement on each of 4 plates. Set several figs next to the duck and spoon the sauce over all.

YIELD: 4 SERVINGS

pan searing duck breasts

I love this two-step approach to cooking duck breasts. The stovetop sear renders the fat and crisps up the skin; finishing it in the oven allows for better temperature control and the skin can continue to crisp without any danger of it burning.

1. To help render as much fat as possible from the duck skin, with a sharp knife score the skin in a crosshatch pattern, without cutting into the flesh.

2. Preheat an ovenproof sauté pan over medium to medium-high heat for 1 minute, then place the breasts skin side down in the pan. Your goal is to render as much of the fat as possible into the pan, leaving the skin crispy and golden. Keep an eye on the skin's progress; if it looks like it is browning faster than it is rendering, turn the heat down. This process should take about 15 minutes.

3. When the skin is browned and crispy, turn the breasts over and finish cooking them in the oven. For me, the perfect doneness for duck is medium to medium-rare, with a little pinkness in the center.

SHELLFISH & FISH

Fishing is a deep, long-standing love of mine. It started with my dad taking me fishing for flounder and bringing our catch home for my mom to cook. I continue this tradition by taking my own children and friends out fishing on the Gulf of Mexico on my boat, *Aldenté*, and I cook what we catch, sometimes right on board. I love to fish for billfish—marlin, swordfish, sailfish, spearfish—but I'm also happy when I pull up my line and find a grouper, tuna, cobia, or snapper on the end. They all make for incredible eating, enjoyed just hours or even minutes after they've been caught.

The recipes in this chapter let the flavor of the fish shine through and many can be on the table in 30 minutes or less. The key is to buy only the best-quality seafood and take care not to overcook it. I grew up eating clams, mussels, and lobsters in New England and so the shrimp, oysters, and crabs that are such a big part of our Gulf Coast diet was a natural fit for me.

brown butter
crab cakes

The very best crab cakes are those made with as little filler as possible, where the crab taste shines through and the cake breaks apart into big crab flakes as you eat it. I wanted to make a crab cake with no bread or cracker crumbs at all, with the added benefit that these are gluten free. My daughters Jilly and Jessie both follow gluten-free diets and have written gluten-free cookbooks together, which has driven me to create some gluten-free recipes.

Enjoy these crab cakes with a simple salad of baby greens and teardrop tomatoes drizzled with olive oil.

1 pound fresh lump crabmeat

¼ cup finely diced onion

2 tablespoons finely diced red bell pepper

2 tablespoons finely diced celery

1 teaspoon minced garlic

¼ cup (½ stick) unsalted butter

4 teaspoons fresh lemon juice

1½ teaspoons Old Bay seasoning

2 tablespoons mayonnaise

½ cup canola oil, for frying

1. Line a small baking sheet or platter with parchment, and set aside.

2. In a medium bowl, pick over the crabmeat and remove any shells or cartilage. Set aside.

3. In an 8-inch sauté pan, combine the onion, bell pepper, celery, garlic, and butter. Over medium-low heat, allow the vegetables to slowly toast in the butter until they are well caramelized and the butter has foamed and begins to brown, 15 to 17 minutes, stirring a few times. Once the butter has browned, remove the pan from the heat and drizzle with the lemon juice.

4. Pour the butter and vegetables over the crabmeat, and add the Old Bay and mayonnaise. Stir well to incorporate the ingredients, making sure the brown butter is spread throughout. Divide the mixture into 4 equal-sized portions, and firmly shape them so they are about the shape and thickness of a hockey puck. Set them on the prepared baking sheet. (You can also use a 3-inch mold or biscuit cutter to shape the cakes. Place the ring on baking sheet and press mixture firmly into it. Remove ring and repeat with the remaining mixture.)

5. Once formed, cover the crab cakes with plastic wrap and refrigerate at least 2 hours and up to overnight to allow the brown butter to solidify.

6. Remove the crab cakes from the refrigerator and set a 12-inch sauté pan over medium-low heat. Heat the oil until hot, then carefully add the crab cakes to the pan, using a flat-edge metal spatula. Cook until the bottoms are well caramelized and the tops are barely warm, about 5 minutes. Turn the cakes over and cook for another 4 to 5 minutes, until golden. Serve immediately.

YIELD: 4 CRAB CAKES, 4 SERVINGS

How is it that these crab cakes stay together without breadcrumbs? Because of the melted butter that is tossed with the crab. When the cakes are refrigerated, that butter coagulates, creating a glue that holds the crab in place. That is why it is important to firmly shape the cakes and to allow them enough time in the refrigerator for the butter to firm up.

crabmeat stuffed shrimp

One of my first restaurant jobs was in high school, working at the Venus de Milo in Swansea, Massachusetts. This is my tribute to one of their most popular dishes—baked shrimp stuffed with crabmeat and topped with buttered Ritz cracker crumbs. I must have made literally thousands of them. The shrimp, crab, and Ritz crackers are still in place, but I've put a Louisiana spin on it, building the stuffing from a sauté of what we call here the Trinity—a mix of chopped onion, celery, and bell pepper. A good dose of my Creole seasoning is added, and it's served drizzled with your choice of Lemon Butter Sauce or Creole Meunière Sauce, both very traditional to New Orleans.

1 pound fresh lump crabmeat, picked over for shells and cartilage

3 teaspoons Emeril's Creole Seasoning (page 108) or other Creole seasoning

8 tablespoons (1 stick) unsalted butter

1 cup finely chopped yellow onion

½ cup minced celery

½ cup minced green bell pepper

¼ cup plus 1 tablespoon finely chopped fresh flat-leaf parsley

1½ tablespoons minced garlic

¼ cup mayonnaise

3 tablespoons fresh lemon juice

2 teaspoons Worcestershire sauce

1⅓ cups crushed Ritz crackers (about 26 crackers)

24 to 28 large shrimp, peeled, leaving tail and first segment attached, deveined, and butterflied

½ teaspoon salt

¼ teaspoon freshly ground black pepper

Lemon wedges, for serving

Lemon Butter Sauce (recipe follows) or Creole Meunière Sauce (page 153), for serving

1. Place the crabmeat in a large bowl and season with 1 teaspoon of the Creole seasoning, tossing the crab very gently to coat. Cover and refrigerate until needed.

2. In a medium skillet, heat 4 tablespoons of the butter over medium-high heat. When the butter begins to sizzle, add the onion, celery, bell pepper, and remaining 2 teaspoons Creole seasoning, and cook, stirring a few times, until the vegetables have softened, about 4 minutes. Add ¼ cup of the parsley and the garlic, and cook, stirring, for 1 minute. Remove from the heat and let cool.

3. Add the sautéed vegetables to the crabmeat and stir gently to combine. Add the mayonnaise, lemon juice, Worcestershire, and ⅓ cup of the cracker crumbs. Stir gently and set aside.

4. Preheat the oven to 375°F, and line a large baking sheet with parchment paper.

5. Season the shrimp with the salt and pepper and arrange them, opened up, evenly spaced on the prepared baking sheet. Working with a spoon or a small scoop, divide the crabmeat filling evenly among the shrimp, about 2 tablespoons per shrimp, mounding the filling and pressing it onto the shrimp.

6. Melt the remaining 4 tablespoons butter and stir it into the remaining 1 cup cracker crumbs until well combined. Using a spoon or your fingers, divide the buttered crumbs evenly over the tops of the shrimp, pressing the crumbs into the filling to help them adhere. Bake until the shrimp are cooked through and the crumbs are golden brown on top, about 15 minutes.

7. Serve hot, with lemon wedges or with either of the sauces lightly drizzled on top. Any extra sauce can be passed at the table.

YIELD: 4 MAIN-COURSE OR 8 FIRST-COURSE SERVINGS

lemon butter sauce

This sauce is a classic. It's also delicious with salmon and chicken.

1 cup dry white wine

1 lemon, quartered and chopped

1 tablespoon minced shallot

½ cup heavy cream

1 cup (2 sticks) plus
1 tablespoon unsalted butter, cut into tablespoons

1 teaspoon kosher salt

⅛ teaspoon freshly ground white pepper

1 tablespoon chopped fresh flat-leaf parsley (optional)

1. Combine the wine, lemon, and shallot in a medium saucepan and bring to a boil. Reduce the heat to medium-low and simmer until reduced by half, about 20 minutes, stirring occasionally and mashing the lemon with the back of a spoon to break into pieces.

2. Add the cream and simmer until reduced by half, about 3 minutes.

3. Whisk in the butter, 1 tablespoon at a time, not adding another piece until the previous one has been completely incorporated. Continue to cook until all the butter is incorporated and the sauce coats the back of a spoon. Do not allow the sauce to come to a boil or it will break. Add the salt and pepper, and whisk to blend.

4. Remove the pan from the heat. Strain the sauce through a fine-mesh strainer into a small bowl, pressing down on the solids with the whisk; discard the solids. Stir in the parsley, if desired, and serve immediately, or cover to keep warm.

YIELD: ABOUT 1¾ CUPS

butterflying shrimp

Stuffed shrimp make for such a special presentation, and butterflying shrimp is so easy to do.

1. Peel the shrimp, leaving the shell on the tail. With a sharp knife, cut along the back of the shrimp.

2. Cut almost all the way through.

3. Open the shrimp up to lie flat.

shrimp stewfée

Born and raised in St. Martinville, along the banks of the Bayou Teche in South Louisiana, food journalist Marcelle Bienvenu worked with me on a number of my cookbooks and is an expert on Louisiana cooking. One day, we were talking about étouffée and she told me about a quicker take on it that she called a stewfée. I loved the sound of it, and the name, and we worked on a version to serve at Emeril's way back when. It's a simple preparation, but it's loaded with flavor.

6 tablespoons (¾ stick) unsalted butter

2 cups chopped onions

1 cup chopped bell pepper

1 cup chopped celery

1 tablespoon minced garlic

¾ teaspoon salt

½ teaspoon cayenne pepper

2 bay leaves

3 tablespoons all-purpose flour

1½ cups Shrimp Stock (page 84)

4 sprigs fresh thyme

1½ pounds medium Gulf shrimp, peeled and deveined

2 teaspoons Emeril's Creole Seasoning (page 108) or other Creole seasoning

1 tablespoon chopped fresh flat-leaf parsley

Hot white rice, for serving

1. In a medium, heavy-bottomed Dutch oven, melt 2 tablespoons of the butter over medium-high heat. Add the onions, bell pepper, and celery, and cook, stirring occasionally, until the vegetables have softened and are lightly golden, about 6 minutes. Add the garlic, salt, cayenne, and bay leaves, and cook, stirring, for 2 minutes. Sprinkle the flour over the vegetables and cook, stirring and scraping the bottom of the pan to keep the flour from sticking, until the flour is lightly golden, 3 to 4 minutes.

2. Add the stock and thyme, and stir to combine. Partially cover the pot, reduce the heat to a simmer, and cook until any floury taste is gone and the sauce is flavorful, about 30 minutes.

3. While the sauce is simmering, place the shrimp in a bowl, add the Creole seasoning, and toss to evenly coat.

4. After 30 minutes, stir the shrimp into the sauce and cook just until they curl and turn pink, 3 to 4 minutes. Stir in the remaining 4 tablespoons butter until they melt and are incorporated, then stir in the parsley and remove from the heat. Remove and discard the thyme sprigs and bay leaves.

5. Serve the stewfée in shallow bowls ladled over a mound of hot white rice.

YIELD: 4 SERVINGS

For flavoring and thickening, this recipe makes use of a shortcut roux. Sprinkle flour over the sautéed vegetables and cook just a few minutes, until lightly golden, before adding stock. It's very important to let the stock simmer for the full 30 minutes to eliminate any remaining raw flour taste.

*To make
a mushroom
broth, place
mushroom stems
and scraps
in a pot with just
enough water
to cover, bring to
a boil, then simmer
for 45 to 60 minutes.
Strain and use.*

•

*Don't ever
buy what are
known as "wet"
scallops; these
have been soaked
in preservative,
which makes
a good sear
impossible. Only
buy dry (or dry-
packed) scallops
or diver scallops.
If the scallops at
your fish counter
aren't labeled,
ask the fishmonger.*

seared scallops
with wild mushrooms, ham, and portobello-truffle emulsion

The town of New Bedford, Massachusetts, is known as the scallop capital of the United States (and in the 1800s it was the center of the whaling industry). It's not surprising that when I was growing up, my mother served us either fried or broiled sea scallops every week (not that I'm complaining!). Now I enjoy them seared to a golden brown. If you're pressed for time, you can do without the Portobello-Truffle Emulsion. But with it, the emulsion provides a funky truffle flavor that pairs beautifully with the sweet scallops and sautéed mushrooms.

4 tablespoons ($\frac{1}{2}$ stick) unsalted butter

4 tablespoons olive oil

1 pound mixed wild mushrooms, such as chanterelles, shiitake, maitake, and/or oyster, cleaned (see page 171) and quartered

$\frac{1}{4}$ cup minced shallots

$\frac{1}{4}$ cup thickly sliced ham, cut into small dice

$\frac{1}{4}$ cup dry sherry

$\frac{1}{4}$ cup mushroom broth (see Essentials, at left) or low-sodium chicken broth

$\frac{1}{3}$ cup heavy cream

1 teaspoon chopped fresh thyme

2 teaspoons salt

$\frac{1}{2}$ teaspoon freshly ground black pepper

12 U10 diver scallops or dry-packed sea scallops (see Essentials, at left)

$\frac{1}{2}$ teaspoon white pepper

2 sprigs fresh tarragon

4 tablespoons Portobello-Truffle Emulsion (page 34, optional), warmed

1. In a large sauté pan, melt 1 tablespoon of the butter over medium-high heat, then add 1 tablespoon of the oil. When hot, add half of the mushrooms, and cook until golden brown on both sides, about 4 minutes. Transfer the mushrooms to a paper towel–lined baking sheet or plate. Add another tablespoon of the butter and oil to the pan, and repeat the process with the remaining mushrooms, also transferring them to paper towels.

2. Add the shallots and ham to the pan, and cook until the shallots are tender, about 1 minute. Return the mushrooms to the pan along with the sherry, broth, cream, and thyme. Season with 1 teaspoon of the salt and the black pepper. Cook, stirring as needed, until most of the liquid has evaporated, about 5 minutes. Set aside and cover to keep warm.

3. Season the scallops on both sides with the remaining 1 teaspoon salt and the white pepper. Heat the remaining 2 tablespoons oil in a 14-inch skillet over high heat. When the pan is hot and the oil just starting to smoke, add the scallops, flat side down. Cook until golden brown, about 2 minutes, then carefully turn them over. Add the remaining 2 tablespoons butter and the tarragon. Baste the scallops with the butter for 1 minute.

4. For each serving, spoon 1 tablespoon of the Portobello-Truffle Emulsion onto the center of a serving plate. Place $\frac{1}{3}$ cup of the mushroom mixture on top of the emulsion, and top with scallops. Serve immediately.

YIELD: 4 SERVINGS

my nod to nobu's miso
black cod

Nobu Matsuhisa has been a colleague and friend of mine for more than 30 years. He is one of my culinary heroes (which I tell him every time I see him!) and one of the finest chefs working today. I met Nobu when he opened his first restaurant, Matsuhisa, in Beverly Hills, which is where I had his miso cod for the first time. It is my absolute favorite Nobu dish, and I have it every time I go to one of his restaurants. This is my version of the dish, a tribute to Nobu. It pairs deliciously with Meril's Super-Quick Cabbage with Bacon (page 199).

½ cup mirin

½ cup sake

¼ cup honey

½ cup white miso paste

1 teaspoon toasted sesame oil

1 (5-gram) package seasoned sea snack (see Essentials, at right), crumbled

2 pounds fresh black cod fillets, cut into 4 equal portions

1. In a small saucepan, combine the mirin, sake, and honey, and bring to a boil over high heat. Reduce the heat to a simmer and cook for 2 minutes, stirring, to dissolve the honey. Remove the pan from the heat and whisk in the miso paste, sesame oil, and crumbled sea snack; let stand for 10 to 15 minutes to cool. Strain the mixture through a fine-mesh strainer, and discard any solids.

2. Place the cod fillets in a zip-top plastic bag, and pour the marinade over the fish. Seal the bag and turn it over several times to make sure the cod is well coated with the marinade. Refrigerate for 24 hours.

3. Preheat the oven to 400°F. Position a rack in the center of the oven and another close to the broiler.

4. Transfer the fish from the marinade to a baking sheet. Roast the fish for 20 minutes on the center rack, then turn on the broiler and move the baking sheet to the upper rack. Cook until the cod is golden brown and caramelized on top, 3 to 5 minutes. Serve immediately.

YIELD: 4 SERVINGS

black cod

Black cod, also known as sablefish and butterfish, isn't at all related to cod. It's fished in the North Pacific and lives in very deep water. To function in this harsh environment, black cod contains a lot of fat, which, as one of its alternative names indicates, yields a rich, almost buttery flavor, with a texture that practically melts in your mouth. You can use black cod as a substitute for Chilean sea bass, which has experienced overfishing.

You must make this with black cod—its texture is key to the success of the dish.

•

Look for seasoned seaweed in the international section of the supermarket; my favorite brand is Wang from Korea. Sold as Crispy Sea Snack, it contains seaweed; salt; and sesame, grapeseed, and olive oils. If you can't find it, substitute seasoned nori sheets.

roasted cedar-plank trout

Larry Forgione is known as the Godfather of American Cuisine, and with good reason. He used local ingredients sourced directly from small producers more than 30 years ago, spurred by his experience working in France, where this was a common practice for restaurants. I first met Larry when he was executive chef at the River Café in Brooklyn, and enjoyed his preparation of a cedar-planked salmon, which he told me he had learned from James Beard. He was a close friend of Jim's and the driving force behind the creation of the James Beard House and James Beard Foundation after his death. Larry and I kept in touch, and I had many memorable meals at An American Place, which he opened in Manhattan in 1983. Larry was an important mentor to me in learning to cook and source locally.

When I was developing recipes for the wood-burning oven in my restaurant NOLA, I thought back to Larry's cedar-planked salmon and used the technique with trout. The dish has been on the menu ever since, served with one of these two sauces. Both are super simple and incredibly delicious. You will need four cedar planks for this.

5 teaspoons vegetable oil, or as needed

8 ounces fresh horseradish root (see Essentials, at left), peeled and finely grated (about 2 cups)

1 tablespoon fresh lemon juice

1 tablespoon fresh orange juice

1/8 teaspoon salt

4 (6-ounce) trout or other firm white fish fillets, such as redfish, pompano, snapper, or drum

1 1/4 teaspoons Emeril's Creole Seasoning (page 108) or other Creole seasoning

2 teaspoons extra-virgin olive oil

Lemon Brown Butter and/or Citrus-Sesame Soy Sauce, for serving (recipes follow)

Chopped green onions, for garnish

1. Preheat the oven to 450°F. Generously oil one side of each of 4 cedar planks with about 1 teaspoon of the vegetable oil and set on a large rimmed baking sheet, oiled side up.

2. Combine the horseradish, juices, and salt. Season the fillets on both sides with the Creole seasoning; set a fillet on each plank. Drizzle 1/2 teaspoon of the olive oil over each. Divide the horseradish crust among the fillets, patting it to cover the tops evenly. Roast until the crust is browned and a knife easily pierces the center of the fillets, 20 to 25 minutes.

3. To serve, drizzle the sauce over the fish, and serve on the planks, sprinkled with green onions.

YIELD: 4 SERVINGS

lemon brown butter

1/4 cup (1/2 stick) unsalted butter

1 tablespoon fresh lemon juice

Melt the butter in a small sauté pan over medium heat. Cook, swirling the pan gently, until the butter smells nutty and is browned on the edges, 2 to 2 1/2 minutes. Swirl in the lemon juice; serve immediately.

YIELD: 1/4 CUP

citrus-sesame soy sauce

2 tablespoons soy sauce

2 tablespoons fresh lemon juice

2 tablespoons fresh orange juice

2 teaspoons toasted sesame oil

In a small bowl, whisk together all the ingredients. Whisk a final time before serving.

YIELD: 1/3 CUP

andouille-crusted redfish
with creole meunière sauce

This recipe has been on the menu since Emeril's opened in 1990 and is still served, as it always has been, with fried shoestring potatoes. Killer! It is absolutely the taste of Louisiana, starting with the redfish, which was almost fished out of existence in the Gulf because of Chef Paul Prudhomme's blackened redfish (its population has since recovered, following a years-long ban on fishing it in Louisiana). It's topped with andouille and served with a savory butter sauce. You'll lick your plate clean!

8 ounces andouille sausage, chopped

8 tablespoons olive oil

1 cup chopped onion

2 tablespoons minced garlic

2 tablespoons chopped fresh flat-leaf parsley

6 tablespoons plain dry breadcrumbs

2½ teaspoons Emeril's Creole Seasoning (page 108) or other Creole seasoning

½ cup finely grated Parmigiano-Reggiano cheese

4 (6- to 8-ounce) redfish, trout, or catfish fillets

Creole Meunière Sauce (see opposite), for serving

1. Preheat the oven to 450°F.

2. Pulse the andouille in a food processor on high until it resembles coarse crumbs.

3. Heat 2 tablespoons of the oil in a medium skillet over medium heat. Add the onion and cook, stirring a few times, until softened, about 5 minutes. Add the garlic and andouille and cook, stirring as needed, until the sausage is browned and its fat has rendered, about 5 minutes. Transfer the mixture to a small bowl and combine with the parsley, breadcrumbs, ½ teaspoon of the Creole seasoning, the Parmigiano, and 4 tablespoons of the oil.

4. Season both sides of each redfish fillet with ¼ teaspoon of the Creole seasoning. Heat the remaining 2 tablespoons oil in a large ovenproof skillet over medium-high heat. Add the redfish, presentation side down, to the skillet, and cook until golden, 3 to 4 minutes.

5. Remove the pan from the heat. Carefully turn the fish over in the pan and generously top each fillet with the andouille mixture, packing it evenly over the fillets. Transfer the pan to the oven and bake just until the fish is cooked through, about 5 minutes.

6. For each serving, spoon some of the sauce over the fillet. Serve immediately.

YIELD: 4 SERVINGS

creole meunière sauce

This sauce is a staple in restaurants throughout New Orleans, served with pan-sautéed or fried fish, shrimp, even soft-shelled crabs. Take a taste and you'll understand why!

½ cup Worcestershire sauce, preferably homemade (recipe follows)

¼ cup chopped onion

2 bay leaves

1 lemon, skin and pith discarded, cut in half

6 tablespoons heavy cream

½ cup (1 stick) cold unsalted butter, cut into tablespoons

1. In a medium saucepan, combine the Worcestershire, onion, bay leaves, and lemon halves, and bring to a boil over medium-high heat. Reduce the heat to a simmer and continue to cook until the liquid is reduced by two-thirds and thickened, about 3 minutes, pressing on the lemons with the back of a spoon to release as much of their juice as possible. Whisk in the cream and simmer 1 minute longer. Whisk in the butter, 1 tablespoon at a time, not adding another piece until the previous one is completely melted and incorporated into the sauce.

2. Remove the pan from the heat, strain the sauce through a fine-mesh strainer into a small pot (discard the solids), and cover to keep warm until ready to serve.

YIELD: ABOUT 1 CUP

adding flavor

Cooking the entire lemon, which I do when making my Worcestershire sauce and the meunière sauce, yields a more pronounced lemon flavor that I like—kind of like that of a preserved lemon.

my homemade worcestershire

2 tablespoons olive oil

6 cups coarsely chopped onions

4 jalapeño peppers, with stems and seeds, chopped (¾ cup)

2 tablespoons minced garlic

2 teaspoons freshly ground black pepper

4 (2-ounce) cans oil-packed anchovy fillets

½ teaspoon whole cloves

2 tablespoons salt

2 medium lemons

4 cups dark corn syrup

2 cups Steen's 100% Pure Cane Syrup

2 quarts distilled white vinegar

4 cups water

12 ounces fresh horseradish root, peeled and grated (about 3 cups)

1. Combine the oil, onions, and jalapeños in a large, heavy-bottomed stockpot over high heat. Cook, stirring, until slightly softened, 2 to 3 minutes. Add the garlic, pepper, anchovies, cloves, salt, lemons (just put them in whole), corn syrup, cane syrup, vinegar, water, and horseradish, and bring to a boil. Reduce the heat to a simmer and let gently bubble, uncovered and stirring occasionally, until the mixture barely coats a wooden spoon, about 6 hours.

2. Strain through a fine-mesh strainer into an airtight container; discard the solids. Let cool to room temperature, then refrigerate. It will keep in the refrigerator for up to 1 month, or you can process it as directed in Step 3 and it will keep in a cool, dark place for up to 1 year. Once opened, it must be refrigerated and will keep for a month.

3. Sterilize 3 pint-size jars and their metal lids according to the manufacturer's instructions. Spoon the hot mixture into the jars, filling to within ½ inch of the rim. With a clean, damp towel, wipe the rims and fit with a hot lid. Tightly screw on the metal ring. Place, without touching, on a rack in a large, deep canning kettle or stockpot of rapidly boiling water; the water should cover the jars by 1 inch. Boil and process for 15 minutes. Using tongs, remove the jars from the water, place on a clean, dry towel, and let cool completely before storing. Test the seals and tighten the rings as needed. If the jars have properly vacuum-sealed, the lids will be concave. (If they aren't, store the jars in the refrigerator and use within a month.) Store in a cool, dark place for at least 2 weeks before using.

YIELD: ABOUT 6 CUPS

portuguese-style cod
with potatoes, kale, and chorizo

This easy pan sauté has all the flavors of my mother's kitchen. I make it with cod, but you could also use scrod, halibut, dorado, or whatever large-flaked white fish looks best at the fish counter.

8 ounces Yellowfin, Russian Banana, Yukon Gold, or other waxy potatoes

2 bay leaves

4 sprigs fresh thyme

3¼ teaspoons salt

5 black peppercorns

2 tablespoons olive oil

8 ounces hot chorizo, cut into ⅛-inch-thick rounds and then quartered

1 cup chopped yellow onion

1 teaspoon minced garlic

1 cup lacinato (Tuscan) kale, stems removed and cut into bite-size pieces (about 1 inch square)

1 cup Vinho Verde or other light dry white wine

1 cup Fish Stock (page 91), Shrimp Stock (page 84), or water

1 cup chopped fresh or canned tomatoes

½ cup pitted mixed black and green Cerignola olives, quartered

1 tablespoon chopped oil-packed anchovy fillets

1 tablespoon drained nonpareil capers

4 (6-ounce) cod fillets

2 tablespoons Wondra or rice flour

3 tablespoons unsalted butter, cut into tablespoons

1. In a medium saucepan, combine the potatoes, bay leaves, 2 sprigs of the thyme, 2 teaspoons of the salt, the peppercorns, and enough cold water to cover everything by 1 inch. Bring to a boil over high heat, then reduce the heat to a simmer and cook the potatoes until fork-tender, about 20 minutes. Let the potatoes cool in the cooking liquid, then cut into quarters and set aside.

2. Heat 1 tablespoon of the oil in a large, high-sided sauté pan over medium-high heat. When hot, add the chorizo and cook for about 1 minute. Add the onion and garlic and cook, stirring, for 2 minutes. Add the kale, wine, and stock, and cook until the liquid has reduced by half, about 5 minutes. Stir in the tomatoes, olives, anchovies, and capers, season with ¼ teaspoon of the salt, and cook for 2 minutes. Remove from the heat.

3. Season the cod fillets on both sides with the remaining 1 teaspoon salt, and dust them with the flour.

4. Heat the remaining 1 tablespoon oil in a large sauté pan over high heat. When hot, add the cod fillets, flesh side up, and cook for 3 to 4 minutes. Carefully flip the cod over and add the butter, the remaining 2 sprigs thyme, and potatoes. As the butter melts, baste the fish and potatoes with it for 2 to 3 minutes.

5. Using a slotted spoon, transfer the fish and potatoes to individual plates or a large platter. Spoon the sauce over the fish. Serve immediately.

YIELD: 4 SERVINGS

The North Atlantic cod population is under serious threat, a combination of overfishing and changes in ocean temperature. Your best bet is U.S.-fished Pacific cod. To keep up to date on sustainable choices when buying fish, consult fishwatch.gov and seawatch.org.

citrus salt–crusted snapper
with chimichurri sauce

This dish makes for an amazing presentation at the table. But why go to all the trouble of building a salt dome around your fish? The salt creates an airtight seal, which keeps the moisture in and cooks the fish evenly. And the salt is first mixed with citrus, so those flavors permeate the fish while it's cooking.

2 whole red snapper or redfish (2 to 2½ pounds each), cleaned and scaled

4 tablespoons olive oil

4 teaspoons Emeril's Creole Seasoning (page 108) or other Creole seasoning

½ cup plus 2 tablespoons fresh lemon juice

1 lemon, cut into 6 slices

1 (3-pound) box kosher salt

⅓ cup fresh lime juice

¼ cup fresh orange juice

¼ cup grated lemon zest

1 tablespoon grated orange zest

1 teaspoon freshly ground black pepper

Chimichurri Sauce (recipe follows), for serving

1. Preheat the oven to 400°F. Line a baking sheet with parchment paper. With a sharp knife, make 5 slits, just deep enough to cut through the skin, at an angle and about 1½ inches apart, on each side of the fish. Rub 1 tablespoon of oil over each side, then season with 1 teaspoon of Creole seasoning. Set on the prepared baking sheet, and drizzle 1 tablespoon of the lemon juice over each fish. Lay the lemon slices on top.

2. In a large bowl, combine the salt with the remaining ½ cup lemon juice, the lime and orange juices, lemon and orange zests, and pepper. Mound one-half evenly over each of the fish and firmly press into the flesh and around the sides, sealing the fish. Bake for 45 minutes.

3. Let the fish cool for 2 minutes. With the back of a heavy spoon, lightly pound the salt crust to crack it open, beginning at the tail end. Carefully pull off the crust and discard. Using a small spatula, carefully remove the flesh from the bone from the top side of the fish. Remove the backbone, then serve the flesh from the bottom side of the fish. Spoon some chimichurri over each serving.

YIELD: 4 SERVINGS

chimichurri sauce

This lively fresh herb sauce is served with steak in Argentina, but also pairs beautifully with chicken and fish and can be used as a marinade. I've layered in heat and smoke by adding a charred jalapeño and smoked paprika. Serve at room temperature.

1 jalapeño or serrano pepper

½ cup extra-virgin olive oil

2 tablespoons good quality sherry vinegar

2 teaspoons grated lemon zest

2 teaspoons chopped fresh oregano

2 teaspoons chopped fresh basil

2 teaspoons chopped fresh mint

¾ teaspoon sea salt

3 cloves garlic, minced

¼ teaspoon smoked hot paprika or crushed red pepper

¾ cup fresh flat-leaf parsley leaves

¾ cup fresh cilantro leaves

1. In a dry cast iron skillet over high heat, char the pepper, using tongs to turn it until the entire outside is blistered. Remove from the heat and let cool.

2. Remove the stem, split the pepper down the center, and remove the seeds. Roughly chop the pepper and put in a blender. Add the remaining ingredients and blend until almost smooth but slightly chunky.

YIELD: 1 CUP

Feel free to experiment by changing the aromatics added to the salt crust— another tasty combination is soy sauce and fresh ginger. Grapefruit juice also works well, and you can add chopped fresh herbs. Use a light hand with the herbs, though, as some, like dill, can overwhelm the delicate flavor of the fish if used in too great a quantity.

slow-roasted salmon
with roasted creamy cauliflower

It was my pleasure and honor to have dined many times at Girardet, Chef Frédy Girardet's Michelin three star–rated restaurant in Crissier, Switzerland. It was there that I had the original version of this dish. I had never experienced fish cooked using this low and slow method, and it was truly a revelation, as was pairing the salmon with a cauliflower puree. This is my tribute to Frédy—he retired almost twenty years ago, but to me he is still the Pope of Fine Cooking.

2 lemons

¾ ounce sprigs fresh thyme (8 to 10 sprigs)

4 (6-ounce) skin-on wild salmon fillets (see Essentials, at right), about 1 inch thick

¼ cup olive oil

½ teaspoon coarse sea salt

½ teaspoon freshly ground white pepper

Roasted Creamy Cauliflower (recipe follows)

1. Preheat the oven to 250°F. Line a baking sheet with parchment paper. Cut one lemon into ⅛-inch-thick slices, and juice the second lemon. Arrange the slices on the prepared baking sheet and place the thyme sprigs on top. Add the salmon fillets, skin side down. Drizzle the lemon juice and oil over the salmon, then sprinkle with the salt and pepper. Place in the oven on the center rack and roast until the salmon is cooked almost all through at the thickest point, about 25 minutes. To check for doneness, make an incision with a sharp knife at the thickest point of a fillet and pull it apart to check for opaqueness; don't cook it beyond medium-rare.

2. To serve, spoon 2 to 3 tablespoons of the cauliflower onto each plate, then gently place a fillet on top. Garnish with the lemon slices and the thyme sprigs, or just the leaves. Serve immediately.

YIELD: 4 SERVINGS

roasted creamy cauliflower

At Girardet, the salmon was served with a cauliflower puree. Here, I added chopped roasted cauliflower for a delicious textural counterpoint to the salmon.

1 small head cauliflower (about 1½ pounds)

1 tablespoon olive oil

Fine sea salt and ground white pepper

2 cups half-and-half

2 tablespoons unsalted butter

1 tablespoon roasted garlic

1. Preheat the oven to 400°F. Cut the cauliflower into small florets (you'll end up with about 5 cups). In a medium bowl, toss half of the cauliflower with the oil, ½ teaspoon salt and ¼ teaspoon pepper until coated. Arrange in a single layer on a baking sheet and roast, stirring occasionally, until golden brown and tender, about 30 minutes.

2. Place the remaining florets in a medium saucepan with the half-and-half, butter, and ½ teaspoon salt and ¼ teaspoon pepper. Simmer over medium heat until the cauliflower is very tender, about 20 minutes. Drain, reserving about 1 cup of the cooking liquid.

3. Place the simmered cauliflower and garlic in a blender. Process into a very smooth puree, adding just enough of the reserved cooking liquid. Transfer to a small, heavy-bottomed saucepan. Chop the roasted cauliflower and fold it into the puree. Adjust the seasonings and keep warm over low heat until ready to use, or store in an airtight container in the refrigerator for up to 4 days. Reheat in a saucepan over low heat.

YIELD: 2½ CUPS; 4 SERVINGS

Don't think of using anything but wild salmon for this. Wild salmon is much leaner than farm-raised, and this low and slow method traps the fish's natural oils, yielding a soft, silky, buttery texture—it practically melts in your mouth.

barbecued salmon

with fried onion rings and andouille-potato hash

I originally developed this recipe for the lunch menu at Emeril's. It was such a big success that it was one of the first dishes we had on the menu at New Orleans Fish House in Las Vegas. The barbecue sauce and gastrique can be made ahead of time.

2 cups cubed (1/2-inch) peeled russet potatoes (about 2 pounds)

3 teaspoons salt

2 tablespoons olive oil

4 ounces andouille sausage, fresh or smoked, crumbled or chopped

1/2 cup minced onion

1 tablespoon chopped garlic

1/2 teaspoon freshly ground black pepper

1/2 teaspoon Emeril's Creole Seasoning (page 108) or other Creole seasoning

1 cup beef stock or low-sodium beef broth

1/2 cup chopped green onions

1 tablespoon unsalted butter

4 (6-ounce) skinless salmon fillets, about 1 inch thick

1/2 cup BBQ Sauce (see opposite)

Fried Onion Rings (see opposite), for garnish

2 tablespoons chopped fresh flat-leaf parsley, for garnish

Spicy Tomato Gastrique, for drizzling (optional; see opposite)

1. Preheat the oven to 350°F. Place the potatoes in a small pot and cover with water. Add 2 teaspoons of the salt and bring to a boil over high heat. Reduce the heat to medium-low and simmer until just tender, 5 to 6 minutes. Drain and set aside to cool.

2. Heat 1 tablespoon of the oil in a 12-inch sauté pan over medium heat. When the oil begins to ripple, add the sausage, onion, and garlic. Cook, stirring as needed, until the sausage is browned and its fat has rendered, 5 to 6 minutes. Increase the heat to high, add the potatoes, and season with 1/2 teaspoon of the salt, 1/4 teaspoon of the pepper, and the Creole seasoning. Continue to cook 2 to 3 minutes longer, until the potatoes begin to brown. Add the stock and bring to a boil. Reduce the heat to low and simmer until most of the liquid has evaporated, about 5 minutes longer. Stir in the green onions and butter until the butter has melted, then remove from the heat. Cover to keep warm.

3. Season the salmon fillets with the remaining 1/2 teaspoon salt and 1/4 teaspoon pepper. Add the remaining 1 tablespoon oil to an ovenproof 12-inch nonstick skillet and set over medium-high heat. Once the oil begins to ripple, add the salmon, presentation side down, and cook until nicely browned, about 3 minutes. Turn the salmon over and brush with the barbecue sauce. Transfer the pan to the oven and cook for 3 minutes for medium-rare (check by inserting a sharp knife in the thickest part of each fillet). Remove from the oven.

4. Divide the andouille potato hash among 4 serving plates, and place a salmon fillet over it. Mound onion rings over the salmon, and sprinkle with the parsley. If using, drizzle the gastrique around the plate, and serve.

YIELD: 4 SERVINGS

bbq sauce

1 cup canned chopped tomatoes, with juices

½ cup water

½ cup chopped onion

1 clove garlic, chopped

3 tablespoons cider vinegar

2 tablespoons dark brown sugar

2 tablespoons molasses

1 tablespoon Creole or coarse-grain mustard

1 tablespoon tomato paste

1 teaspoon salt

½ teaspoon freshly ground black pepper

1. Combine all the ingredients in a small saucepan and bring to a boil. Reduce the heat to a simmer and continue to cook, stirring as needed, for 30 minutes to let the flavors develop. Remove from the heat and set aside to cool slightly.

2. Transfer the sauce to a blender or food processor and process on high until smooth, about 1 minute. Use or store in an airtight container in the refrigerator for up to 2 weeks or in the freezer for up to 6 months.

YIELD: ABOUT 2 CUPS

fried onion rings

2 cups vegetable oil, for frying

½ cup all-purpose flour

½ teaspoon salt

¼ teaspoon freshly ground black pepper

1 large onion, thinly sliced and pulled apart into rings

1. Preheat the oil in a heavy-bottomed pot to 350°F.

2. Combine the flour, salt, and pepper in a small bowl. Dredge the onion rings in the flour to fully coat and shake off any excess.

3. Working in batches, fry the onion rings in the hot oil until lightly browned and crisp, 1 to 2 minutes, stirring as needed. Using a slotted spoon, transfer them to paper towels to drain. Serve immediately.

YIELD: ABOUT 2 CUPS

spicy tomato gastrique

¾ cup sugar

6 tablespoons hot sauce (I like Crystal for this)

5½ tablespoons cider vinegar

1 tablespoon Creole or coarse-grain mustard

1 tablespoon tomato paste

½ teaspoon salt

¼ teaspoon crushed red pepper

Combine all the ingredients in a small saucepan and whisk to combine. Bring to a boil, reduce the heat to a simmer, and cook until it becomes thick and syrupy, 12 to 15 minutes. Remove from the heat and set aside to cool to room temperature. If not using the day it is made, store in an airtight container in the refrigerator for up to 1 month. If the sauce gets too thick, thin it with water.

YIELD: ABOUT 1 CUP

wild vs. farm-raised salmon

When I cook salmon, I only cook wild-caught. The flavor and texture is vastly superior to that of farm-raised salmon, no doubt about it. However, I recognize that wild salmon is a lot more expensive than farm-raised and is not always available, to which I say, enjoy it as a treat. But if you are going to use farm-raised salmon, know that not all farm-raised salmon are the same; you should take it upon yourself to know where the salmon you are buying came from and the methods that are used by that particular company and their sustainability, all of which your fishmonger should be able to tell you.

seared sesame-crusted tuna
with sake-ponzu vinaigrette on spicy greens

In the late summer, early fall, the tuna begin to run out by the big oil rigs in the Gulf of Mexico. Tuna are wonderful fighting fish and, at 100 to 200 pounds each, bringing one in is like pulling in a refrigerator. When I catch a tuna, I like to enjoy it right on the boat as sashimi, and the rest gets set on ice until we get onto shore.

There are a lot of flavors working together in this dish but the taste of the fresh tuna shines through and brings it all together. The preparation is simple and fast; DO NOT overcook the tuna!

1½ pounds sushi-grade tuna loin, as fresh as possible

1½ teaspoons salt

1 teaspoon wasabi powder

¼ cup mixed black and white sesame seeds (or you can use all white, if you prefer)

2 tablespoons peanut oil

3 tablespoons sake

3 tablespoons ponzu

3 tablespoons fresh lime juice

1 tablespoon mirin

2 teaspoons fish sauce, preferably Vietnamese

2 teaspoons sugar

2 teaspoons toasted sesame oil

4 to 6 cups spicy mixed greens, such as mizuna

Carrot-Jalapeño Pickle, for serving (page 164)

Fried Wontons, for serving (page 164)

1. Using a very sharp knife, remove the skin, if necessary, from the tuna, then cut into 4 rectangular blocks by cutting the loin in half lengthwise and then in half crosswise. Season the pieces evenly with the salt and wasabi on all sides. Mix the sesame seeds on a shallow plate and press the pieces of tuna into them, fully and evenly coating the tuna on all sides.

2. In a medium nonstick sauté pan, heat the peanut oil over medium-high heat. When hot, add two of the tuna blocks to the pan, and sear 30 to 35 seconds per side (all the sides, not just top and bottom). Transfer them to a platter and repeat with the remaining tuna. When the tuna is cool enough to handle, use a very sharp knife to cut it crosswise into ¼- to ½-inch-thick slices.

3. In a small bowl, whisk together the sake, ponzu, lime juice, mirin, fish sauce, sugar, and sesame oil. The dressing can be made a day in advance and refrigerated in an airtight container.

4. Toss the greens in about half of the ponzu vinaigrette. For each serving, place about 1 cup of the greens on a plate, shingle 5 slices of tuna over the greens, spoon 1 tablespoon of the Carrot-Jalapeño Pickle over the tuna, place about ½ cup of the wontons on top of the greens, and spoon the rest of the dressing over the top.

YIELD: 4 TO 6 SERVINGS

(continued)

ponzu

Also sold as *ponzu shoyu*, it is a sauce used in Japanese cooking that is made from mirin, rice vinegar, and yuzu juice. Yuzu is a hybrid citrus fruit whose lineage includes the satsuma, which is grown throughout South Louisiana. The sauce is sweet-salty-acidic, with tones of lime and orange. I like using it with grilled and raw fish and as a dressing for salads.

The success of this rests on the shoulders of the tuna. If you can't get a beautiful piece of sushi-grade tuna from a fishmonger you trust, don't make it.

carrot-jalapeño pickle

This is also delicious added to sandwiches and as a garnish for noodle dishes.

2 jalapeño peppers, thinly shaved crosswise using a mandoline or very sharp knife

2 medium carrots, thinly shaved into rounds using a mandoline

½ teaspoon kosher salt

½ cup unseasoned rice vinegar

¼ cup fresh lime juice

3 tablespoons sugar

1½ teaspoons Vietnamese chili garlic sauce (*tuong ot toi*)

1. Place the jalapeños and carrots in a nonreactive bowl, sprinkle with the salt, and toss to combine.

2. Combine the vinegar, lime juice, and sugar in a small saucepan, and bring to a boil over medium-high heat. Cook, stirring, until the sugar has dissolved, about 1 minute. Remove from the heat and stir in the chili garlic sauce. Pour the vinegar mixture over the jalapeños and carrots, and let sit at room temperature for at least 1 hour in an airtight container before serving. This will keep in the refrigerator for up to 1 month.

YIELD: 1 CUP

fried wontons

Nori komi furikake is a Japanese rice seasoning that contains seaweed, sesame seeds, salt, and sugar. It's available in Asian food markets. If you can't find it, you can substitute crumbled seaweed snack.

Vegetable oil, for frying

16 spring roll wrappers, cut into ⅛-inch-wide strips

3 tablespoons nori komi furikake

In a large sauté pan, add oil to a depth of ½ to 1 inch, and heat it over medium-high heat. When the oil is hot, add one-third of the spring roll strips and fry until golden brown, 30 to 45 seconds. Using a slotted spoon, transfer them to a paper towel–lined plate to drain. Immediately season each batch with 1 tablespoon of the nori. Repeat with the remaining spring roll strips and seasoning, and set aside until ready to use.

YIELD: 6 SERVINGS

pan searing tuna

This is a perfect treatment for fresh tuna that develops a flavorful, crunchy crust while leaving the center a beautiful red. Only do this if you can get sushi-grade tuna. The success of the dish hinges on the quality of the tuna.

1. Sprinkle the tuna steaks with salt and wasabi powder, then dredge them on all sides in a mixture of black and white sesame seeds. Be sure to fully coat the fish.

2. In a hot nonstick pan over medium-high heat, sear the tuna no more than 30 to 35 seconds on all sides before removing to a platter.

PASTA & RICE

Growing up, pasta meant spaghetti and meatballs or a baked pasta dish in my house. The beauty of pasta is how quickly it cooks up, making it an essential choice for weekday cooks. In this chapter you'll find recipes like Meril's Linguine with Littleneck Clam Sauce (page 177) and Spaghetti for Mario (page 168), with sauces that can be prepared in about the same time it takes the pasta to cook to al dente. I also share long-simmering sauces that can be made the night before or enjoyed on the weekend, such as Pappardelle with White Wine–Braised Rabbit, Dijon, and Fresh Herbs (page 174).

Many rice dishes qualify as comfort food, satisfying both body and soul. My mom had a very nice repertoire of cold rice salads, including one made with *bachalau* (salt cod) and another with carrots and peas. Occasionally she would make her own version of paella, with fresh fava beans and a little chorizo. You'll find my favorites here, including Killer Red Beans and Rice (page 185) and EJ's Fried Rice (page 186).

spaghetti for mario

I've known Mario Batali since our *Food Network* days together. He is a dear friend. Our wives are friends, our kids are friends. For a time, we would alternate having Sunday suppers at each other's house with our families. There are many dishes I associate with Mario, but I first had a version of this one at his restaurant, Babbo, in New York City. It had me scratching my head afterward, thinking, "Man, what was that?" There is something about the combination of the cauliflower, anchovies, garlic, and walnuts that makes this out of sight.

1 head cauliflower, cut into florets and thick stems discarded

¾ cup walnut halves or pieces

1 (2-ounce) tin oil-packed anchovy fillets

5 cloves garlic, peeled

2 cups packed baby arugula

1 cup packed fresh flat-leaf parsley leaves

½ cup extra-virgin olive oil

¾ teaspoon crushed red pepper

¼ cup grated Parmigiano-Reggiano cheese, plus more for serving

Finely grated zest of 1 lemon

1 pound spaghetti

Salt and freshly ground black pepper

Toasted Breadcrumbs (recipe follows), for serving

1. Pulse the cauliflower florets in a food processor until they resemble coarse crumbs, with some pieces about the size of a pea or slightly smaller. Transfer to a bowl and set aside.

2. To the food processor (no need to clean out the bowl), add the walnuts, anchovy fillets with their oil, garlic, arugula, parsley, ¼ cup of the oil, and the red pepper. Pulse until the mixture comes together to form a coarse paste. Add the cheese and lemon zest, and pulse briefly to combine. Set aside.

3. Bring a large pot of water to a boil and season generously with salt—it should taste like seawater. Add the spaghetti and cook until it is al dente, usually 8 to 9 minutes. Drain the pasta, reserving 2 cups of the pasta water.

4. While the pasta is cooking, heat a 14-inch skillet over high heat with the remaining ¼ cup oil. When the oil is very hot, add the cauliflower and cook, stirring frequently, until it begins to brown around the edges and smells nutty, 5 to 6 minutes. Stir in the arugula pesto and cook briefly, then remove the pan from the heat.

5. Return the skillet to medium-high heat and add the drained pasta and 1 cup of the reserved pasta water. Using tongs, toss the pasta with the cauliflower and pesto, adding more of the pasta water as necessary to form a sauce that just coats the pasta. Season with salt and pepper to taste, then serve immediately in pasta bowls, garnished with the Toasted Breadcrumbs and additional cheese.

YIELD: 4 TO 6 SERVINGS

toasted breadcrumbs

2 tablespoons olive oil or unsalted butter

¼ teaspoon salt

2 cups coarse dry breadcrumbs or panko

Heat the oil in a small nonstick skillet over medium heat. Add the breadcrumbs and salt and cook, stirring, until browned and crisp, about 5 minutes.

YIELD: 2 CUPS

A whole tin of anchovies? Believe me, it's not too much; in fact, I've been known to add more, as with the garlic. Make the recipe once as written, then tweak it to suit your own particular tastes.

•

The starchy pasta water is a key ingredient, acting as a thickener for the sauce.

fresh pasta with homemade tasso and smoked mushrooms

I've been making a version of this since my days at Commander's Palace, when I had to sneak a table-top grill into the kitchen and smoke the mushrooms when Dick Brennan went home between lunch and dinner because I wasn't allowed to have a smoker in the Garden District of New Orleans. The dish is still on my menu at Emeril's, and there would be a riot if I tried to take it off. What I do like to do is change it up a bit sometimes, adding crawfish when they're in season. Shrimp would also work well.

For making both the mushrooms and the tasso, you'll need a stovetop smoker (like I describe on page 53, Steps 2 and 3). And if you're going to make your own tasso, plan ahead, as the pork mixture needs to marinate in its spice mix for at least three days before smoking.

1 pound fresh lasagna sheets, cut into ½-inch-wide strips, or fresh pasta of your choice (linguine, pappardelle, etc.)

2 tablespoons olive oil

4 ounces Homemade Tasso (see opposite), cut into ¾-inch dice

2 cups packed baby spinach (2½ ounces)

2 tablespoons minced shallot

1 tablespoon minced garlic

½ cup Marsala

Smoked Mushrooms (see opposite)

1 cup heavy cream

¼ cup (½ stick) unsalted butter, cut into small cubes

¼ cup grated Parmigiano-Reggiano cheese

1. In a large pot of salted boiling water, cook the pasta until it is just al dente, about 7 minutes. Drain the pasta in a colander, reserving ½ cup of the pasta water.

2. Heat the oil in a large high-sided sauté pan over medium heat. Add the tasso and cook for 1 minute. Add the spinach and cook, stirring, until it wilts, 1 to 2 minutes. Add the shallot and garlic, and cook 1 minute longer, stirring. Add the Marsala and cook until it reduces by half. Add the mushrooms, cream, and reserved pasta water, and simmer until the sauce thickens, about 3 minutes.

Whisk in the butter cubes one at a time, waiting until each one is fully incorporated into the sauce before adding the next. Add the pasta to the pan and toss until it is coated with the sauce.

3. Serve the pasta immediately topped with the cheese.

YIELD: 4 SERVINGS

homemade tasso

A specialty of South Louisiana, tasso is a spicy smoked pork used primarily as a seasoning in other dishes. If you don't want to make your own and it's not available locally, tasso is easy to order online. For the wood chips, I like to use hickory, pecan, or apple.

7 tablespoons paprika

5 tablespoons granulated onion

3 tablespoons salt

2 tablespoons plus 1 teaspoon freshly ground black pepper

2 tablespoons cayenne pepper

1 tablespoon plus 2 teaspoons garlic powder

1 (3½- to 4-pound) boneless pork butt, trimmed of fat and cut into 1-inch-thick slices

1. In a large shallow bowl, combine all the spices to blend well. Working with one slice of pork at a time, place it in the spice mixture, pressing the mixture into the meat so that it is very well coated. Transfer the slice to a piece of plastic wrap and wrap tightly. Place all of the pork "packages" in a zip-top plastic bag and refrigerate for at least 3 days and up to 1 week.

2. Set up a stovetop smoker or other home smoker according to the manufacturer's instructions with the wood chips. Place the slices of pork in a single layer on the rack in the smoker, leaving enough space for the smoke to circulate around them. (Depending on the size of your smoker, you may have to do this in batches.) Heat the stovetop smoker over medium heat and, once the smoker begins to smoke, cover it and continue to cook the tasso over medium heat, undisturbed, for 25 to 30 minutes. (For an electric or outdoor smoker, keep the temperature in the smoker at 175° to 200°F and smoke up to 2 hours.) An instant-read thermometer inserted into the center of the meat should register about 190°F.

3. Remove the tasso from the smoker and let cool. Use as desired (it will keep up to 2 days in the refrigerator), or wrap the individual pieces of tasso tightly with plastic wrap and then again in freezer paper and freeze for up to 6 months.

YIELD: 3½ TO 4 POUNDS

smoked mushrooms

You can use any kind of smoking wood chip for this but I think hickory yields the best flavor, by far. These mushrooms are also delicious added to soups and omelets, used as a pizza topping, or included in a grilled cheese sandwich. Don't use portobellos, as they will turn the pasta black because of their gills.

1 pound mixed fresh mushrooms, such as button, shiitake, oyster, cremini, and/or chanterelle, trimmed and cleaned

3 tablespoons olive oil

1 teaspoon salt

½ teaspoon coarsely ground black pepper

3 sprigs fresh thyme

1. In a large bowl, combine all the ingredients and mix well.

2. Prepare a stovetop smoker according to the manufacturer's instructions with the wood chips. Place the mushrooms on the grill pan and partially cover the smoker, leaving the lid askew by 1 inch. Place over medium-high heat. When it begins to smoke, close the lid completely and cook until the mushrooms are tender and completely smoked, about 10 minutes.

3. Turn off the heat and let the mushrooms absorb the remaining smoke for 5 minutes longer.

4. Remove the mushrooms from the smoker and discard the thyme. The mushrooms will keep in an airtight container in the refrigerator up to 1 week.

YIELD: ABOUT 2 CUPS

cleaning mushrooms

Not all mushrooms are created equal when it comes to cleaning them. Clean chanterelles by washing them in a bowl of cool water, using a paring knife to trim the stem and any dried pieces, then dry them on a towel. Remove the entire stem from shiitakes and wipe their caps clean. For maitakes and oyster mushrooms, trim away any tough parts of their stems and give them a quick wipe. In fact, mushrooms that look pretty clean can just be brushed with a pastry brush to remove any traces of dirt, if necessary.

spaghetti carbonara
with fresh duck eggs

Carbonara is quick and easy to make. I love to throw it together for the family. To me, it's real comfort food. I make it using only the yolks from duck eggs—it yields deeper flavor and beautiful color. If duck eggs aren't available, you can use chicken eggs, but please make sure they are farm-fresh and organic. Be sure to have a pepper grinder on hand—freshly ground black pepper is a key flavor component in this dish. Any leftovers will reheat beautifully in the microwave—it only takes about 1 minute.

4 large duck egg yolks, beaten
(use the highest-quality, freshest eggs)

1 teaspoon freshly ground black pepper

1/4 teaspoon sea salt

3/4 cup freshly grated Parmigiano-Reggiano cheese, plus more for serving

1 tablespoon chopped fresh flat-leaf parsley

1/2 pound thickly sliced pancetta or guanciale

3 tablespoons minced shallot

1 tablespoon minced garlic

1 pound spaghetti, cooked until al dente and drained, reserving 3/4 cup pasta water

1/2 cup fresh peas, blanched 2 to 3 minutes, or frozen, thawed

1. In a large bowl, briskly whisk together the eggs, pepper, salt, cheese, and parsley until well combined. Set aside.

2. In a large sauté pan over medium heat, cook the pancetta, stirring as needed, until crispy, about 6 minutes. Add the shallot and garlic, and cook, stirring, for 1 minute. Add the cooked pasta, reserved pasta water, and peas, and toss well, coating the pasta fully with the hot fat. Cook, stirring to keep the pasta from sticking to the pan, until most of the water has evaporated, about 1 minute.

3. Add half of the pasta to the bowl and quickly toss it with the egg mixture. This will temper the egg yolks so they do not get scrambled from the heat of the pasta but instead will end up evenly coating the strands of pasta. Working quickly, add the remaining pasta to the bowl and toss until everything is thoroughly combined.

4. Portion the pasta into warm shallow bowls and offer a pepper grinder and more grated cheese, if desired.

YIELD: 4 TO 6 SERVINGS

pancetta and guanciale

These two pork products are both cured but not smoked bacons—pancetta is made from the pork belly and *guanciale* from the pork jowl or cheek. Both have a more acidic flavor and cook differently than bacon. *Guanciale* is usually less salty than pancetta, and pancetta is usually chewier than both bacon and *guanciale*. Imported Italian *guanciale* is very fatty and should have a melt-in-your-mouth feel. You can substitute smoked bacon for either in this recipe, but be sure to use a high-quality slab bacon and know that the flavor profile will be different.

Cooking the pasta with the rendered fat for a minute really infuses it with the flavor of the pancetta or guanciale.

pappardelle

with white wine–braised rabbit, dijon, and fresh herbs

This is essentially a play on the classic coq au vin, prepared instead with rabbit and white wine. The Chablis adds a delicious mineral note to the sauce. This is a favorite of my friend Sammy Hagar, when he eats at Delmonico's.

2 large rabbits (about 3 pounds each), cut into serving pieces

$\frac{1}{2}$ cup Dijon mustard

1 teaspoon salt

$\frac{1}{2}$ teaspoon freshly ground black pepper

1 cup plus 1 tablespoon all-purpose flour

4 tablespoons ($\frac{1}{2}$ stick) unsalted butter

2 tablespoons grapeseed or olive oil

1 large yellow onion, cut into $\frac{1}{2}$-inch dice (about 2 cups)

1 knob celery root, peeled and cut into $\frac{1}{2}$-inch dice (about 2 cups)

3 cups French Chablis or other dry white wine

2 sprigs fresh rosemary

2 sprigs fresh thyme

1 sprig fresh basil

1 bay leaf

1 pound pappardelle, linguine, or wide egg noodles

$\frac{1}{3}$ cup crème fraîche

2 tablespoons finely chopped fresh flat-leaf parsley

1. Coat the rabbit pieces evenly with the mustard and sprinkle with the salt and pepper. Dredge the pieces in 1 cup of the flour, coating them completely and tapping off any excess.

2. Melt 2 tablespoons of the butter with 1 tablespoon of the oil in a large Dutch oven or other heavy-bottomed pot over medium-high heat. When the butter sizzles, add the rabbit pieces and sear until very crisp and golden brown on all sides, about 15 minutes total. Transfer to a platter as they are browned. You may need to do this in batches.

3. Reduce the heat to medium and melt the remaining 2 tablespoons butter with the remaining 1 tablespoon oil. Add the onion and celery root, and cook, stirring occasionally, until softened, 5 to 7 minutes. Stir in the remaining 1 tablespoon flour. Add the wine and bring to a boil, scraping up any browned bits from the bottom of the pan. Return the rabbit pieces to the pan, along with the herbs; cover, reduce the heat to low, and cook until the rabbit is tender, 35 to 45 minutes.

4. When the rabbit is just about done, cook the pasta in a large pot of boiling salted water according to package directions until just al dente. Drain, return to the pot, and cover to keep warm.

5. Remove the Dutch oven from the heat. Remove and discard the bay leaf and herb sprigs, then stir in the crème fraîche and parsley.

6. Portion the pasta onto plates or into large shallow bowls and top with a generous ladleful of sauce and several pieces of rabbit.

YIELD: 4 TO 6 SERVINGS

Also known as celeriac, celery root is a variety of celery grown for its root. When buying, look for one that feels heavy for its size.

•

Because of its decidedly not smooth surface, celery root can be awkward to peel. First, trim the root and stem ends with a paring knife, then run a Y-shaped vegetable peeler over the knobby surface until you get down to the smooth, white portion of the root.

meril's linguine
with littleneck clam sauce

This is my daughter Meril's favorite pasta dish, and it'll become one of yours, too. Start to finish, you can have it on the table in 20 minutes. Round out the meal with crusty bread and a green salad.

1 pound linguine or spaghetti

3 tablespoons extra-virgin olive oil

1 cup chopped onion

2 tablespoons minced garlic

$1/4$ teaspoon crushed red pepper, plus more to taste

$1/4$ teaspoon freshly ground black pepper

2 pounds littleneck clams, scrubbed, discarding any that won't close

1 cup dry white wine

1 cup clam juice

3 tablespoons unsalted butter

2 tablespoons chopped fresh flat-leaf parsley

Salt

1. Bring a large pot of salted water to a boil. Add the linguine and cook until just al dente, 8 to 9 minutes. Remove the pot from the heat and allow the pasta to sit in the water 30 seconds longer. Remove $1/2$ cup pasta water from the pot and set aside. Drain the pasta.

2. Set a 14-inch skillet on the stovetop with its lid nearby. If you don't have a lid, use another 14-inch skillet as the top. Add the oil to the skillet and heat it gently over medium heat. Add the onion, garlic, red pepper, and black pepper, and cook, stirring a few times, until the onion is softened and the garlic fragrant, about 5 minutes.

3. Add the clams and wine to the pan, increase the heat to high, and cook for 3 minutes. Add the clam juice and cover the skillet. Steam the clams, shaking the pan intermittently, until all the clams have opened, 10 to 12 minutes. Discard any that aren't opened.

4. Add the pasta to the skillet along with the reserved pasta water, the butter, and parsley, and cook until the pasta is warmed through and coated with the sauce. Season with salt and additional red pepper to taste. Serve immediately, making sure the servings have equal amounts of clams.

YIELD: 4 TO 6 SERVINGS

Store clams in the refrigerator in a colander set in a bowl, covered with ice. It is important that the bowl be deep enough so that when the ice melts, the clams don't make contact with the water. None of this purging business, leaving clams to soak in water you've added cornmeal to, supposedly to get them to spit out any sand. In fact, if you leave clams in water, you'll kill them (believe it or not, they'll drown).

seafood fideuà

I've traveled to Spain many times, including family trips to the island of Ibiza, and this is one of my very favorite recipes from that part of the world. *Fideuà* is a cousin of paella, traditionally made in a paella pan but instead of rice, it's made with a pasta called *fideo* that is toasted in hot olive oil. It's then further cooked with wine and fish stock, with the catch of the day (or whatever's looking good at your local fish counter) added in. *Fideuà* is served with a big dollop of intensely garlicky allioli plopped on top to be stirred in. When I make this, I think of the small restaurants that line the beaches in Ibiza and the neighboring island of Formentera—nothing more than shacks with wooden tables set out front—turning out pan after pan of *fideuà* cooked over an open fire with seafood that came straight off the fishing boats. Enjoy with a glass of Albariño white wine.

8 ounces large shrimp, peeled and deveined

1 to 1½ pounds white-fleshed fish fillets, such as halibut, cod, haddock, or grouper, cut into 2-inch pieces

3 tablespoons extra-virgin olive oil, plus more for frying

3½ teaspoons kosher salt

2 teaspoons smoked sweet paprika

¼ teaspoon freshly ground black pepper

1 pound fideo pasta or cappellini, broken into ½-inch pieces

2 cups finely chopped onions

⅔ cup chopped mixed red and green bell peppers

½ cup finely chopped celery

3 tablespoons minced garlic

½ cup diced cured Spanish chorizo

1 teaspoon crushed red pepper

4 tablespoons finely chopped fresh flat-leaf parsley

¾ teaspoon loosely packed saffron threads

1 cup dry white wine, preferably Portuguese or Spanish (Vinho Verde works well)

6 cups Fish Stock or Shrimp Stock (page 91 or 84)

1 to 1½ pounds cherrystone clams (18 to 20 clams), scrubbed well, discarding any that won't close

Allioli, for serving (see opposite)

1. In a medium bowl, place the shrimp, fish, 1 tablespoon of the oil, ¾ teaspoon of the salt, ½ teaspoon of the paprika, and the black pepper, and toss until the seafood is thoroughly coated with the oil and spices.

2. Preheat the oven to 400°F. Line a large heatproof bowl with paper towels and have it ready near the stovetop.

3. In a paella pan or 14-inch ovenproof skillet, pour in oil to come ¼ inch up the side (about ½ cup) and heat over medium-high heat. When the oil starts to shimmer, add the pasta and cook, stirring and tossing frequently, until it is golden brown. Take care not to let the pasta burn; it cooks quickly once it begins to brown. Using a wooden spoon or metal spatula, transfer the pasta to the prepared bowl and set aside. (You may need to wipe the skillet with a paper towel to remove any stubborn pieces of pasta clinging to the pan.)

4. Add the remaining 2 tablespoons oil to the skillet and the onions, bell peppers, celery, garlic, and chorizo. Season with ¼ teaspoon of the salt and the red pepper, and cook, stirring a few times, until the onions are softened, 4 to 6 minutes. Add 2 tablespoons of the parsley and the saffron, and cook for 1 minute. Add the wine and stock, and bring to a gentle simmer. Cook for 5 minutes to allow the flavors to come together. Add the remaining 2½ teaspoons salt and 1½ teaspoons paprika and taste; the stock should be well seasoned; if not, add more salt to taste.

5. Add the browned pasta to the simmering stock and cook, stirring frequently, until it returns to a boil and the pasta expands and absorbs some of the liquid; it should be thickened but still somewhat soupy, about 3 minutes. Add the clams and cook until they begin to open, about 2 minutes. Discard any that aren't opened. Add 2 tablespoons of the Allioli and stir well to incorporate it into the sauce. Nestle the fish and shrimp down into the pasta, arranging them evenly over the entire pan.

6. Transfer the skillet to the oven and cook until the pasta has absorbed almost all of the liquid (it may appear just a bit jiggly in the center) and the surface is crispy, 8 to 10 minutes. Set aside, loosely covered, for 10 minutes before serving.

7. Serve hot, garnished with the remaining 2 tablespoons parsley and with the remaining Allioli passed at the table.

YIELD: 8 TO 10 SERVINGS

allioli

This is traditional with *fideuà* but is also a delicious alternative to ketchup for French fries.

2 tablespoons minced garlic

1 teaspoon kosher salt

2 large egg yolks, at room temperature

2 teaspoons fresh lemon juice

1 cup mild olive oil

Mash the garlic and salt into a paste by using the side of a chef's knife and repeatedly pressing it back and forth on a wooden cutting board. Transfer to a food processor and add the egg yolks and lemon juice. Process to combine. While the motor is running, add the oil through the lid in a thin, steady stream until a smooth, thick emulsion is formed. If the allioli breaks, add a few drops of room-temperature water and stir to help the emulsion come back together. Taste and adjust the seasoning if necessary. Store in an airtight container in the refrigerator up to several days.

YIELD: ABOUT 1¼ CUPS

fideo pasta

Using Italian pasta for comparison, fideo pasta varies in thickness from that of angel hair or cappellini to spaghetti and is sold in coils (or "nests") or cut into 1-inch lengths, perfect for making *fideuà*. You can also find it sold under the name *fidelini*. I love to make *fideuà* with squid-ink fideo (*fideuà de tinta de calamar*). If you can't find fideo in your supermarket, substitute cappellini broken into short lengths or shop for it online.

penne with pompano, fresh tomatoes, and basil

With all the culinary challenge shows on television now, everyone is used to the idea of the ingredient challenge, the competitors given a box of ingredients and told to make a dish. But this is something home cooks come up against all the time; you aren't able to go to the store and you need to pull dinner together from what you have.

That is essentially what this dish is. I love to fish, and whenever I am able, I'm on my boat fishing the Gulf. One day, I caught an African pompano. Working with what I had onboard, this is how we enjoyed it that evening. Unlike the reality challenges, there is nothing exotic here, but that's part of the magic—you can prepare a deeply flavored dish using simple techniques and a few ordinary ingredients.

8 ounces penne pasta

3 tablespoons extra-virgin olive oil

1 cup diced yellow onion

1 tablespoon minced garlic

4 cups chopped vine-ripened tomatoes, preferably heirloom

Sea salt and freshly ground black pepper

¼ cup fresh basil chiffonade (see Essentials, page 37)

½ cup grated Parmigiano-Reggiano cheese, plus more for garnish

4 skinless pompano fillets

1 teaspoon Emeril's Creole Seasoning (page 108) or other Creole seasoning

Small fresh basil leaves, for garnish

1. Bring a large pot of salted water to a boil and cook the pasta until al dente, about 10 minutes. Drain, saving ½ cup of the pasta water, and return the pasta to the pot. Set aside.

2. In a large sauté pan, heat 2 tablespoons of the oil over medium-high heat. When hot, add the onion and garlic, and cook, stirring a few times, until softened, 3 to 4 minutes. Add the tomatoes, 2 teaspoons salt, and 1 teaspoon pepper, and cook until the tomatoes begin to break down, about 5 minutes. Add the reserved pasta water and cook, stirring as needed, until the sauce begins to thicken, about 10 minutes. Reduce the heat to medium-low, stir in the basil and cheese, and let simmer for 5 minutes. Add the pasta to the pan and toss to coat. Remove from the heat and set aside, covered.

3. Heat another large sauté pan over medium-high heat until hot, then add remaining 1 tablespoon oil. Lightly season the fish on both sides with Creole seasoning, and place the fillets in the hot pan. Cook until golden brown, about 2 minutes per side. Transfer the fish to a paper towel–lined plate.

4. Serve the pasta on plates or in shallow bowls, topped with a pompano fillet and sprinkled with more grated Parmigiano and basil leaves.

YIELD: 4 SERVINGS

In a recipe this simple, the starchy pasta water plays a crucial role, adding additional salt for seasoning and helping to thicken the sauce.

Instead of pompano, you can make this with trout, flounder, or snapper.

herbed pancetta-potato
gnocchi with pink vodka sauce

This is a dish I love to prepare on the weekends with my children EJ and Meril. Gnocchi are not hard to make and you get such phenomenal flavor from homemade. Instead of pancetta, you can use prosciutto, andouille, or chorizo (I peel the skin off and let the meat crumble), or you can leave it out entirely if you want to go vegetarian. This is a delicious bowl of comfort.

2 ounces thinly sliced pancetta

1½ pounds waxy potatoes, such as Yukon Gold (see Essentials, at right)

2 tablespoons olive oil

1 teaspoon kosher salt

¼ teaspoon freshly ground white pepper

¼ cup grated Parmigiano-Reggiano cheese, plus more for garnish

1 tablespoon chopped fresh basil

1 tablespoon chopped fresh chives

1 large egg plus 1 large egg yolk, whisked together

1½ cups all-purpose flour, or more, if needed

Pink Vodka Sauce (page 184)

Small fresh basil leaves, for garnish

1. Preheat the oven to 400°F.

2. In a small nonstick sauté pan over medium heat, render the fat from the pancetta. Once the pancetta is crispy, transfer it to paper towels to drain. Discard the fat and finely chop the pancetta. Set aside.

3. Rub the potatoes all over with the oil, and season with half of the salt and pepper. Place on a baking sheet and bake until tender, 1 to 1½ hours. Remove from the oven and cool completely. Peel the potatoes and discard the skins.

4. On a clean work surface, evenly mash the potatoes using a fork, then season with the remaining salt and pepper. Add the pancetta, cheese, herbs, and eggs and mix well. Add 1¼ cups plus 2 tablespoons of the flour and work this very gently into the potatoes to form a dough that is damp but not tacky to the touch.

5. Sprinkle the remaining 2 tablespoons flour on the work surface. Cut the dough into four portions. Gently roll each portion into a cylinder about 1 inch thick. Cut each rope into ½-inch pieces. Roll each piece lightly using the tines of a fork to create shallow ridges; the ridges will help the sauce adhere to the gnocchi. See the tutorial on page 184.

6. Bring a large pot of salted water to a boil. Working in small batches, add the gnocchi to the water and cook until the dumplings float to the top, 1 to 2 minutes. Remove the gnocchi using a slotted spoon and place on a large rimmed baking sheet to cool.

7. If necessary, reheat the vodka sauce in a large sauté pan over medium-high heat. Transfer the gnocchi to the sauce and cook until they are just heated through. Serve on a large platter sprinkled with more cheese and basil leaves.

YIELD: 6 TO 8 SERVINGS

(continued)

I call for waxy potatoes in this recipe but you'll also get great results with russet potatoes.

•

Some folks boil the potatoes when making gnocchi but I believe you get a better texture when they are baked.

•

Don't use a blender or food processor to mix up the dough for gnocchi or you'll end up with a gummy mess.

pink vodka sauce

¼ cup olive oil

2 cups chopped yellow onions

1½ teaspoons salt

Pinch of crushed red pepper

2 tablespoons minced garlic

2 (14.5-ounce) cans crushed tomatoes

½ cup vodka

1 cup heavy cream

1 to 2 tablespoons fresh basil chiffonade (see Essentials, page 37)

¼ cup grated Parmigiano-Reggiano cheese

1. In a large skillet, heat the oil over medium heat. When hot, add the onions, salt, and red pepper, and cook, stirring, until the onions are soft and golden, about 5 minutes. Add the garlic and cook until fragrant, about 30 seconds. Add the tomatoes and cook, stirring, until thick, about 8 minutes. Add the vodka; cook until the sauce is reduced by half, 3 to 4 minutes. Stir in the cream and cook until the sauce thickens, 4 to 5 minutes. Use immediately or let cool and store in an airtight container in the refrigerator for up to 1 week or in the freezer for 6 months.

2. Right before serving, stir in the basil and sprinkle the cheese over the sauce.

YIELD: 4 SERVINGS

making gnocchi

Gnocchi are best served the day they are made but can be refrigerated for a day or frozen up to two months.

1. Using a fork, mash the scooped-out flesh from the baked potatoes on a clean work surface until it's all of an even texture.

2. Season the potatoes, then add the pancetta, cheese, herbs, and eggs and mix well.

3. Be careful to add just enough flour, otherwise your gnocchi will be dense. Work the flour gently into the potatoes to form a dough that is damp but not tacky to the touch. Don't overwork the dough.

4. Cut the dough into four portions and roll each into a long rope about 1 inch thick.

5. Cut each rope across into ½-inch pieces. With the fork, roll each piece to elongate it and give it shallow ridges.

ESSENTIAL EMERIL

killer red beans and rice

Red beans and rice is quintessential New Orleans comfort food. It's the kind of dish that can easily feed a crowd and is deeply satisfying. I talked to a lot of grandmas about their red beans and rice and from my conversations developed my own take. The flavors are unbelievable.

2 tablespoons olive oil

1 smoked ham hock, skin scored in several places

4 cups chopped onions

1 cup chopped green bell peppers

1 cup chopped celery

3 tablespoons minced garlic

2 bay leaves

1 tablespoon Emeril's Creole Seasoning (page 108) or other Creole seasoning

1 teaspoon dried thyme

$3/4$ teaspoon cayenne pepper

6 cups Emeril's Pork Stock (recipe follows), Rich Chicken Stock (page 68), or store-bought low-sodium chicken broth

4 cups water

1 pound dried red kidney beans, picked over

1 pound smoked pork sausage, cut into $1/2$-inch-thick rounds

$1/2$ pound smoked ham, cut into 1-inch cubes

Salt

Hot white rice, for serving

Chopped green onions, for garnish

Louisiana hot sauce, for serving

1. Heat a large, heavy-bottomed Dutch oven over medium-high heat and add the oil. When hot, add the ham hock, onions, bell peppers, and celery, and cook, stirring occasionally, until the vegetables are soft and lightly golden, about 15 minutes.

2. Add the garlic, bay leaves, Creole seasoning, thyme, and cayenne, and cook, stirring, for 2 minutes longer. Add the stock and water, and bring to a boil. Reduce the heat to a low simmer, partially cover the pan, and cook for 1 hour.

3. Rinse the beans well under cool running water. Drain, then stir them into the pot. Partially cover and continue to cook at a low simmer, stirring occasionally, for another $1/2$ hours.

4. Add the sausage and ham to the pot, cover partially, and cook until the beans are tender and creamy and the meat on the ham hock is tender enough to pull from the bone, 1 to $1/2$ hours longer. Taste and adjust the seasonings if necessary.

5. Serve the beans in large shallow bowls ladled over a mound of hot rice and garnished with green onions. Pass the hot sauce at the table for guests to use to their liking.

YIELD: 6 TO 8 SERVINGS

emeril's pork stock

$3/2$ pounds pork bones, shoulder bones, country ribs, or other meaty pork parts

$2/2$ pounds smoked pork tails, hocks, or necks

8 quarts water

6 black peppercorns

2 sprigs fresh flat-leaf parsley

1 sprig fresh thyme

1 bay leaf

1 clove garlic, peeled

2 onions, quartered

2 ribs celery, roughly chopped

2 carrots, roughly chopped

1. Heat a large stockpot over medium-high heat, then add the pork bones and cook in batches until golden brown on all sides, 5 to 6 minutes. Add the smoked pork and water, and bring to a boil. Reduce the heat to a simmer and cook, skimming off any scum from the surface, for 3 hours.

2. Prepare a bouquet garni by wrapping the peppercorns, parsley, thyme, bay leaf, and garlic in cheesecloth. Once the stock has cooked for 3 hours, add the bouquet garni, onions, celery, and carrots, and simmer the stock for another $1/2$ hours.

3. Strain the stock through a colander into another large pot or heatproof container. If there are any bits still floating in the stock, strain it again, using cheesecloth or a fine-mesh strainer. Use the stock immediately, or cool it rapidly and store it in airtight containers in the refrigerator for several days or in the freezer for up to 6 months.

YIELD: 4 QUARTS

ej's fried rice

My son, EJ, has strong opinions, right down to what he wants in his fried rice, which is one of his favorite dishes. EJ likes sweet Chinese sausage, but you can use any kind of sausage, maple-cured ham or bacon, poultry, or tofu for your protein.

3 tablespoons vegetable or canola oil

3 large eggs, lightly beaten

2 pinches of salt

2 tablespoons minced green onions (green part only)

1 tablespoon minced garlic

1 tablespoon minced peeled fresh ginger

$^2/_3$ cup diced red onion

4 ounces Chinese sausage (*lap xu'ong*), diced

1 small baby bok choy, root end trimmed away and sliced across into $^1/_2$-inch-wide strips (about $1^1/_2$ cups sliced)

$^1/_2$ cup diced blanched green beans

1 cup small broccoli florets, blanched until crisp-tender

1 red bell pepper, seeded and cut into 1-inch squares

$^1/_2$ cup frozen edamame or baby lima beans, thawed

$^1/_2$ cup fresh or thawed frozen green peas

6 cups cold cooked jasmine rice

5 tablespoons soy sauce, or to taste

1 tablespoon toasted sesame oil

$^2/_3$ cup thinly sliced green onions (green and white parts)

1. Heat a large wok over high heat until very hot. Add 1 tablespoon of the vegetable oil and swirl to coat the pan, then add the eggs and salt, and tilt the pan while stirring and scraping the eggs continually with a heat-resistant rubber spatula until they are just softly set, about 30 seconds. Using the spatula, chop the eggs against the side of the pan repeatedly to cut into small pieces. Quickly scrape the cooked eggs into a dish and set aside.

2. Working quickly, add the remaining 2 tablespoons vegetable oil to the wok and, when hot, add the minced green onions, garlic, and ginger, and stir-fry until fragrant, 15 to 30 seconds. Add the red onion and sausage, and cook briefly, 30 to 60 seconds, stirring constantly. One at a time and stirring for about 10 seconds between each addition, add the bok choy, green beans, broccoli, bell pepper, edamame, and peas, then cook, stirring, until softened slightly.

3. Add the rice and cook, stirring, until it begins to stick to the pan, about 1 minute. Immediately add the soy sauce and sesame oil and cook, stirring, until the rice is evenly coated with the mixture and warmed through. Add the reserved cooked eggs and stir until heated through, about 1 minute. Add the sliced green onions, stirring until fragrant, about 10 seconds. Serve immediately.

YIELD: 6 TO 8 SERVINGS

how to stir-fry

This technique can be used for fried rice or any kind of stir-fry, with your choice of ingredients. If you have a wok, use it; otherwise, a large sauté pan with slanted sides will work.

1. The key to stir-fry is having your ingredients measured, prepped, and ready to go. Cut ingredients into similar sizes so they cook evenly, and blanch harder vegetables so they cook faster.

2. Preheat the pan over high heat before swirling in oil. For this stir-fry, eggs are added first. If you are using another protein, precook it at this point and remove from the pan.

3. Add the aromatics, sausage, and vegetables as directed in your recipe.

4. Add the rice, stirring to break up any clumps. It works best to use cold rice.

5. Add flavorings like soy sauce and sesame oil. Heat, then add your protein back to the pan along with the sliced green onions.

1

2

3

4

5

paella
with chicken, chorizo, clams, and shrimp

This recipe brings back memories of being in Valencia, the paella capital of the world, with my son, EJ, to see our favorite soccer team, Real Madrid. We hooked up with my good friend Gonzalo and his two sons beforehand to eat at one of the paella shacks there, the paella cooked in pans over open fires out front. As we sat down, we realized the entire Real Madrid team was there, digging into paella, too. It was an unforgettable day.

2 teaspoons salt

1 teaspoon freshly ground black pepper

1 teaspoon smoked hot paprika

6 bone-in skin-on chicken thighs (about 2 pounds), skin trimmed but not removed

1/2 cup extra-virgin olive oil

1 1/2 cups chopped yellow onion

3/4 cup chopped green bell pepper

3/4 cup chopped celery

2 tablespoons minced garlic

8 ounces chorizo, chopped

5 bay leaves

3 1/2 cups Rich Chicken Stock (page 68) or store-bought low-sodium chicken broth

1/2 teaspoon saffron threads

2 cups Valencia (also called *bomba*), Arborio, or other short-grain rice

1 (14.5-ounce) can diced tomatoes, with juices

2 teaspoons Worcestershire sauce

1 teaspoon hot sauce

18 to 24 clams, scrubbed

18 to 24 medium shrimp (about 3/4 pound), tails left on, peeled and deveined

1/4 cup chopped fresh flat-leaf parsley, for garnish

8 lemon wedges, for serving

1. Preheat the oven to 325°F.

2. Combine the salt, black pepper, and paprika in a small container. Using a meat cleaver, cut the chicken thighs in half across the bone (see Essentials) and sprinkle with the spice mix. Heat the oil in a paella pan or ovenproof 14-inch skillet over medium heat until it ripples; add the chicken, skin side down, and brown for 8 minutes. Turn the chicken skin side up and brown the other side, about 3 minutes. Remove the chicken from the pan.

3. Add the onion, bell pepper, celery, garlic, chorizo, and bay leaves to the pan, and cook, stirring, for 5 minutes. Meanwhile, combine the stock and saffron in a small saucepan and bring to a boil.

4. Add the rice to the paella pan and stir to coat it very well in the oil; toast the rice for 2 minutes. Stir in the tomatoes and cook, stirring as needed, until the liquid has evaporated. Add the hot stock, Worcestershire, and hot sauce, and stir to combine. Return the chicken pieces and any accumulated juices to the pan along with the clams, seam side up. Bring the broth to a boil over medium-high heat and continue to boil until enough liquid has evaporated so that the liquid is even with the surface of the rice and the mixture is no longer soupy, about 8 minutes. Some liquid should still remain.

5. Nestle the shrimp into the pan and bake, uncovered, in the oven for 25 minutes.

6. Remove the paella from the oven. Cover with aluminum foil and allow it to steam an additional 5 to 10 minutes before serving.

7. Right before serving, stir the paella and sprinkle with the parsley. Serve in large shallow bowls with a wedge of lemon.

YIELD: 8 SERVINGS

If you don't own a cleaver, ask the butcher to cut the chicken thighs in half. It's important because it allows the chicken to cook faster so that it is done at about the same time as the shrimp and clams.

•

Follow my recipe, and you will end up with the prize of paella—the socarrat. This is a layer of crunchy brown rice at the bottom of the pan.

triple truffle risotto

My present to Sammy and Kari Hagar when they got married twenty years ago was a bag of fresh truffles, which I brought with me and used in multiple dishes I prepared at their reception, including a risotto. I've re-created that risotto here but in a less expensive form, using truffle oil, truffle paste, and truffle butter—the choice of white or black truffles is yours. The flavor is phenomenal. And if you're feeling flush and they're in season, by all means, finish this with very thin shavings of fresh truffle showered over the top. You can offer smaller servings as an indulgent first course, enjoy it as the main event, accompanied with a salad, or serve the risotto as a side dish— it pairs beautifully with roasted meats.

6 cups Rich Chicken Stock (page 68)
or store-bought low-sodium chicken broth

3 tablespoons unsalted butter

1 medium onion, finely chopped

1½ cups Arborio rice

½ cup dry white wine

3 ounces truffle butter

¼ cup heavy cream

½ cup finely grated Parmigiano-Reggiano cheese

Salt and freshly ground black pepper

2 teaspoons truffle paste, or more to taste

2 tablespoons truffle oil, plus more for garnish, if desired

Finely shaved fresh truffle (optional)

1. In a medium saucepan, bring the broth to a simmer over low heat.

2. In a wide, heavy-bottomed saucepan, melt the butter over medium heat. When it begins to sizzle, add the onion and cook, stirring a few times, until tender, about 5 minutes. Add the rice and cook, stirring constantly, until it is opaque and coated with the butter, 1 to 2 minutes.

3. Increase the heat to medium-high and add the wine. Cook, stirring, until the rice has absorbed the wine. Add 1 cup of the simmering stock and stir frequently until it is absorbed into the rice. Continue to add the stock in ½-cup increments, stirring frequently and not adding any more until the last addition has been absorbed. Add the stock in this manner until the rice is tender but still has some bite to it, usually 15 to 20 minutes. The last addition of stock should just absorb into the rice.

4. Add half of the truffle butter, the cream, and cheese, and stir to mix well. Season to taste with salt and pepper. Stir in the truffle paste and truffle oil.

5. Serve immediately in wide shallow bowls, topped with an additional dollop of the remaining truffle butter, a drizzle of truffle oil, if desired, and some freshly cracked black pepper. If you are lucky enough to have a fresh truffle available, garnish the risotto with a pile of paper-thin shavings.

**YIELD: 4 MAIN-COURSE
OR 6 FIRST-COURSE SERVINGS**

truffle products

When purchasing truffle oil, truffle butter, or truffle paste, you need to read the label carefully. A lot of what is available is infused with a synthetically manufactured aroma and flavor that approximate those of real white or black truffles. Check the ingredients. Believe me, if it contains real truffles in some form—actual bits of truffles or truffle juice—you'll know it. If the only mention of truffles is "truffle aroma" or "truffle essence," it's synthetic.

Success with risotto is all about the slow addition of the simmering stock to the rice. Rice has its own life, especially Arborio, and you need to pay attention to its absorption of the stock, not adding more until what is in the pot has been pulled into the swelling grains of rice.

The finished risotto shouldn't be at all soupy or overly wet. If it seems a bit dry, thin it with a little water before serving.

lobster & saffron risotto

Growing up in Massachusetts, I've enjoyed my share of Maine lobsters, but down here on the Gulf of Mexico, the Caribbean spiny lobster is king. Whatever kind of lobster you have access to, you're going to want to make this. I love deep-sea fishing, and at the holidays I have a special get-together for the boat captains I go out with; I always make this risotto for them.

2 cups roughly chopped ripe tomatoes (see Essentials, at right)

2$\frac{1}{2}$ cups dry white wine

2$\frac{1}{2}$ quarts plus $\frac{1}{2}$ cup water

1 cup thinly sliced onion

3 black peppercorns

2 sprigs fresh tarragon

2 (1$\frac{1}{2}$-pound) live lobsters

1 bay leaf

2 tablespoons olive oil

2 tablespoons unsalted butter

$\frac{1}{2}$ cup finely chopped onion

$\frac{1}{2}$ cup minced shallots

$\frac{1}{2}$ packet or vial saffron threads (.25 gram or .00875 ounce)

1$\frac{1}{2}$ cups Arborio rice

1$\frac{1}{4}$ teaspoons kosher salt

$\frac{1}{4}$ teaspoon freshly ground black pepper

$\frac{1}{4}$ cup heavy cream

$\frac{1}{2}$ cup fresh green peas, blanched in boiling water 2 to 3 minutes, or frozen peas, thawed

$\frac{1}{2}$ cup grated Parmigiano-Reggiano cheese, plus extra for serving

Extra-virgin olive oil, for serving

1. Fill a large bowl with ice water and set it on the counter.

2. In a large, heavy-bottomed Dutch oven with a tight-fitting lid, combine the tomatoes, 2 cups of the wine, the $\frac{1}{2}$ cup water, sliced onion, peppercorns, and tarragon. Bring to a boil over high heat, reduce the heat to a simmer, and cook for 15 minutes.

3. Cover the pot and raise the heat back to high. Wait a couple of minutes to let the steam build in the pot, then add the lobsters to the pot; cover the pot immediately. Steam the lobsters until they are bright red and you can pull out the long feelers on the head with no resistance, about 13 minutes. Using tongs, immediately plunge the lobsters into the ice water and let cool for 5 minutes.

4. Remove the lobsters from the ice water and set on a rimmed baking sheet. Using a knife or kitchen shears, remove the lobster meat from the tail and claws (see Cracking a Lobster, page 194). Chop the meat into bite-size pieces. You should have about 2 cups of lobster meat; set aside.

5. Remove and discard all the spongy stuff remaining in the shells, then rinse the shells, including the heads. Place the shells back in the pot with the lobster steaming liquid. Add the remaining 2$\frac{1}{2}$ quarts of water and the bay leaf. Bring to a boil over high heat, then reduce the heat to medium-low and simmer, uncovered, for 1 hour. Strain the lobster stock through a fine-mesh strainer lined with cheesecloth. Discard the solids.

6. Transfer the stock to a clean saucepan and return to a simmer. Reduce the stock until you have about 6 cups remaining—this is the amount you will need to cook the rice. Cover and keep warm.

(continued)

Using fresh tomatoes is key to the final flavor of this risotto— please don't use canned.

•

When you use an expensive ingredient like lobster, you want to get the most out of it. I do that here by adding water and the lobster shells to the liquid the lobsters were steamed in and reducing that into a concentrated lobster stock, which is used to cook the rice.

7. In a wide, heavy-bottomed saucepan, heat the oil and butter together over medium-high heat. When the butter starts to sizzle, add the chopped onion, shallots, and saffron, and cook, stirring a few times, until the vegetables are soft and lightly golden, 4 to 6 minutes. Add the rice and cook until opaque, stirring to coat each and every grain with oil and butter. Add the remaining ½ cup wine and cook until it has evaporated. Stir in the salt and pepper.

8. Add 1 cup of the simmering lobster stock to the pan, and stir frequently until it is absorbed into the rice. Continue to add the stock in ½-cup increments, stirring frequently and not adding any more until the last addition has been absorbed. Add the stock in this manner until the rice is tender but still has some bite to it, usually 15 to 20 minutes. You will probably use all 6 cups of the stock. The last addition of stock should just absorb into the rice; the finished risotto shouldn't be at all soupy or overly wet. If the risotto seems a bit too dry, it can be thinned out with a little water before serving.

9. Stir in the cream, peas, reserved lobster meat, and cheese; taste and adjust the seasonings, if necessary.

10. Serve the risotto in shallow pasta bowls. Sprinkle each serving with a little extra cheese, freshly cracked black pepper, and a drizzle of extra-virgin olive oil. Serve immediately.

YIELD: 6 SERVINGS

cracking a lobster

It is so much more economical to steam lobsters and pick out the meat yourself rather than buy already picked lobster meat. Add the lobster meat to the risotto right before serving to preserve its tender texture.

1. With your hands, break the lobster into pieces: Twist off the claws and separate the head from the tail.

2. Break the claws apart at all the joints.

3. With a knife or kitchen shears, cut open the shells of the claws and remove the meat.

4. Cut down the center of the underside of the tail, then, with your hands, grab the tail on both sides and crack the shell back, to release the meat.

SIDES & SALADS

When I was growing up, my mother never needed to nag me to eat my vegetables. We had a vegetable garden out back and I loved that you could pick something and eat it right then and there or walk into the kitchen and cook it into something delicious. Honestly, I can make a meal just out of sides. And it seems right that home for me now is in the South, where the side dish is king. Sit down to dinner here and you'll find at least three vegetables alongside your main course, maybe even four or five. I've filled this chapter with my very favorite vegetables and salads, dishes I turn to again and again for family and friends. They are easy to prepare and full of flavor and good nutrition.

collard greens

I love braising greens in beer—it's the perfect match for the smoke-on-smoke flavor of the ham hocks and bacon.

1 (1½-pound) smoked ham hock

12 ounces thick-sliced bacon (about 10 strips), chopped

1 tablespoon vegetable oil

1 cup chopped onion

2 tablespoons chopped garlic

2 (12-ounce) bottles beer

1 tablespoon hot sauce, plus more to taste

2 teaspoons salt, plus more to taste

1½ teaspoons freshly ground black pepper, plus more to taste

½ teaspoon crushed red pepper, plus more to taste

6 large bunches dark greens (about 1 pound each), such as collards, kale, mustard, or a mix, stems cut away, washed well, and cut into 2-inch pieces

1. Add the ham hock to a pot small enough to hold it and cover with water. Bring to a boil over medium heat, reduce the heat to a simmer, and cover. Cook until the meat is fork-tender, about 1 hour.

2. In a large Dutch oven or other large, heavy-bottomed pot, combine the bacon and oil, and cook, stirring as needed, over medium-low heat until the bacon begins to render some fat. Add the onion and garlic, and cook, stirring as needed, until the onion is softened, about 5 minutes. Stir in the beer, hot sauce, salt, and black and red pepper. Bring to a boil, then add the greens one large handful at a time until the pot is filled. Cook, stirring as needed, until the greens wilt, then repeat with the remaining greens.

3. When all of the greens have been added, add the ham hock (reserve the liquid for another purpose; also, see Infusing Flavor, at right). Reduce the heat to a simmer, cover, and cook, stirring as needed, until the greens are very tender, 35 to 40 minutes longer. Taste, and adjust the seasonings. Remove the ham hock and separate the meat from the bone and skin. Return the meat to the pot, stir into the greens, and serve.

YIELD: 6 TO 8 SERVINGS

infusing flavor

Pick a light or amber beer for this; you don't want anything too dark or bitter. If you prefer, you can use water or chicken broth instead. Another option is to use some of the water from simmering the ham hock. But be careful when adding it—a little goes a long way in regard to flavor; some people find it too salty, but I love it.

meril's super-quick cabbage with bacon

Cabbage in the microwave? You bet. This is one of my favorite ways to prepare it for my family. And it's just as good the next day, eaten cold right out of the fridge, like a crunchy salad. In fact, my daughter Meril calls it "lettuce" because the texture is like romaine. The quick cook time in the microwave keeps the cabbage crisp and fresh-tasting, and it's coated with just enough of the bacon drippings and olive oil to give it phenomenal flavor.

½ pound sliced bacon, cut across into ½-inch strips

1 large head green cabbage, cored and coarsely shredded

1 large yellow onion, halved and thinly sliced lengthwise

2 tablespoons olive oil

1½ teaspoons salt

¾ teaspoon freshly ground black pepper

1. Place the bacon in a microwavable bowl and cook, stirring every 90 seconds, until crispy, about 7 minutes total. Remove from the microwave and, using a slotted spoon, transfer the crispy bacon to paper towels to drain. Reserve about ¼ cup of the drippings and save any remaining drippings for later use.

2. Combine the cabbage and onion in a large microwavable bowl, drizzle with the reserved bacon drippings and the oil, and sprinkle with the salt and pepper. Toss well to combine. Cover the bowl tightly with plastic wrap and microwave for 4 minutes, undisturbed.

3. Remove the bowl from the microwave, uncover, and stir well to combine. Add the crispy bacon to the bowl, stir, and serve.

YIELD: 6 TO 8 SERVINGS

bacon fat

If you're making bacon, always save those drippings, like you would rendered duck fat. Keep them in an airtight container in the fridge and use them to sear meat, sauté vegetables, or add to cornbread batter to give a hint of bacon flavor.

sweet potato soufflé
with maple sugar and pecans

Sweet potatoes are very popular in the South, usually prepared in a casserole. I wanted something a little more special and came up with the idea of a soufflé topped with pecans and maple sugar. This puffs up beautifully without the use of a collar. I love it with My Brined Roast Chicken (page 119), Creole Duck Breasts with Sweet & Sour Figs (page 136), and Turkey Roulade (page 116). It's a treat for the holidays.

½ cup (1 stick) unsalted butter, melted

1 cup pecan pieces

1½ tablespoons maple sugar

¾ teaspoon salt

3 cups mashed sweet potatoes (see Essentials, at right)

1 cup half-and-half

½ cup firmly packed dark brown sugar

¼ teaspoon freshly ground black pepper

¼ teaspoon freshly grated nutmeg

⅛ teaspoon ground cloves

6 large egg whites, at room temperature

½ teaspoon cream of tartar

1. Preheat the oven to 425°F. Grease the bottom and sides of a 4-quart soufflé dish with 1 tablespoon of the melted butter.

2. Roughly chop the pecan pieces and toss them with 1 tablespoon of the melted butter, the maple sugar, and ¼ teaspoon of the salt. Set aside.

3. In a large bowl, combine the mashed sweet potatoes, half-and-half, brown sugar, remaining 6 tablespoons melted butter, remaining ½ teaspoon salt, the pepper, nutmeg, and cloves. Whisk together until smooth. Set aside.

4. In the medium bowl with an electric mixer on medium-high speed, whip the egg whites until foamy, then add the cream of tartar. Continue to whip the whites to soft peaks. With a rubber spatula, fold the whites into the sweet potato mixture, making sure the whites are fully incorporated (see Essentials, at right). Transfer the mixture to the soufflé dish, sprinkle the top with the sugared pecans, and bake on the bottom rack until puffed and golden brown on top, 40 to 45 minutes.

5. Bring the soufflé to the table immediately so everyone can admire it, then spoon out to serve.

YIELD: 6 TO 8 SERVINGS

essentials

To cook the mashed sweet potatoes, you can boil 3 large sweet potatoes in lightly salted water until they're tender. Or, you can roast them in a preheated 375°F oven until a knife inserted in the center goes in without any resistance, about 1 hour, then peel and mash.

•

When folding in the whipped egg whites, try to maintain as much of their aeration as possible while combining with the sweet potatoes.

love potatoes

This got its name because every time I make it, my family says, "Oh, I love those potatoes!" It's kind of a cross between Lyonnaise potatoes (sliced potatoes and onions pan-fried in butter) and hash browns; the potatoes develop a golden-brown crunch that is just super good. You can make this with waxy potatoes, if you want, but russets brown much better.

6 tablespoons canola oil

3 (12-ounce) russet potatoes, cut into ⅛-inch slices (6 cups)

Salt and freshly ground white pepper

2 tablespoons unsalted butter

2 medium yellow onions, thinly sliced lengthwise (4 cups)

2 teaspoons snipped chives, for garnish (optional)

Sour cream, for garnish (optional)

1. Heat 2 tablespoons of the oil in a large nonstick sauté pan over medium-high heat and start to arrange a layer of overlapping potato slices over the bottom of the pan in concentric circles. Season the potatoes with ⅛ teaspoon each of salt and pepper, and cook for 1 to 2 minutes. Sprinkle 1 tablespoon of the oil over the top, then add a second layer of potatoes, season the same way, and let cook for 1 to 2 minutes. Repeat this process until you have 4 layers of potatoes.

2. Reduce the heat to medium-low and cook the potatoes, gently shaking the pan to keep them from sticking, until the bottom layer of potatoes begins to caramelize and turn golden brown, about 5 minutes. Using a rubber spatula, turn the potatoes over and cook, gently shaking the pan, until that bottom layer turns golden, about another 5 minutes. Continue to cook and flip the potatoes until all of the potatoes are golden brown, about another 15 minutes.

3. Add the butter to the pan in one piece and let it melt. Arrange half the onions over the potatoes. Season with ⅛ teaspoon each of the salt and pepper. Flip the potatoes on top of the onions so the onions are cooking on the bottom of the pan. Cook the onions for 2 to 3 minutes, then add the remaining onions to the pan and season in the same way. Continue to cook and flip the potatoes and onions until the onions begin to caramelize, about 10 minutes longer. Garnish with chives and sour cream, if desired, and serve.

YIELD: 4 TO 6 SERVINGS

proper browning

This dish is all about getting the potatoes brown and crunchy, and there are three secrets to making that happen. First, the potatoes need to be sliced as thin as possible. Use a mandoline, if you have one. Next, pat the slices as dry as you can with paper towels. Finally, don't add the onions till the end. Onions contain a lot of water; if you add them earlier, they'll lose their water to the pan, which will interfere with the browning of the potatoes.

salt-roasted beets

I am a huge beet fan—I love them roasted, pickled, cold, in soups, or sliced in salads. This method is a great way to prepare them; when you roast beets without a salt crust, you can sometimes end up with a dirt flavor that masks their taste. Each beet is packed in its own salt crust to which aromatics have been added. The crust keeps in the moisture and transfers those flavorings to the beets. Another benefit to this method is that it's less messy; any oozing beet juices are absorbed by the salt. It's important that the beets be the same size so they cook evenly. If need be, cut larger beets in half before packing them in the salt. Serve these sliced as a side dish with any meat, fish, or poultry entrée; add them to a salad; or serve chilled and drizzled with a simple vinaigrette.

8 large egg whites

6 cups kosher salt

¼ cup fresh orange juice

2 tablespoons fresh thyme leaves

2 pounds beets in assorted colors, approximately the same size

3 tablespoons extra-virgin olive oil

½ teaspoon coarse sea salt

Freshly ground black pepper

1. Preheat the oven to 400°F. Line a baking sheet with parchment paper or aluminum foil.

2. In a medium bowl, combine the egg whites, kosher salt, orange juice, and thyme. Pack the salt mixture onto each beet; you should easily be able to mold it around each beet using your hands. Place the salt-encrusted beets on the prepared baking sheet, making sure they do not touch. Bake until the crust is golden brown, 45 to 50 minutes.

3. Remove the baking sheet from the oven and let the beets cool for about 10 minutes. Remove the salt crust by tapping on it with a fork and cracking it open. Using a paper towel, gently rub the skin off. Slice the beets into ½-inch-thick wedges and toss them with the oil, sea salt, and pepper to taste. Serve immediately or store in an airtight container in the refrigerator for up to 4 days.

YIELD: 4 SERVINGS

salt roasting

This technique will work with any root vegetable; I particularly like parsnips, rutabagas, and turnips. You can also flavor the salt in any way you like, using whatever herb, spice, and/or juice you prefer in place of the ones used here; just use them in the same proportions. The flavored salt should have the consistency of wet sand.

stuffed eggplant
with roasted red pepper coulis for roger

Chef Roger Vergé had a magical way with eggplant; it's also a favorite vegetable in New Orleans and Creole cooking. So when it came to creating a dish to offer in tribute to Roger, who was a mentor and whose cooking at his restaurant Moulin de Mougins in Provence gave me so much pleasure, the choice was obvious. It's equally delicious warm or at room temperature.

4 medium eggplants (about 3 pounds total)

8 tablespoons extra-virgin olive oil

³/₄ teaspoon kosher salt

1 medium onion, finely chopped

3 oil-packed anchovy fillets, minced (2 teaspoons)

¹/₂ teaspoon crushed red pepper

2 tablespoons minced garlic

1 red bell pepper, roasted, peeled, seeded, and chopped (¹/₂ cup)

¹/₂ cup chopped pitted oil-cured olives

2 tablespoons minced drained nonpareil capers

2 tablespoons red wine vinegar

¹/₄ cup chopped fresh basil

2 tablespoons chopped fresh mint

5 tablespoons coarse plain dry breadcrumbs

10 ounces French feta cheese, crumbled

Roasted Red Pepper Coulis (page 206), for serving

Small fresh basil leaves, for serving

1. Preheat the oven to 400°F. Line a large baking sheet with parchment paper or aluminum foil.

2. Halve the eggplants lengthwise and, using a sharp paring knife, score the flesh in a crosshatch pattern, cutting as deeply as possible without piercing the skin. Set them, cut side up, on the prepared baking sheet. Brush the cut sides with about 3 tablespoons of the oil. Sprinkle with the salt. Roast until the flesh is very tender and the tops are golden brown, 35 to 40 minutes. Set aside until cool enough to handle.

3. Use a spoon to remove the eggplant flesh while leaving a shell ¹/₈ to ¹/₄ inch thick. Coarsely chop the flesh—you should have about 3 cups. Choose 6 of the nicest shells and discard the others, scraping any remaining flesh from the skins.

4. Heat 2 tablespoons of the oil in a large nonstick skillet over medium-high heat. Add the onion, anchovies, and crushed red pepper, and cook, stirring as needed, until the onion is soft and lightly golden, 4 to 6 minutes. Add the garlic and cook, stirring, for 2 minutes. Add the eggplant and cook, stirring, until it is soft and any extra liquid has evaporated, about 4 minutes. Stir in the roasted pepper, olives, and capers, and cook 1 to 2 minutes longer.

5. Remove the pan from the heat and stir in the vinegar, basil, mint, and 2 tablespoons of the breadcrumbs. Let cool briefly, then gently stir in 6 ounces of the feta.

6. Divide the filling evenly among the 6 eggplant shells and sprinkle the top of each with ¹/₂ tablespoon of the breadcrumbs. Drizzle the top of each with ¹/₂ tablespoon of the oil. Bake until the eggplants are heated through and the crumbs are crispy and golden brown on top, about 30 minutes. Serve warm or at room temperature with the Roasted Red Pepper Coulis drizzled over the eggplant and the remaining feta and the basil sprinkled on top.

YIELD: 6 SERVINGS

(continued)

You can serve this as an entrée (to make it vegetarian, leave off the anchovies), as a side dish, or as part of an antipasti spread.

roasted red pepper coulis

4 red bell peppers

2 tablespoons olive oil

1 medium onion, finely chopped

4 cloves garlic, minced

½ teaspoon crushed red pepper

½ cup Rich Chicken Stock (page 68) or store-bought low-sodium chicken broth

2 to 4 tablespoons heavy cream, as needed

Salt

A few drops of fresh lemon juice

1. Roast the whole peppers until they are completely black and charred all over. Place them in a paper bag and close tightly. Let them steam for 15 to 20 minutes to loosen the skins. When the peppers are cool enough to handle, rub off their blackened skins. Try to do this without running them under water, as this will wash away much of the charry pepper flavor. Remove the stems, inner cores, and seeds, then tear the peppers into strips and set aside.

2. In a medium saucepan, heat the oil over medium heat. Add the onion and cook until tender, about 5 minutes, stirring as needed. Add the roasted peppers, garlic, and crushed red pepper, and cook 1 to 2 minutes. Add the broth and bring to a simmer. Let simmer until the peppers are very tender and most of the liquid has evaporated, 10 to 15 minutes.

3. Transfer the contents of the pan to a blender and add cream as needed to form a very smooth puree. Return the sauce to the saucepan and season with salt and lemon juice to taste. Keep warm until ready to serve. This will keep in an airtight container in the refrigerator for up to 1 week. Reheat gently before serving.

YIELD: ABOUT 2 CUPS

roasting red peppers

To roast the peppers, you can place them directly on a stovetop gas burner or on a gas or charcoal grill, turning them for even charring. Or rub the peppers all over with olive oil and broil them about 5 inches away from the heat source, turning them frequently.

roger vergé

When I was starting out, there were two chefs at the forefront of modern French cuisine, or nouvelle cuisine— Roger Vergé and Paul Bocuse. Nouvelle cuisine was a conscious step away from traditional classic French cooking, with its intricate techniques and rich sauce-centric dishes, to preparations that showcase and build from the inherent flavors of the ingredients being used. Emphasis is on sourcing the highest quality ingredients possible and learning how to coax the most, best flavor from them. I read and cooked my way through everything Chef Bocuse and Vergé wrote, in particular Roger's *Cuisine of the Sun*, which set out his philosophy of flavor.

I would later eat at Chef Vergé's three Michelin star–rated restaurant, Moulin de Mougins, in Provence many times. The food was a revelation, an education, particularly the vegetables, which Roger had an expert hand with. It was a valuable lesson in respecting the ingredients and developing the knowledge to maximize their flavor, not muddy it. I respected Roger so much, I sent one of my own chefs, Bernard Carmouche, to work in his kitchen for two months.

Roger came to Emeril's several times and it was a treat and an honor to be able to cook for him. He was one of the nicest men you could possibly meet, a true gentleman, and was so generous with his knowledge over the years. I learned much from Roger, from how to handle a simple eggplant to how to perfect a foie gras terrine.

lemon-garlic crusted cauliflower

Here is a unique way to roast a whole cauliflower—the crispy, intensely flavored crust is delicious.

3 quarts water

Kosher salt

1 head cauliflower (1 to 1½ pounds), leaves removed and stem end trimmed flush

½ cup plus 1 tablespoon plain, fine, dry breadcrumbs, preferably homemade

½ cup extra-virgin olive oil, plus more for drizzling (optional)

⅓ cup fresh lemon juice

⅓ cup finely grated Parmigiano-Reggiano cheese

2 tablespoons minced garlic

2 large oil-packed anchovy fillets, mashed to a paste (about 1 teaspoon)

¾ teaspoon finely grated lemon zest

½ teaspoon freshly ground black pepper

1 lemon, sliced crosswise into ⅓-inch-thick slices

1. Bring the water to a boil in a large saucepan or stockpot. Stir in ¼ cup salt and add the cauliflower—the water should completely cover the cauliflower. Cook for 5 minutes, then transfer to a plate to cool. Preheat the oven to 400°F and line a small baking sheet with aluminum foil.

2. In a small bowl, combine ½ cup of the breadcrumbs, the oil, lemon juice, cheese, garlic, anchovies, lemon zest, pepper, and 1¼ teaspoons salt. Stir until the mixture is thoroughly combined and a wet paste is formed.

3. Once the cauliflower is cool, pat well on all sides with paper towels to remove any trace of water. Position the lemon slices in a single even layer in the center of the baking sheet. Place the cauliflower on the lemon slices. Spoon the breadcrumb mixture on the cauliflower and, using your hands, pat it evenly over the top and down the sides. Sprinkle the remaining 1 tablespoon breadcrumbs evenly over the cauliflower. Roast the cauliflower until it is golden brown and very fragrant and the crust is crispy, 35 to 40 minutes.

4. Remove from the oven and set aside to cool briefly before slicing into wedges to serve. Serve drizzled with additional extra-virgin olive oil, if desired.

YIELD: 6 SERVINGS

blanching cauliflower

It can take a long time to get cauliflower to cook through to the center. Blanching the head before roasting it jump-starts the cooking. When this is done, the cauliflower will still be crisp-tender.

curry acorn squash

I'm always looking for new ways to prepare winter squash, and this dish really knocks it out of the park. It's a perfect partner for any kind of roast meat or poultry.

2 acorn squash (about 3 pounds total)

3 tablespoons unsalted butter or ghee, melted, or vegetable oil

1/2 teaspoon salt

1/4 teaspoon turmeric

1/8 teaspoon ground cloves

1/8 teaspoon ground cinnamon

1/8 teaspoon ground fennel seeds

1/8 teaspoon ground cumin

1/8 teaspoon crushed red pepper

Curry Ghee (recipe follows), for serving

1. Preheat the oven to 450°F.

2. Halve the squash lengthwise and remove and discard the seeds. Cut each piece in half lengthwise and place, cut side up, in a casserole dish or on a rimmed baking sheet.

3. In a small bowl, combine the melted butter, salt, and spices, and brush all over the cut sides of the squash. Roast until fork-tender, 45 to 55 minutes.

4. Remove the squash from the oven and drizzle with the Curry Ghee. Serve immediately.

YIELD: 4 SERVINGS

curry ghee

Ghee (clarified butter) is a staple of Indian cooking, and you can buy it in jars at Indian food stores. If you would like to make your own, see the tutorial on page 243 for how to clarify butter.

6 tablespoons ghee or unsalted butter, melted

1/2 cup minced onion

1/4 cup chopped fresh cilantro

1/2 teaspoon curry powder

1/4 teaspoon crushed red pepper

1/4 teaspoon salt

Combine all the ingredients in a small sauté pan and cook over low heat until the onion is softened, about 10 minutes, stirring as needed. Remove from the heat and keep warm until needed.

YIELD: ABOUT 1/3 CUP

roasted zucchini,
summer squash, shallots, and garlic
with balsamic vinaigrette

Once the squash get going in my garden in the summer, there is no stopping them. Here's a great way to make use of the surplus. You can serve this as a side dish or offer it up as part of an antipasti platter.

2 heads garlic

9 tablespoons plus 1 teaspoon extra-virgin olive oil

8 ounces shallots, peeled

1½ pounds small to medium zucchini (see Essentials, at left)

1½ pounds small to medium summer squash

2 red bell peppers

¼ teaspoon freshly ground black pepper

¼ cup chopped fresh flat-leaf parsley leaves

3 oil-packed anchovy fillets, minced

2 tablespoons drained nonpareil capers

¼ cup balsamic vinegar

1½ teaspoons kosher salt

½ teaspoon crushed red pepper

1. Preheat the oven to 350°F. Cut a piece of aluminum foil to measure approximately 5 x 4 inches.

2. Slice off the top quarter of each head of garlic and place the garlic, cut side up, on the foil. Drizzle 1 teaspoon of the oil over the garlic and enclose in the foil. Transfer the pouch to a baking sheet and roast until the cloves are soft and golden brown, about 1 hour. Remove from the oven and set aside. Increase the oven temperature to 450°F.

3. Halve or quarter the shallots as necessary so that they are similar sizes, leaving the root end intact. Smaller shallots can be left whole. Add the shallots, zucchini, squash, and bell peppers to

a large bowl and season with the black pepper. Drizzle 4 tablespoons of the oil over the vegetables and toss to coat. Arrange the vegetables in a single layer on a rimmed baking sheet, and roast for 20 minutes.

4. In a small bowl, combine the parsley, anchovies, capers, vinegar, salt, and crushed red pepper. Whisk in the remaining 5 tablespoons oil, and set aside.

5. Remove the shallots from the baking sheet and set aside in a large bowl.

6. Turn the squash and peppers over and continue to roast until lightly browned, about another 10 minutes. Remove the peppers to a small bowl, cover with plastic wrap, and let steam until cool enough to handle. Let the squash cool on the baking sheet.

7. Open the pouch of garlic and squeeze the garlic out of their skins, gently pressing on each head with your fingers to expel the soft cloves into the bowl with the roasted shallots. Trim the ends of the squash and discard. Cut the squash into 1-inch pieces and add to the bowl with the shallots and garlic. Remove and discard the stems, skin, and most of the seeds from the peppers, then chop them into 1-inch pieces and add to the bowl.

8. Pour the balsamic vinaigrette over the vegetables and toss gently to combine. Set aside at room temperature until ready to serve (up to several hours), stirring intermittently. You can also make this the day before and refrigerate in an airtight container. Reheat gently in the microwave before serving.

YIELD: 6 TO 8 SERVINGS

cheddar, bacon, apple, and pecan
spoonbread

This is not your mama's spoonbread. Chock-full of flavor, it is insanely good served with any kind of poultry.

1 tablespoon unsalted butter, softened

3 tablespoons fine-ground cornmeal

4 ounces sliced bacon (4 to 6 strips)

½ cup finely chopped onion

¼ cup finely chopped celery

2 cups diced cored apples (2 medium apples; don't peel them)

½ cup chopped lightly toasted pecans (see Essentials, page 227)

Salt and freshly ground black pepper

2 cups whole milk

⅔ cup heavy cream

⅔ cup buttermilk

1 cup stone-ground cornmeal

6 ounces Cheddar cheese, grated (about 1½ cups)

6 large eggs, at room temperature, separated

1 teaspoon fresh thyme leaves

1 teaspoon baking soda

1 teaspoon baking powder

1 teaspoon sugar

Pinch of cream of tartar

1. Butter a 9 x 13-inch baking dish with the butter. Add the fine cornmeal to the dish and tilt the dish to coat the bottom and sides with the cornmeal. Set aside.

2. In a medium skillet over medium heat, cook the bacon until crisp. Transfer the bacon to paper towels to drain. When cool enough to handle, crumble the bacon into small pieces. Set aside.

3. To the bacon drippings in the skillet, add the onion and celery, and cook over medium-high heat, stirring a few times, until the vegetables are softened, about 4 minutes. Increase the heat to high, add the apples, and continue to cook, stirring occasionally, until the onion is lightly caramelized and the apples softened, another 4 minutes. Remove from the heat and set aside until cooled. Stir in the pecans and bacon and season lightly with ¼ teaspoon salt and a pinch of pepper.

4. Combine the milk, cream, buttermilk, and 1½ teaspoons salt and ¾ teaspoon pepper in a medium saucepan and bring just to a boil. Whisk in the stone-ground cornmeal and cook, stirring constantly, until the mixture thickens, 2 to 3 minutes. Remove from the heat and transfer the cornmeal mixture to a heatproof bowl. Stir in the cheese and set the bowl aside until the mixture is lukewarm, usually 10 to 15 minutes, stirring frequently to prevent a skin from forming.

5. Preheat the oven to 350°F.

6. In a small bowl, lightly beat the egg yolks. Stir the yolks, thyme, baking soda, and baking powder into the cooled cornmeal mixture. Stir in the sautéed apple mixture.

7. Combine the egg whites, sugar, and cream of tartar in a large bowl and beat with an electric mixer on high speed until stiff peaks form. Working with a large rubber spatula, carefully fold one-third of the whites into the cornmeal mixture to lighten it. Add the remaining whites and gently fold in until the whites are incorporated but still fluffy.

8. Transfer the mixture to the prepared baking dish and bake until the spoonbread is puffed and golden brown on top and a knife inserted into the center comes out clean, 35 to 40 minutes. Serve immediately.

YIELD: 8 TO 10 SERVINGS

Make sure you whip the egg whites to stiff peaks and then fold them in as gently as you can to keep them fluffy. You want to preserve as much of that aeration as possible to offset the density of the heavier ingredients.

•

This is also delicious made with pears, and you can substitute walnuts for the pecans and swap in smoked Gouda for some of the Cheddar.

wild mushroom
bread pudding

I love dessert bread puddings, so why not create one that is savory to serve as a side dish? This is beyond decadent, and because it's so rich, it's a perfect choice for a party buffet. Serve it alongside Creole Duck Breasts with Sweet & Sour Figs (page 136), or any kind of roast meat or poultry.

8 tablespoons (1 stick) unsalted butter

2 medium onions, julienned

1½ teaspoons salt

1½ pounds mixed wild mushrooms, such as shiitake, oyster, chanterelles, wood ear, or lobster, cleaned (see Cleaning Mushrooms, page 171) and sliced

2 teaspoons minced garlic

½ cup brandy

5 large eggs

3 cups heavy cream

1 cup milk

1½ teaspoons Worcestershire sauce

2 teaspoons minced fresh thyme

¾ teaspoon freshly ground black pepper

¾ pound stale crusty bread, such as peasant, sourdough, or ciabatta, cut into 1-inch cubes (8 to 10 cups, depending on the density of the bread)

¾ cup grated Gouda cheese

¾ cup grated Fontina cheese

⅓ pound smooth duck liver pâté

1. In a large sauté pan over medium-high heat, melt 2 tablespoons of the butter. When it begins to foam, add the onions and ⅛ teaspoon of the salt and cook, stirring as necessary, until they are golden brown and soft, about 10 minutes. Transfer the onions to a heatproof bowl and set aside.

2. To the hot skillet, add 2 more tablespoons butter and, when melted, add half the mushrooms, half the garlic, and ⅛ teaspoon of the salt. Cook, stirring occasionally, until the mushrooms are golden brown, about 4 minutes. Transfer the mushrooms to the bowl with the onions, then repeat with another 2 tablespoons butter, the remaining mushrooms and garlic, and ⅛ teaspoon of the salt.

3. Return the onions and sautéed mushrooms to the pan and add the brandy, scraping up any browned bits from the bottom of the pan and cooking until the brandy is nearly evaporated. Remove from the heat.

4. In a large bowl, whisk together the eggs, cream, milk, Worcestershire, thyme, the remaining 1⅛ teaspoons salt, and the pepper. Add the bread cubes and stir to combine. Allow the bread to sit in the cream mixture until it has softened, 10 to 20 minutes (see Essentials, at left).

5. Preheat the oven to 350°F. Grease a 9 x 13-inch baking dish with 1 tablespoon of the butter.

6. Stir the sautéed onions and mushrooms and grated cheeses into the bread mixture until well combined, then pour everything into the prepared baking dish. Cut the pâté into small pieces and tuck them down into the bread mixture, spacing them evenly. Cut the remaining 1 tablespoon butter into small pieces and dot the top of the pudding with them. Bake in the center of the oven until the bread pudding is set, golden brown, and crispy on top, about 55 minutes. Remove from the oven and cool briefly before serving.

YIELD: 10 TO 12 SERVINGS

As with a sweet bread pudding, the key to success is allowing enough time for the bread to fully absorb the egg and cream mixture. The bread should be spongy all the way through. That will translate into a golden puffiness and creamy interior in the heat of the oven.

watercress and celery salad

One of my very favorite places in New York City is Ristorante Sant Ambroeus on Madison Avenue, an old-school Italian restaurant and pastry shop. Their menu usually includes a celery salad, which you might think sounds pretty boring. But they respect the vegetable and give it the attention it needs to have its delicate flavor shine, peeling the ribs before slicing them very thinly. I wanted to include a salad in this book that showcases celery in the same way. Be careful to add just enough vinaigrette to lightly coat the celery, onion, and watercress.

3 large ribs celery, peeled top to bottom with a vegetable peeler, removing all fibrous strings

½ small red onion, thinly sliced

4 ounces (1 bag or 2 bunches) watercress, stems trimmed

¼ cup fresh lemon juice

1 teaspoon Dijon mustard

1 teaspoon nonpareil capers (not salt-packed; do not drain)

½ cup extra-virgin olive oil

½ cup Parmigiano-Reggiano cheese shavings

2 ounces (about 20 slices) thinly sliced cacciatorini or Felino, Genoa, or hard salami, julienned

Sea salt and freshly ground black pepper

1. Using a mandoline, shave the celery paper thin.

2. Bring a medium pot of salted water to a boil. Fill a medium bowl with ice water. Blanch the celery for 30 seconds. Drain the celery in a colander and immediately transfer it to the ice water. As soon as the celery is cool, drain and transfer to paper towels to remove any excess water. Dry the bowl. Add the celery, onion, and watercress, and toss well.

3. In a small bowl, combine the lemon juice, mustard, and capers. Using a fork or whisk, stir until the mixture is homogenized. Slowly drizzle in the oil, constantly whisking until it thickens.

4. Pour the vinaigrette over the celery and watercress, and toss well. Add the cheese and salami, season to taste with salt and pepper, and toss again. Divide the salad among 4 cold salad plates, and serve immediately.

YIELD: 4 SERVINGS

watercress

In the 1970s and '80s, just about every restaurant in America had watercress on the menu—as a garnish, in salads, everywhere. In the 1990s, it dropped out of sight, but now it seems to be making a comeback. Watercress, a species of nasturtium that grows wild alongside streams, has a distinctive peppery bite and crunch and is packed with nutrients, including vitamins A and C, iron, and calcium. It's not as easy to find in markets as it once was; make sure what you buy looks fresh and happy. If it's wilted, don't bother. To prep watercress, all you need to do is trim away the heaviest part of the stems.

crispy okra with grape tomatoes and garlic

This is how my wife and I like to prepare okra at home. When roasted like this, the slime factor of okra is seriously diminished and it becomes crisp around the edges. If you like your okra crunchy, this is an easier and less messy alternative to frying it. Look for small okra pods; they're more tender. Serve as a side dish or tapas-style with drinks before dinner.

1 pound fresh okra pods, tough part of stem ends trimmed and pods cut in half lengthwise

6 ounces grape tomatoes

8 cloves garlic, thinly sliced

6 sprigs fresh thyme

1 teaspoon kosher salt

¼ teaspoon freshly ground black pepper

3 tablespoons olive oil

Extra-virgin olive oil, for serving (optional)

Sea or kosher salt, for serving (optional)

1. Preheat the oven to 425°F. Line a large baking sheet with parchment paper.

2. Place all of the ingredients in a large bowl, except the extra-virgin olive oil and sea salt, and toss until well blended. Arrange on the prepared baking sheet in a single layer and roast until the okra is crisp around the edges and lightly caramelized, about 30 minutes.

3. Remove from the oven and let cool briefly before serving. If you like, serve the okra and tomatoes drizzled with extra-virgin olive oil and sprinkled with sea salt.

YIELD: 4 TO 6 SERVINGS

classic caesar salad

My family craves this salad and I make it for them at least once a week, using a wooden bowl made from Vermont maple that is dedicated only to this salad. Like a cast iron skillet, I feel that the bowl has built up a flavor patina that adds something special to the final taste of the salad. I love making this salad because it's really built from the ground up, starting with mashing the garlic cloves with the salt, then the other ingredients being added and worked in one at a time, and finally tossing it together with the lettuce and croutons.

3 cloves garlic, peeled

1/4 teaspoon salt

3 oil-packed anchovy fillets

1 tablespoon Dijon mustard

1 teaspoon Worcestershire sauce

1 large egg yolk

Juice from 1/2 lemon (about 2 tablespoons)

1/4 cup vegetable oil

2 tablespoons extra-virgin olive oil

2 tablespoons plus 1/2 cup finely grated finely grated Parmigiano-Reggiano cheese

1/4 teaspoon freshly ground black pepper

3 dashes hot sauce (optional)

1 large head romaine lettuce (about 1 1/2 pounds), bottom trimmed, leaves washed, spun dry, and torn into 1/2-inch pieces (about 3 quarts)

2 cups Garlic Croutons (recipe follows)

1. Place the garlic cloves and salt in a large wooden bowl. Using the tines of a dinner fork, mash the garlic with the salt against the side of the bowl until it begins to exude juices, about 3 minutes. Add the anchovies and continue to mash until a paste is formed, about 3 minutes longer. Continue using the fork and mix in, one at a time, the mustard, Worcestershire, egg yolk, and lemon juice.

2. Begin mixing vigorously with the fork and add a few drops of the vegetable oil. Continue to mix while slowly adding drops of the oil until about half of the vegetable oil is incorporated. At this point you can add the remaining vegetable oil in a slow, steady stream, whisking all the while.

3. Whisk in the olive oil. Stir in 2 tablespoons of the cheese, the pepper, and hot sauce, if desired. Add the lettuce, croutons, and remaining 1/2 cup cheese and toss gently to coat the croutons and lettuce with the dressing. Serve immediately.

YIELD: 4 SERVINGS

garlic croutons

4 tablespoons olive oil

4 cloves garlic, smashed

1 (16- to 20-inch) baguette, cut into 1/2-inch cubes

1. Preheat the oven to 350°F.

2. Add 2 tablespoons of the oil and 2 cloves of the garlic to a 12-inch sauté pan. Set it over medium-low heat until the garlic sizzles at a gentle simmer. Add half the bread cubes and toss in the garlic oil until well coated and lightly toasted, about 1 minute. Transfer the cubes to a baking sheet. Repeat with the remaining ingredients.

3. Spread the cubes out in a single layer. Bake the croutons until golden, 18 to 20 minutes, stirring as needed. Set aside to cool. Use or store in an airtight container at room temperature until ready to use or up to 2 weeks.

YIELD: ABOUT 8 CUPS

make it a meal

If you want to turn this into a main-course salad, add the protein of your choice—chicken, steak, and shrimp are all good choices.

radish, watercress, and apple salad

I love radishes so much that I'll cook them on their own with a little salt and pepper, basting them with butter until they're soft; they end up with a flavor similar to turnips. In this salad, the heat and bite of the radishes shine through. This is delicious with the red radishes you usually find in the supermarket, but there are lots of different varieties you can seek out at farmers' markets—yellow, white, black, purple, green.

1 cup distilled white vinegar

2 cups water

1 1/2 tablespoons salt

1 bunch radishes (about 8 ounces), trimmed and quartered

12 ounces watercress, any tough stems trimmed and discarded

1 cucumber (about 8 ounces), cut in half lengthwise, seeded, and cut on the diagonal into 1/8-inch-thick slices

1 small Granny Smith apple, cored and cut into julienne or thin slices (leave the peel on)

3 ounces ricotta salata cheese, finely grated (about 1/2 cup)

5 tablespoons Champagne Vinaigrette (recipe follows)

Kosher salt and freshly ground black pepper (optional)

1. Fill a small bowl with ice water.

2. In a small saucepan, combine the vinegar, water, and salt, and bring to a boil. Add the radishes and blanch for 30 seconds. Remove them with a slotted spoon and transfer to the ice water. Once they are cooled, drain and pat dry.

3. In a medium bowl, combine the radishes, watercress, cucumber, apple, and ricotta salata, and toss with the vinaigrette. Taste, season with salt and pepper, if necessary, and serve immediately.

YIELD: 4 SERVINGS

blanching radishes

Blanching the radishes in the boiling vinegar solution fixes their bright color and tames any harshness while also highlighting the radish flavor.

champagne vinaigrette

2 tablespoons Champagne vinegar

1 tablespoon Dijon mustard

1 teaspoon honey

1/2 teaspoon salt

1/2 teaspoon freshly ground black pepper

1/2 cup vegetable oil

In a small bowl, combine the vinegar, mustard, honey, salt, and pepper. While whisking constantly, slowly drizzle the oil into the vinegar mixture until the oil is completely incorporated and the vinaigrette is smooth and emulsified.

YIELD: 1/2 CUP

washington avenue salad

This salad is my homage to the Commander's Palace house salad, which I made a gazillion times during my time there. Over the years, I've tweaked it to suit my own tastes, including adding mustard and sour cream to make the dressing creamy.

8 cups torn hearts of romaine lettuce

6 strips bacon, crisp-cooked and crumbled

4 large eggs, hard-boiled, peeled, and coarsely chopped

1/3 cup finely grated Parmigiano-Reggiano cheese

2 cups Garlic Croutons (page 218)

Black Peppercorn Dressing (recipe follows)

In a large bowl, combine the romaine, crumbled bacon, chopped eggs, cheese, and croutons. Add enough of the dressing to lightly coat the salad, and toss gently but thoroughly to combine. Divide the salad among 4 chilled salad plates, and serve immediately.

YIELD: 4 SERVINGS

black peppercorn dressing

1/4 cup white wine vinegar

1 clove garlic, minced

3 tablespoons minced shallot

1 large egg

1/2 teaspoon Dijon mustard

3/4 cup vegetable, canola, or grapeseed oil

1/2 cup olive oil

2 tablespoons sour cream

2 teaspoons coarsely ground black pepper

1 teaspoon salt

1/2 teaspoon Emeril's Creole Seasoning (page 108) or other Creole seasoning

Add the vinegar, garlic, shallot, egg, and mustard to a blender, and puree until smooth. With the motor running, add each of the oils in a thin but steady stream through the lid, processing until the mixture forms a smooth, thick emulsion. Transfer to a small bowl and whisk in the sour cream, pepper, salt, and Creole seasoning. Refrigerate until ready to use.

YIELD: 2 CUPS

Save your extra-virgin olive oil for another use; you want the more neutral flavor of regular pure olive oil for this.

watermelon, heirloom tomato, and
burrata salad

A combination of crisp watermelon, meaty tomatoes, sweet onions, and fresh herbs topped with burrata cheese, this salad is the best that summer has to offer. It may seem like an odd idea, but really, it's not. Watermelon and vine-ripened tomatoes come into season at the same time, and the burrata, which provides a creamy contrast, is a play on the classic combination of tomatoes and mozzarella.

6 cups mâche (see Essentials, at right)

3 cups diced (1-inch) seedless watermelon

1 cup tomatoes, cut into halves, quarters, or wedges (I prefer heirlooms for this—use cherry tomatoes or regular-size tomatoes or a mix, whatever you have available)

½ cup thinly sliced sweet onion, such as Vidalia

1 tablespoon fresh basil chiffonade (see Essentials, page 37)

1 tablespoon fresh mint chiffonade

Fresh Herb and Red Wine Vinaigrette (recipe follows)

1 (8-ounce) ball burrata cheese, divided into 4 to 6 pieces, or 4 to 6 (2-ounce) burratini

Sea salt and coarsely ground black pepper

Extra-virgin olive oil, for drizzling

1. In a large bowl, combine the mâche, watermelon, tomatoes, onion, and herbs. Toss the salad with all of the vinaigrette.

2. Divide the salad among 4 to 6 salad plates. Place the burrata on top of each, season with salt and pepper to taste, and give each salad a drizzle of oil. Serve immediately.

YIELD: 4 TO 6 SERVINGS

fresh herb and red wine vinaigrette

This lively dressing also pairs well with spinach, spring greens, and mesclun.

½ cup olive oil

¼ cup red wine vinegar

2 tablespoons pomegranate jam (currant jam also works well)

¼ teaspoon salt

⅛ teaspoon freshly ground black pepper

2 teaspoons chopped fresh mint

1 teaspoon chopped fresh basil

In a small bowl, combine all the ingredients and whisk together well. This will keep in an airtight container in the refrigerator for up to 1 week.

YIELD: ABOUT ¾ CUP

burrata

Burrata originated in Puglia, Italy, to use up leftover bits of mozzarella. It is made by forming a piece of stretched mozzarella into a pouch, then filling it with a mixture of fresh cream and strings of mozzarella curd. The result is a cheese that looks like a ball of mozzarella but when broken open reveals its creamy contents (the name derives from *burro*, or butter, which gives you an idea of its richness). Burrata can be made from buffalo's milk or cow's milk and is sold in 2-, 4-, 8-, and 16-ounce pieces; the 2-ounce pieces are called burratini. Use burrata soon after purchasing it; it's a fresh cheese not meant to be stored for any length of time.

I prefer mâche for this, but you can substitute baby arugula or field greens.

•

Toss the salad with the dressing immediately before serving, as the mâche will begin to wilt as soon as the vinaigrette hits it. If you want to offer this as part of a buffet, keep the vinaigrette separate and allow diners to spoon it over their own salads.

kale salad with crisped
pancetta, golden raisins, and pine nuts

The incredible popularity of kale today is no surprise to me. I grew up eating braised kale and kale soup and have always loved it. I wanted this salad to have crunch and saltiness and a bit of sweetness, but without adding sugar. The result is incredibly yummy, a hearty, healthy salad you can enjoy as a side or main course.

3 cups cubed (1-inch) crusty bread, such as ciabatta

4 tablespoons olive oil

$1/8$ teaspoon table salt

$1/8$ teaspoon freshly ground black pepper

1 bunch lacinato (Tuscan) kale (10 to 12 ounces), washed well and tough stems removed

1 ounce thinly sliced pancetta, cut across into thin strips

2 oil-packed anchovy fillets, minced

$1/2$ teaspoon minced garlic

$1/2$ teaspoon kosher salt, plus more to taste

3 tablespoons fresh lemon juice

1 tablespoon minced shallot

2 teaspoons honey

$1/2$ teaspoon Dijon mustard

$1/4$ teaspoon crushed red pepper

$1/4$ cup extra-virgin olive oil

$1/4$ cup vegetable or canola oil

$1/3$ cup golden raisins

$1/3$ cup pine nuts, lightly toasted (see Essentials, at left)

1. Preheat the oven to 325°F. Line a small baking sheet with parchment paper.

2. Place the bread cubes on the baking sheet and drizzle with 3 tablespoons of the oil. Season with the table salt and black pepper and toss with your hands to evenly distribute the oil and seasonings. Arrange the cubes in a single layer on the sheet and bake until golden and crispy, about 15 minutes. Remove from the oven and let cool. Once cool, transfer to a zip-top plastic bag and seal. Using a rolling pin or the palms of your hands, crush the croutons against the counter to make irregularly sized coarse breadcrumbs. Set aside until you are ready to serve the salad.

3. Working with several leaves of kale at a time, pile them on one another, then roll them up lengthwise and, using a sharp knife, cut crosswise as thinly as you can to form ribbons. Place in a salad bowl, cover with a damp cloth or paper towel, and refrigerate until you are ready to serve the salad.

4. Heat the remaining 1 tablespoon oil in a medium nonstick skillet over medium heat until hot. Add the pancetta strips and cook, stirring to evenly distribute, until golden and crispy. Transfer to paper towels to drain until completely cool. Once cool, place the pancetta on a cutting board and roughly chop to form small pieces. Set aside.

5. On the cutting board, mash the anchovy fillets together with the garlic and kosher salt with the side of a chef's knife until it forms a smooth paste. Transfer to a small bowl and whisk in the lemon juice, shallot, honey, mustard, and crushed red pepper. While whisking, drizzle in the extra-virgin olive oil, then the vegetable oil in a slow, steady stream until the mixture thickens into an emulsion. Taste, and adjust the seasonings, if necessary.

6. When ready to serve the salad, toss the kale with the pancetta, raisins, pine nuts, and enough of the dressing to coat. Taste, and adjust the seasonings if necessary. Serve on 4 salad plates, garnished with crisp crouton crumbles.

YIELD: 4 SERVINGS

shredded brussels sprouts and
quinoa salad

The key to Brussels sprouts having a delicious nutty flavor is to not overcook them. This salad takes that taste and amps it up with the addition of quinoa and walnuts.

2 pounds Brussels sprouts (see Essentials, at right), root ends trimmed

1/2 cup red or white quinoa

1 cup vegetable broth

Pinch plus 1/2 teaspoon salt

1/4 cup red wine vinegar

3 tablespoons chopped shallot

1 tablespoon not too finely grated lemon zest

2 teaspoons minced garlic

6 tablespoons extra-virgin olive oil

1/4 teaspoon freshly ground black pepper

1 tablespoon chopped fresh flat-leaf parsley

1 cup walnut halves, toasted (see Essentials, at right) and chopped

1. Bring a large saucepan of salted water to a boil over medium-high heat. Fill a large bowl with ice water. Add the Brussels sprouts to the pan and cook until the water returns to a boil, about 3 minutes. Transfer them with a slotted spoon to the ice water. Once the Brussels sprouts are cool enough to handle, drain and set aside.

2. Add the quinoa to an 8-inch sauté pan and toast over medium heat, stirring as needed, until it begins to crackle, about 2 minutes. Remove from the heat.

3. In a small saucepan, combine the broth, pinch of salt, and toasted quinoa. Bring to a boil, then reduce the heat to low, cover, and simmer for 12 minutes (the timing is important here). Remove from the heat and let it steam an additional 5 minutes. All of the liquid should be absorbed at this point;

if some remains, drain it off. Fluff the quinoa with a fork and set aside, uncovered.

4. In a small bowl, combine the vinegar, shallot, lemon zest, and garlic, and whisk to combine. Slowly pour in the oil as you whisk to make a vinaigrette. Stir in the remaining 1/2 teaspoon salt, the pepper, parsley, and walnuts.

5. Thinly slice the Brussels sprouts from top to bottom (parallel to the core, lengthwise) and add to a medium bowl with the quinoa and vinaigrette. Toss to combine. Taste for salt and pepper. Serve immediately, or cover and refrigerate up to 1 day, though the sprouts will lose some of their crispness and the color will change slightly.

YIELD: 6 TO 8 SERVINGS

quinoa

Ten years ago, very few people had ever heard of quinoa, let alone knew how to pronounce it (keen-wah). Now it's everywhere, and for good reason. This ancient grain (actually a seed), which was sacred to the Incas and considered by them to be the "mother of all grains," is a nutritional powerhouse. It's one of the few plant foods that is a complete protein, meaning it contains all the essential amino acids. It's also gluten-free. White quinoa is the most common type sold, but there is also red and black quinoa.

Quinoa has a bitter outer coating that needs to be removed before it's cooked. When you buy quinoa, check the package to see if the producer has already rinsed the grains. If not, pour it into a fine-mesh strainer and rinse under cool running water for several minutes, rubbing the grains as you do. Don't skip toasting the quinoa before cooking—it heightens its nutty flavor.

Select Brussels sprouts about the same size so they cook evenly. Watch the timing on the sprouts. The worst thing you can do is overcook Brussels sprouts, which brings out their cabbagey quality.

•

It's best to toast walnut (and pecan) halves, then chop them; if you toast them chopped, you run a greater risk of burning them. Place on a baking sheet in a 350°F oven until you just start to smell their nutty fragrance.

hearts of palm salad with
jumbo lump crabmeat and honey tangerine vinaigrette

Hearts of palm are the tender inner core of the cabbage palm and have a flavor reminiscent of artichokes. I've always loved them, so much so that once, in the early days of Emeril's, I had some harvested and shipped unprocessed from Costa Rica, so I could show my staff how to break it down and ready it for preparation. That entire week we offered different hearts of palm dishes, including salads like this one. This is a substantial, easy, and refreshing salad that will make a big impression.

4 honey tangerines or satsuma oranges, peel and pith removed

Additional fresh honey tangerine juice as needed

¼ cup Champagne vinegar or white wine vinegar

1 teaspoon finely grated tangerine zest

⅓ cup grapeseed or canola oil

½ teaspoon coarse sea salt

¼ teaspoon freshly ground black pepper

1 pound fresh jumbo lump crabmeat, picked over for cartilage and shells

3 tablespoons chopped fresh chives

1 tablespoon chopped fresh basil

5 ounces baby spinach

1 (14-ounce) jar hearts of palm, drained and cut into ½-inch-thick rounds

1. Working over a bowl, section the tangerines (see Sectioning Citrus, opposite), catching the juice for the vinaigrette. Place the sections in a medium bowl. Squeeze the tangerine peels over the bowl; they contain a lot of juice. Pour the juice into a measuring cup and add more juice to measure ½ cup. Pour the juice in a small saucepan and bring to a boil over high heat. Reduce the tangerine juice by half. Set aside to cool.

2. In a small bowl, combine the reduced juice, vinegar, and zest. Whisking, add the oil in a slow, steady stream until emulsified. Whisk in the salt and pepper and set aside.

3. In a medium bowl, combine the crabmeat with the chives, basil, and 2 tablespoons of the vinaigrette. In a separate medium bowl,

toss the spinach with about 2 tablespoons of the vinaigrette—it should just lightly coat the leaves. Add the hearts of palm and tangerine sections, and very gently toss together, taking care not to break the sections.

4. Divide the spinach-tangerine mixture among 4 salad plates. Divide the crabmeat among the plates, setting it in the center of each salad. Drizzle each with any remaining vinaigrette. Serve immediately.

YIELD: 4 SERVINGS

sectioning citrus

This technique can be used with any kind of citrus to remove the peel, pith, and chewy membranes between the sections.

1. Cut across the top and bottom of the citrus fruit and sit it flat on the cutting board. You want to slice the fruit so you completely remove the peel and woolly pith below it, taking as little of the flesh as possible. Continue cutting away the peel and pith, slicing down along the side of the fruit.

2. In the photo for Step 1, looking at the top of the fruit, you will see a pinwheel effect. The lighter colored lines are the membranes that separate the individual citrus sections. Take your knife and cut out each section, slicing snug up against the membrane on either side.

3. You now have juicy, vibrantly colored sections to add to your salad, As you continue to cut them out, periodically pour the juice that will accumulate on the cutting board into a small bowl and add it to the vinaigrette.

1

2

3

grilled calamari salad with fresh tomatoes, olives, and roasted red peppers

This terrific salad takes its flavor profile from the Mediterranean. With a zing of heat and smoke from the crushed red pepper and smoked paprika and a pleasing edge of acid from the lemon, vinegar, and capers, it's savory, crunchy, and aromatic. Served over toasted bread, it makes for a filling light dinner.

1½ pounds cleaned squid, bodies and tentacles

½ cup extra-virgin olive oil, plus more for brushing

1 tablespoon fresh lemon juice

2 teaspoons minced fresh oregano

2 cloves garlic, smashed

1 cup chopped fresh tomatoes

¾ cup pitted mixed olives, roughly chopped

¼ cup finely diced roasted red peppers

¼ cup finely diced red onion

¼ cup finely diced celery

¼ cup celery leaves

¼ cup red wine vinegar

2 tablespoons nonpareil capers

1 teaspoon grated lemon zest

1 teaspoon crushed red pepper

¼ teaspoon smoked hot paprika

1 loaf ciabatta bread

Salt and freshly ground black pepper

Chopped fresh flat-leaf parsley, for garnish

1. In a large bowl, combine the squid with ¼ cup of the oil, the lemon juice, oregano, and garlic. Cover and refrigerate for 1 hour.

2. In a small bowl, combine the tomatoes, olives, roasted peppers, onion, celery and celery leaves, vinegar, the remaining ¼ cup oil, the capers, lemon zest, crushed red pepper, and paprika, and set aside.

3. Remove the squid from the refrigerator.

4. Preheat a grill or grill pan over high heat.

5. Grill the squid until slightly golden on both sides and opaque all the way through, about 3 minutes. Remove the squid to a cutting board and slice the bodies across into ⅛-inch rings. Slice the tentacles in half if they are large. Immediately transfer the squid to the bowl with the tomato and olive mixture, and toss to combine. Allow the salad to sit, either at room temperature or refrigerated, for about 15 minutes before serving.

6. Slice the ciabatta bread into 1-inch-thick slices and brush each slice on one side with olive oil. Season the same side with salt and pepper to taste. Transfer the bread to the grill or grill pan, oiled side down, and cook until the bread is toasted and golden brown, 8 to 10 minutes.

7. Portion the salad onto plates, garnish with a sprinkling of parsley, and serve with the toasted bread on the side. The salad can be kept overnight, but the texture of the squid will change somewhat because of the acid from the lemon juice and vinegar. It's best eaten the day it is prepared, slightly chilled or at room temperature.

YIELD: 2 TO 3 LIGHT MAIN-COURSE OR 4 TO 6 FIRST-COURSE SERVINGS

cooking squid

If you're going to grill the squid outside, put them in a grill basket to cook. If cooking on a grill pan, be sure not to crowd them so they can get good and crispy— you may have to cook the calamari in several batches to do this. And while a nice char adds flavor, don't let the calamari get deeply scorched—it will taste bitter.

BREAKFAST & BRUNCH

Talk to me about breakfast and I'll talk to you about eggs. They are a savory blank canvas you can take in most any direction you like. I wanted to take the egg to new heights and have created special dishes with mind-blowing flavors that your family and guests will never forget. From creamy scrambled eggs with a double shot of aromatic truffle to fried eggs on a rich and crispy bed of shredded potatoes and homemade duck confit. If you like a bit of sweet for breakfast, nothing beats my blueberry beignets, crunchy and tender all at once. To wash it all down, I've included a selection of favorite cocktails tailor-made for the flavors of breakfast.

creamy double-truffle
scrambled eggs

Truffles and eggs are an amazing combination. At the restaurant during truffle season, I will put a couple dozen eggs in a paper sack along with a fresh truffle. After a few days, the flavor of the truffle will have penetrated the shells and infused the eggs inside. But fresh truffles aren't always available, and when they are, they're very expensive. So for this dish, we used truffle butter and truffle salt, with great results.

8 large eggs

¼ cup heavy cream

1 tablespoon unsalted butter

2 tablespoons truffle butter (see Truffle Products, page 190), at room temperature

Truffle salt

Freshly ground white pepper

2 tablespoons snipped fresh chives (optional)

1. In a medium bowl, vigorously whisk together the eggs and cream to incorporate some air.

2. Melt the unsalted butter in a 12-inch nonstick sauté pan over medium heat. When the butter begins to sizzle, add the eggs and cook undisturbed until they begin to set around the edges, about 10 seconds. Begin folding the eggs into one another by scraping gently back and forth with a heatproof rubber spatula, continuing to stir until the eggs are softly set, about 2 minutes.

3. Add the truffle butter, remove the pan from the heat, and continue to stir until the butter is fully incorporated (it melts quickly; you just need to stir to distribute evenly). Season the eggs with truffle salt and pepper to taste, and transfer to a warm serving platter. Garnish with the chives, if desired, and serve immediately.

YIELD: 4 SERVINGS

making scrambled eggs

Scrambling eggs is simple, so why a tutorial? Because simplicity doesn't ensure success if you have bad technique. I've eaten a lot of bad scrambled eggs in my travels, eggs that weren't so much scrambled as cooked on contact with a hot pan. This method yields delicious, softly set, truly scrambled eggs.

1. For the best texture, it's important to give the eggs and cream a really good whisking to incorporate as much air as possible.

2. Use a nonstick pan, if you have one. Melt the butter over medium heat—and no higher! Add the eggs to the pan and let them cook, undisturbed, until they are set all along the outer edge, then take a rubber spatula and scrape it back and forth through the eggs.

3. Continue to stir in this way until the eggs are cooked the way you prefer them. I like my scrambled eggs as shown here, with nice, large, soft curds. Serve the eggs on warm plates, otherwise they'll get cold on the way to the table.

1

2

3

duck confit
rösti potatoes with fried eggs

In the early days of Emeril's, there were two gentlemen who visited the restaurant on a regular basis. Every Friday they would come in for lunch and ask that I make them something that wasn't on the menu. At some point, I came up with this dish for them and their weekly request changed from "Can you make us something not on the menu?" to "Can you make us that *rösti* again?" I guarantee your family and friends will be asking you the same question after you make this for them.

1 large onion, peeled

2 russet potatoes (about 1½ pounds total)

2 teaspoons plus a pinch salt

½ teaspoon plus a pinch freshly ground black pepper

Roughly shredded meat from Duck Confit (page 134)

3 tablespoons rendered duck fat (you can steal it from the confit)

2 tablespoons unsalted butter

6 large eggs

½ cup sour cream

2 tablespoons chopped fresh chives

1 teaspoon fresh lemon juice

2 teaspoons roughly chopped fresh flat-leaf parsley, for garnish

1. Grate the onion over a small bowl, using the largest holes on a box grater. Transfer it to a fine-mesh strainer and gently press down to remove excess water.

2. Peel the potatoes, then, using the largest holes on a box grater or a food processor, coarsely grate them. Transfer the grated potatoes to the strainer, set over a bowl, and press on them to release as much of the liquid as possible. After the starch has settled to the bottom of the bowl (this only takes a minute or two and you will get a few tablespoons or so of liquid), carefully pour off the clear liquid, reserving the starch (see Essentials, at left). Add the grated potatoes to the starch in the bowl, along with the grated onion, salt, and pepper. Add the shreded duck meat, and toss to combine everything well.

3. Preheat the oven to 400°F.

4. Heat a 12-inch nonstick skillet over medium-high heat and add the duck fat. Add the potato mixture to the pan, patting it down gently, and cook for 5 minutes without touching it so it has the chance to form a nice golden-brown crust. Carefully flip the cake over, like a pancake (if the cake breaks into separate pieces, don't worry—just press the pieces back together to form a solid cake), and continue to cook until it is golden brown and crisp on the other side, about another 12 minutes.

5. Transfer the potato cake to a baking sheet and place in the oven until the potatoes are fully cooked, about 10 minutes. Transfer the *rösti* to a clean cutting board, cut into 6 wedges, and place a wedge on 6 serving plates.

6. In a medium nonstick sauté pan, melt 1 tablespoon of the butter over medium heat. When it starts to sizzle, break 3 of the eggs into the pan, keeping them apart, and fry the way you or your guests like them. When done, place an egg on top of a wedge of the potato cake. Repeat with the remaining butter and eggs.

7. In a small bowl, whisk the sour cream, chives, lemon juice, and a pinch of salt and pepper together. Place a dollop on each potato wedge next to the fried egg. Sprinkle with a generous pinch of parsley, and serve immediately.

YIELD: 6 SERVINGS

The starch added back to the potatoes will help them stay in place when you flip the pancake.

shoyu pork loco moco
for sam choy

Loco moco is a comfort food staple and traditional breakfast dish in Hawaii. Some cooks will serve the rice with fried sausage links (usually Portuguese sausage) on top, while others will chop up the sausage and add it to the rice. One thing is constant: It is always rice served with some sort of meat, an egg, and gravy.

It was my good friend Sam Choy who originally introduced me to loco moco. Sam and I have fished together, cooked together, golfed together, and done many charity dinners together. As a tribute to him, here is my version of loco moco, served over Filipino-style garlic fried rice.

5 tablespoons peanut oil

2½ to 3 pounds boneless pork butt, trimmed of excess fat and cut into 2- to 3-inch pieces

4 cloves garlic, smashed

1 cup plus 2 tablespoons soy sauce

1 cup firmly packed light brown sugar

1 cup Rich Chicken Stock (page 68) or store-bought low-sodium chicken broth

4 thick slices fresh ginger, peeled and bruised

8 ounces (1 link) chorizo, sliced into quarters lengthwise and then cut crosswise into thin pieces

⅓ cup minced garlic

6 cups cold cooked jasmine rice (make it at least a day ahead)

½ cup thinly sliced green onions

3 tablespoons unsalted butter

6 large eggs

Salt and freshly ground black pepper

1. Heat 2 tablespoons of the oil in a small enameled Dutch oven (see Essentials, at right) over medium-high heat until very hot. Sear the pork in batches until nicely browned, 3 to 4 minutes per side. As the pork browns, transfer it to a plate. Once it has all been browned, return the pork to the pot and add the smashed garlic, stirring to combine. Add 1 cup of the soy sauce, the brown sugar, stock, and ginger, and cook, stirring, until the sugar is dissolved and the liquid comes to a boil. Reduce the heat to a steady simmer and cook, uncovered, turning and rearranging the pork as needed so that it cooks evenly in the liquid, until the pork is very tender and the sauce has reduced to a thickened syrupy consistency, about 1 hour to 1 hour and 15 minutes. Cover, remove from the heat, and keep warm until ready to serve.

2. Heat the remaining 3 tablespoons oil in a large nonstick skillet or wok over medium-high heat. When hot, add the chorizo and cook, stirring, until browned around the edges, 3 to 4 minutes. Add the minced garlic and continue to cook, stirring constantly, until the garlic is lightly golden and toasted, 2 to 3 minutes. Crumble the rice into the pan, increase the heat to high, and cook, tossing and stirring constantly, until the rice is heated through. Add the remaining 2 tablespoons soy sauce and toss until thoroughly combined. Sprinkle the green onions over the rice and remove the pan from the heat while you cook the eggs.

3. Heat a large nonstick skillet over medium heat. Add half of the butter and, when it has melted, add 3 of the eggs and cook as you prefer (I like mine sunny-side up). Season lightly with salt and pepper and transfer to a plate while you cook the remaining eggs with the remaining butter.

4. When ready to serve, divide the rice evenly among 6 serving plates or shallow bowls and portion the shoyu pork evenly over the rice. Drizzle each plate with some of the shoyu "gravy" and top each plate with an egg. Serve immediately.

YIELD: 6 SERVINGS

Chinese sausage or Filipino langonesa sausage can be substituted for the chorizo.

•

The size of the Dutch oven is key to the success of this dish. You want it to be just large enough that all the pork will fit in a single layer. The pork cooks, uncovered, for an hour or more in not very much liquid, so you want to slow down the rate of evaporation.

239

corned beef hash
with eggs and classic hollandaise sauce

This is one of my favorite breakfast dishes of all time—I absolutely love corned beef hash. It's also a great way to use up leftover roast meat; feel free to swap out the corned beef for roast beef or roast pork.

8 tablespoons (1 stick) unsalted butter

1 cup finely chopped onion

1 cup finely chopped green bell pepper

½ teaspoon salt, plus more for seasoning

2 tablespoons minced garlic

4 cups finely chopped or shredded corned beef

1 tablespoon chopped fresh flat-leaf parsley

1 tablespoon whole-grain mustard

2 pounds russet potatoes, peeled and cut into ¼-inch dice

½ teaspoon freshly ground black pepper, plus more for seasoning

¼ cup heavy cream

2 tablespoons hot sauce

4 large eggs

Classic Hollandaise Sauce, for serving (page 242)

1. Melt 4 tablespoons of the butter in a large nonstick skillet over medium heat. Add the onion, bell pepper, and ¼ teaspoon of the salt, and cook until softened, about 5 minutes, stirring as needed. Add the garlic and corned beef, increase the heat to medium-high, and cook until the onion is lightly browned, about another 5 minutes. Transfer to a bowl, add the parsley, mustard, potatoes, pepper, and remaining ¼ teaspoon salt, and toss to combine.

2. Add 2 tablespoons of the butter to the skillet and melt over medium heat. Add the corned beef mixture and cook for 5 minutes, pressing the mixture against the bottom of the skillet with a metal spatula and shaking the pan to prevent sticking. Increase the heat to medium-high and cook for another 10 minutes, continuing to press on the mixture and shake the pan to help form a crust.

3. Using the edge of the spatula, cut the mixture into 4 quarters and flip each piece over. Cut the remaining 2 tablespoons butter into small pieces and place them all around the edge of the pan. Cook the other side of the hash for 10 minutes, pressing down on it and shaking the pan. Turn the wedges again and drizzle in the cream and hot sauce. Once the cream and hot sauce have been absorbed by the mixture, with the back of a large spoon, press to make 4 evenly spaced wells in the hash. Crack an egg into each well. Season the eggs with salt and pepper, cover the pan, and cook for 4 minutes. Remove the pan from the heat.

4. Place a portion of the hash with its egg on each of 4 serving plates, spoon over some hollandaise, and serve immediately. Any remaining hollandaise can be served on the side in a small pitcher.

YIELD: 4 SERVINGS

(continued)

Though you can certainly use corned beef from the deli, leftover corned beef brisket will yield the best results because it's more moist.

•

If you have leftover baked or boiled potatoes on hand, use them instead—they work great in this dish! The crust will form quicker and you can cut the amount of cream in half.

classic hollandaise sauce

Hollandaise can be finicky and does not reheat well, so it needs to be prepared close to serving time. You can have everything ready to go (clarified butter kept in a warm spot, a pot of hot water, lemon squeezed, yolks and water in a bowl), then put the sauce together quickly right before serving.

¾ cup (1½ sticks) unsalted butter

2 large egg yolks

2 tablespoons plus 2 teaspoons water

2 teaspoons fresh lemon juice

½ teaspoon salt

Pinch of cayenne pepper

1. Clarify the butter. Melt it in a small saucepan over medium-low heat. Skim away the foam as it forms on the surface of the melted butter. When the heavier milk solids sink to the bottom of the pan, remove the pan from the heat. Using a small ladle, carefully transfer the clear clarified butter to a small heatproof container such as a liquid measuring cup, leaving the milk solids behind (see tutorial, opposite). Keep the clarified butter warm until ready to use. When making hollandaise, you must use the clarified butter while it is liquid.

2. In a small heatproof bowl (it should be large enough to set over a pot of simmering water without touching the water), combine the egg yolks and 2 tablespoons of the water. Set the bowl over simmering water and whisk constantly until the yolks have thickened and, when you pull the whisk out of the bowl, fall back on themselves in ribbons, about 3 minutes, but be careful not to overcook the yolks.

3. Remove the bowl from the heat and whisk in the lemon juice and salt.

4. Dampen a kitchen towel and arrange in a small ring on the counter. Set the bowl of yolks on top of the towel to steady it. With a whisk in one hand (your right hand if you are right handed) and a small ladle in the other, begin to drizzle in the clarified butter drop by drop while whisking vigorously. Repeat this several times. When you see the sauce noticeably thicken, you can then begin to drizzle in the remaining butter in a slow, steady stream while continuing to whisk all the while. When half the butter has been incorporated, whisk in the remaining 2 teaspoons water, then whisk in the remaining clarified butter (still in a slow, steady stream) and the cayenne. Serve immediately or keep the sauce warm by positioning it near the stove, over a warm water bath, or on a warming shelf (but never over a flame) until you are ready to serve.

YIELD: ABOUT 1 CUP

hollandaise help

When making the hollandaise, use a metal whisk to beat the yolks. Also, while beating, think about incorporating air, not just beating the eggs together. The more air that is incorporated into the yolks, the lighter the sauce will be.

If at any point while you are whisking in the clarified butter you think that the sauce may be starting to break (maybe because it's too hot or there isn't enough liquid), whisk in a small ice cube until melted and incorporated, then continue along. That should fix it.

clarifying butter

I think most folks think of butter as they would olive oil, as a single ingredient that can't be broken down any further. But butter consists of three parts: butterfat, milk proteins, and water. The milk proteins will begin to brown and burn if heated for very long; for that reason, butter isn't used for high-temperature cooking. But when butter is clarified, two things happen: As the butter is gently heated, the water evaporates and the milk solids separate from the butterfat. That pure butterfat is clarified butter (also called ghee in Indian cooking). With the milk solids removed, clarified butter can be heated to a much higher temperature before it begins to break down. Also, because the water has been evaporated, when used to make sauces like hollandaise, it yields a thicker final result.

1. Place the butter in a heavy-bottomed saucepan and melt over medium-low heat. The foam you see forming on the top is the whey protein.

2. Skim the foam off with a spoon.

3. As the butter continues to heat, the heavier milk solids will sink to the bottom of the pan, leaving a clear yellow liquid on top, the pure butterfat.

4. Remove the pan from the heat and carefully ladle the butterfat off, leaving the milk solids behind in the pan. This is the clarified butter.

veal grillades
with stone-ground cheddar grits soufflé

Grillades is a wonderful New Orleans brunch classic that can be made the day before and warmed up the next morning. It's delicious with plain grits, but I highly recommend that you serve it with the light and airy Stone-Ground Cheddar Grits Soufflé.

Salt and freshly ground black pepper

¾ teaspoon cayenne pepper

2 pounds thinly sliced veal or beef round steak

¾ cup all-purpose flour

¼ cup plus 2 tablespoons vegetable oil, or more as needed for browning meat

2 tablespoons unsalted butter

2 cups finely chopped onions

1 cup finely chopped celery

1 cup finely chopped mixed red and green bell peppers

½ cup minced shallots

3 tablespoons minced garlic

2 cayenne peppers, minced

6 to 8 sprigs fresh thyme

3 bay leaves

3 cups peeled, seeded, and chopped fresh or canned tomatoes

1 cup dry red wine

4 cups beef stock or low-sodium beef broth

3 tablespoons chopped fresh flat-leaf parsley

Stone-Ground Cheddar Grits Soufflé (see opposite), for serving

1. Preheat the oven to 325°F. In a small bowl, combine 2½ teaspoons salt, 1 teaspoon black pepper, and the cayenne. Cut the veal into roughly 3-inch pieces. Place the pieces between two pieces of plastic wrap or waxed paper. Using the smooth side of a meat mallet, pound the pieces until they have a thickness of about ⅛ inch. Season the meat on both sides with the salt mixture, then lightly dredge in the flour on both sides, shaking to remove any excess.

2. Heat a large Dutch oven over medium-high heat and add ¼ cup of the oil. When hot, brown the meat in batches, 2 to 3 minutes per side. Transfer it to a baking sheet, and add more oil to the Dutch oven as necessary. When all the meat is browned, add the remaining oil and the butter to the drippings in the pot. Add the onions, celery, and bell peppers, and cook, scraping up any browned bits from the bottom of the pot, until the vegetables are softened, about 4 minutes. Add the shallots and garlic, and cook until fragrant, 30 seconds to 1 minute.

Add the cayenne peppers, thyme, bay leaves, and tomatoes, and cook for 2 minutes, then add the wine, stock, and 1½ teaspoons salt, and bring to a boil. Return the meat to the pot and return to a boil. Cover, place in the oven, and cook, stirring occasionally, until the meat is fork-tender, about 2 hours. (The grillades can be prepared up to this point a day ahead. Let cool to room temperature, then refrigerate. Reheat the next day in a 325°F oven.)

3. Remove from the oven and gently stir in the parsley. You can serve the grillades in a wide shallow bowl over the grits or on a plate with the grits alongside.

YIELD: 4 TO 6 SERVINGS

stone-ground
cheddar grits soufflé

The perfect partner for grillades! This can be prepared in advance through Step 3.

4 cups water

4 cups milk

1½ teaspoons salt

¾ teaspoon finely ground white pepper

1 cup stone-ground white grits

4 tablespoons (½ stick) unsalted butter

1½ cups chopped green onions (about 1 bunch)

3 cloves garlic, minced

8 ounces white Cheddar cheese, coarsely grated (2 cups)

6 large eggs, separated, at room temperature

¼ cup half-and-half

⅛ teaspoon cream of tartar

1. Combine the water, milk, salt, and pepper in a large saucepan, and bring to a boil over high heat. Whisk in the grits all at once and return to a boil. Reduce the heat to low, partially cover the pan, and cook until the grits are smooth and creamy, usually 1½ to 2 hours, stirring occasionally at first and more frequently near the end of cooking. Transfer the grits to a large heatproof bowl and set aside to cool for 15 to 20 minutes, stirring frequently to prevent a skin from forming.

2. In a small skillet, melt 3 tablespoons of the butter, then add the green onions and garlic, and cook, stirring a few times, until softened and fragrant, 3 to 4 minutes. Stir the sautéed green onions and garlic and the cheese into the grits. Taste, and adjust the seasonings if necessary.

3. In a small bowl, whisk together the egg yolks and half-and-half; stir into the grits. (You can prepare the recipe up to this point a day ahead, if you like, and refrigerate. Pull the grits and the egg whites out of the fridge in the morning and bring to room temperature before proceeding.)

4. Preheat the oven to 350°F and grease a 9 x 13-inch baking or gratin dish with the remaining 1 tablespoon butter.

5. In a large bowl with an electric mixer on high speed, beat the egg whites with the cream of tartar until stiff peaks form. Using a rubber spatula, gently fold one-third of the whites into the grits to lighten the mixture, then gently fold in the remaining whites until they are incorporated but still fluffy, taking care not to overmix.

6. Transfer the batter to the prepared baking dish, smoothing the top with the spatula, and bake in the lower third of the oven until the soufflé is golden brown and risen and a tester inserted in the center comes out clean, 50 to 60 minutes. Serve immediately.

YIELD: 8 TO 10 SERVINGS

pounding the cutlets

When you are pounding out the pieces of veal, you're not just pounding them to the same thickness for even cooking, you're also tenderizing them, breaking down the muscle fibers.

blueberry
beignets

This is basically a sweet fritter batter. You can substitute raspberries or cut-up strawberries, but there is something about blueberries that makes these awesome.

1 cup fresh blueberries, picked over for stems

¼ cup granulated sugar

2 large eggs, lightly beaten

1 cup half-and-half

1¾ cups bleached all-purpose flour

1 teaspoon baking powder

½ teaspoon salt

Vegetable oil, for frying

1½ cups confectioners' sugar, plus more for dusting as needed

1. In a medium bowl, combine the blueberries and granulated sugar and lightly mash together with a fork. Stir in the eggs and half-and-half.

2. In a large bowl, combine the flour, baking powder, and salt. Make a well in the center, pour in the blueberry mixture, and whisk until combined. Allow the mixture to rest 10 minutes before frying.

3. Pour enough oil to come to the maximum line in an electric fryer or halfway up the side of a deep, large, heavy-bottomed pot (see Essentials, at right). Heat the oil to 360°F.

4. Using a 2-tablespoon scoop, carefully drop the batter into the hot oil, cooking 4 to 6 beignets at a time; don't crowd them. If using a deep fryer, shake the basket to loosen the beignets from the bottom if they're sticking. Cook the beignets until golden, about 6 minutes. If you're frying them in a pot, the beignets will sink to the bottom, then float up to the top, where you can turn them for even coloring.

5. Using a slotted spoon, tongs, or a spider, transfer the fried beignets to paper towels to drain briefly, then add to a large bowl along with the confectioners' sugar, and toss to coat. Set the beignets on a serving platter. Repeat the process with the remaining batter.

6. To serve, dust the beignets a final time with confectioners' sugar, and serve hot.

YIELD: ABOUT 18

malassadas
(portuguese doughnuts)

Every Sunday, my mom would give me money to go to the local Portuguese bakery down the street to buy *malassadas* for the family. I bought them by the half dozen and they were put in a brown paper sack; they'd still be warm when I got them home. When we were testing this recipe, my brother, Mark, had one and got teary-eyed—for us, *malassadas* are the taste of our childhood.

Malassadas are similar to New Orleans beignets, but softer and more tender. They can be cut into any shape, which is part of their charm. The most important thing is that they be generously covered with cinnamon sugar while they are still hot. And, like beignets, they are best eaten right after coming out of the fryer.

Vegetable oil, for frying and oiling bowl

1 (¼-ounce) envelope active dry yeast

1½ cups plus ½ teaspoon sugar

2 tablespoons warm water (110° to 115°F)

3 large eggs, at room temperature

2 tablespoons unsalted butter, melted

½ cup whole milk, at room temperature

½ cup half-and-half, at room temperature

½ teaspoon salt

4¼ cups all-purpose flour, plus more for rolling out dough

1 teaspoon ground cinnamon

1. Oil a large bowl and set aside.

2. In a small bowl, combine the yeast, ½ teaspoon sugar, and warm water. Stir to combine, then set aside until the yeast is foamy, 5 to 10 minutes (if it doesn't foam, the yeast is no longer active and you'll need to start again with fresh yeast).

3. In the bowl of a stand mixer fitted with the whisk attachment, beat the eggs and ½ cup of the sugar on high speed until very thick and pale yellow in color, about 6 minutes. Change the mixer attachment to the dough hook and turn the mixer to low speed. Little by little, add in this order, one at a time, the yeast mixture, melted butter, milk, half-and-half, and salt. Add the flour 1 cup at a time, beating after each addition, just until you can't see the flour anymore, until you have added all 4¼ cups. Continue to mix the dough until it forms a soft dough that pulls away from the side of the bowl and climbs up the dough hook. Transfer the dough (it should be soft and slightly sticky) to the oiled bowl, cover with plastic wrap or a damp kitchen towel, and set it in a warm, draft-free place until it has doubled in size, 1½ to 2 hours (see Essentials, at left).

4. Turn the dough out onto a lightly floured work surface (such as a large cutting board). Dust the top of the dough lightly with flour. Using a rolling pin, roll the dough out into a roughly rectangular shape about 12 x 17 inches and about ½ inch thick. Place a piece of plastic wrap lightly on top of the dough and transfer the dough to a draft-free place; let it rise until it has doubled in size, about 1 hour.

5. Fill a deep, heavy-bottomed pot halfway with oil and heat to 360° to 375°F, or preheat an electric fryer according to the manufacturer's instructions. Place the remaining 1 cup sugar in a medium bowl, and stir in the cinnamon.

6. Using a sharp knife, cut the dough into rectangles about 2 x 4 inches. Don't worry about trimming the edges so that everything is pretty—you want these to look rustic and homemade. Using floured hands, pat the dough down a bit to flatten it. Fry the dough in batches (be sure not to crowd them) until golden brown, turning them so that they brown evenly on both sides, 3 to 4 minutes total. Drain briefly on paper towels, then dredge the doughnuts in the cinnamon sugar until generously coated. Enjoy as soon as possible!

YIELD: 2½ TO 3 DOZEN

portuguese
sweet bread

I learned how to make this bread when I worked at the local Portuguese bakery in high school. It's delicious sliced warm out of the oven or toasted the next day. You can use it for sandwiches, but because it's sweet, it doesn't go with everything—turkey and roast chicken are great partners. And it makes amazing French toast. Even though we usually bought this from the bakery, I always thought my mom's homemade was the best.

1 tablespoon active dry yeast

¼ cup warm water (110° to 115°F)

¾ cup plus 1 teaspoon sugar

½ cup milk

¼ cup (½ stick) unsalted butter, at room temperature, plus more for greasing pan

1 teaspoon salt

3 large eggs, plus 1 large egg, lightly beaten with 1 teaspoon water, for glaze

4 to 4½ cups all-purpose flour, plus more for kneading

Vegetable oil, for greasing bowl

1. In a small bowl, combine the yeast, warm water, and 1 teaspoon of the sugar. Stir to dissolve the yeast, then set aside until foamy, usually 5 to 10 minutes. (If it does not get foamy, that means the yeast is no longer active; throw it out and start again with a fresh package of yeast.)

2. Heat the milk in a small saucepan until it just comes to a boil. Add the butter and salt, and swirl until it melts into the milk.

3. In the bowl of a stand mixer fitted with the dough hook, beat the 3 eggs with the remaining ¾ cup sugar on high speed until lightened in color and foamy. Reduce the speed to low and add the milk mixture, then the yeast mixture. Increase the speed

to medium and add the flour 1 cup at a time until you have added 4 cups. Add the last ½ cup of flour a bit at a time, adding only enough so that the dough forms a ball that is stiff enough to come away from the side of the bowl and climb up the dough hook. The dough will be sticky.

4. Turn the dough out onto a lightly floured work surface and knead, adding a sprinkling of flour as needed to prevent the dough from sticking to the surface and your hands, until the dough is smooth and elastic, usually about 10 minutes. The dough will remain slightly tacky to the touch. Lightly oil a large bowl and place the dough in it, turning to coat all sides. Cover with plastic wrap or a damp kitchen towel and set in a warm, draft-free place until the dough has doubled in size, 2 to 3 hours.

5. Remove the dough from the bowl and punch it down to remove any air bubbles. Shape the dough into a smooth ball, tucking the outer edges underneath it and pinching them to seal the seam. Place the dough in a buttered 7-inch round baking pan (a small springform pan will work if you do not have a small baking round). Cover lightly with plastic wrap or a damp kitchen towel and set in a warm, draft-free place until the dough has doubled in size and the top has risen just above the top of the pan, 1 to 1½ hours.

6. Preheat the oven to 350°F.

7. Brush the top of the dough with the beaten egg wash and bake in the center of the oven until it is deep amber brown on top and an instant-read thermometer inserted into the center of the bread registers 190°F, 45 to 55 minutes. Remove from the oven and set the pan on a wire rack to cool for 15 minutes, then remove the bread from the pan and continue to cool. The bread can be served warm or cooled completely, wrapped in plastic wrap, and used as needed for up to several days.

YIELD: 1 LARGE ROUND LOAF, 4 TO 6 SERVINGS

To get the proper texture (crumb), be sure to let the dough rise completely both times.

•

You can do like the Portuguese bakers do at holiday time—right before putting the bread in the oven, take five or six raw eggs in their shells and push them halfway down into the dough. When the bread is done, the eggs will be, too!

Left to right: Iced Café with Tequila Coffee Liqueur and Nocello, Champagne Cocktail, Black Pepper Bloody Mary, and Rumchata Punch

champagne
cocktail

Try this very elegant drink the next time you have brunch at home. The subtle flavor notes from the bitters combine with the Grand Marnier and Cognac to make this refreshing Champagne cocktail complex and interesting.

1 sugar cube

3 to 4 drops of Peychaud's or Angostura bitters

$1/2$ ounce (1 tablespoon) Grand Marnier

$1/2$ ounce (1 tablespoon) Cognac or brandy

1 ounce (2 tablespoons) fresh orange juice

4 to 6 ounces ($1/2$ to $3/4$ cup) chilled brut Champagne

1 strip orange zest, for garnish

Place the sugar cube in the bottom of a Champagne flute and drip the bitters onto the sugar. Add the Grand Marnier, Cognac, and orange juice to the glass, then slowly pour in the Champagne to fill. Garnish with the orange zest, and serve immediately.

YIELD: 1 SERVING

black pepper
bloody mary

The surprising addition of anchovy fillets to the bloody Mary mix provides another layer of complexity to a very tasty and satisfying drink. No need for any extra hot sauce in this bloody Mary—the spice is all in the mix.

2 oil-packed anchovy fillets

$2^{1}/_{4}$ teaspoons prepared horseradish

2 tablespoons minced celery

1 tablespoon chopped celery leaves

2 tablespoons plus 2 teaspoons Worcestershire sauce

$2^{1}/_{4}$ teaspoons Tabasco sauce (don't substitute another hot sauce for the Tabasco; you want its vinegar notes for this)

Juice from $1/2$ lemon (about 2 tablespoons)

$1^{3}/_{4}$ cups tomato juice

$1^{1}/_{4}$ teaspoons freshly ground black pepper

$1/2$ teaspoon celery salt

$1/4$ teaspoon kosher salt

Ice cubes

6 ounces ($3/4$ cup) vodka

Pickled green beans, for serving

3 celery hearts, for serving

3 thin slices lemon, for serving

1. Add the anchovies, horseradish, celery, celery leaves, Worcestershire, Tabasco, and lemon juice to a blender with enough tomato juice to cover the blade. Blend on high for 15 seconds. Add the remaining tomato juice and continue to blend 20 seconds longer. Stir in the pepper, celery salt, and kosher salt. This bloody Mary mix will keep in an airtight container in the refrigerator for up to 2 weeks.

2. Fill a cocktail shaker with ice, then add the vodka and bloody Mary mix and shake well.

3. Strain over fresh ice into 3 (10-ounce) glasses, and serve each with a pickled green bean, celery heart, and lemon slice.

YIELD: 3 SERVINGS

rumchata
punch

This is a riff on Brandy Milk Punch, a New Orleans favorite. Many people complain about the fat and calories of a regular milk punch, which often contains both milk and heavy cream. This is made with vanilla almond milk, which has half the calories and zero fat. Horchata rum is a cream liqueur that is a super-popular ingredient to use in cocktails, which is great because I love it!

3 cups chilled vanilla almond milk

10 ounces (1¼ cups) horchata rum, preferably Rumchata

4 ounces (½ cup) crème de cacao

2 ounces (¼ cup) Kahlúa

1 quart crushed ice

Freshly grated nutmeg, for garnish

Freshly grated cinnamon, for garnish

In a large pitcher, combine the almond milk, rum, crème de cacao, Kahlúa, and ice. Stir well. Divide evenly among 4 small glasses or single old-fashioned glasses, sprinkle grated nutmeg and cinnamon over the top of each, and serve immediately.

YIELD: 4 SERVINGS

iced café
with tequila coffee liqueur and nocello

Patrón XO Cafe is a coffee-flavored tequila-based liqueur that is delicious sipped on its own. Couple it with the flavors of walnut and hazelnut in Nocello, one of my favorite liqueurs, and you have the perfect spiked iced coffee.

Ice cubes

1 ounce (2 tablespoons) cold-brewed coffee concentrate, such as Cool Brew

1½ ounces (3 tablespoons) water

1½ ounces (3 tablespoons) Patrón XO Cafe

¾ ounce (1½ tablespoons) Nocello

¾ ounce (1½ tablespoons) heavy cream

Fill a rocks glass with ice cubes. Add the coffee concentrate, water, Patrón, and Nocello. Hold an inverted spoon over the glass. Pour the cream over the back of the spoon into the glass so that it floats. Serve immediately.

YIELD: 1 SERVING

Desserts

When I was growing up, it wasn't enough just to eat my dessert. I wanted to know how to *make* it, so much so that I took a cake decorating class. I learned how to pipe swags and roses just like those on the cakes sold in the Portuguese bakery where I worked. The desserts you'll find in this chapter are truly showstoppers. Some are over-the-top makeovers of homey classics, like White Chocolate Bread Pudding with Macadamia Caramel Sauce (page 283), others are re-imaginings of favorite sweets, like Reese's-inspired Mile-High Icebox Chocolate–Peanut Butter Pie (page 267) in a gluten-free peanut butter cookie crust. Along the way, you'll learn a lot of great techniques. And for those times when your sweet tooth is on holiday or you want to try something different, I give you tips on putting together a cheese board, with recipes for a few of my favorite go-alongs.

caramel tomato

Chef Alain Passard has been cooking modern French cuisine at its finest at his three Michelin-star restaurant Arpège in Paris for more than 25 years, and I've been lucky to have eaten there many times. This is my salute to Chef Passard—I tried to re-create the flavors while simplifying the technique.

2 medium firm, vine-ripened tomatoes (about ¾ pound)

1 cup sugar

¼ cup water

4 tablespoons heavy cream

2 tablespoons cold unsalted butter, chopped

Finely grated zest from 1 orange (about 1 teaspoon)

2 tablespoons fresh orange juice

¼ cup chopped salted dry-roasted pistachios

Vanilla-bean ice cream, for serving

2 to 4 sprigs fresh mint, for garnish

caramel tomato step-by-step

1. The tomatoes must be peeled. The easiest way to do this is to cut an X in the bottom of each one and blanch them in a pot of boiling water for 10 seconds.

2. With a slotted spoon, transfer the tomatoes to a bowl of ice water. When they are cool enough to handle, peel away the skins.

3. Cut each tomato in half and use the tip of the knife or your finger to remove the seeds. Pat each one dry and set aside. It's very important to remove all the seeds and to get the tomatoes as dry as possible before adding them to the caramel.

4. To start the caramel, stir the sugar and water together in a sauté pan; the mixture should look like wet sand.

5. Place the pan over medium heat. Swirl the pan occasionally until the sugar dissolves, then cook the sugar without stirring it; doing so once the sugar has become liquid can cause it to crystallize.

6. When the sugar cooks to an amber color, swirl the pan, then add half the cream.

7. Add the butter and orange zest and juice. Stir together until smooth.

8. Add the tomatoes to the caramel, cut side down, in a single layer. When the sauce begins to bubble, baste them with the sauce for 30 to 60 seconds.

9. Using a slotted spoon, transfer the tomatoes to small serving plates, then finish the sauce by whisking in the remaining cream and half the pistachios; bring to a gentle boil over medium heat, cook until the sauce is smooth, about 1 minute, and spoon around the tomatoes and ice cream. Serve garnished with pistachios and mint (see photo at left).

YIELD: 2 TO 4 SERVINGS

3

4

5

6

7

8

banana cream pie
with caramel and chocolate drizzles

This pie has been on the menu since the day Emeril's opened and is our signature dessert. At the restaurant, we pipe the whipped cream onto each individual slice just before serving, but feel free to spread the whipped cream over the top of the whole pie, as shown here.

4 cups heavy cream

1½ cups whole milk

1½ cups plus 2 teaspoons granulated sugar

1 vanilla bean, split in half lengthwise

3 large egg yolks

2 large eggs

½ cup cornstarch

Graham Cracker Crust (page 262)

3 pounds (about 9) firm but ripe bananas, peeled and cut crosswise into ½-inch-thick slices

½ teaspoon vanilla extract

Caramel Sauce (page 262), warm

Chocolate Sauce (page 262), warm

Shaved bittersweet chocolate, for garnish (page 268)

Confectioners' sugar, for garnish

Fresh mint sprigs or leaves, for garnish (optional)

1. Combine 2 cups of the cream, the milk, and ½ cup of the granulated sugar in a large, heavy-bottomed saucepan. With the point of a paring knife, scrape the seeds from the vanilla bean into the pan, then add the bean. Bring the mixture to a gentle boil over medium heat, whisking to dissolve the sugar. Remove the pan from the heat. Remove the vanilla bean.

2. In a medium bowl, combine the egg yolks, whole eggs, cornstarch, and 1 cup of the granulated sugar; whisk until pale yellow in color. Whisk 1 cup of the hot cream mixture into the egg mixture until fully combined. Gradually add the egg mixture to the hot cream mixture in a steady stream, whisking constantly. Place the pan back over medium heat and bring to a simmer, stirring constantly with a wooden spoon to cook the cornstarch and thicken the mixture, about 5 minutes. (The mixture may separate slightly; if so, remove from the heat and beat with an electric mixer on medium speed until thick and smooth.) Strain through a fine-mesh strainer into a clean bowl. Cover with plastic wrap, pressing it down against the surface to prevent a skin from forming. Refrigerate for at least 4 hours or overnight.

3. To assemble the pie, spread ½ cup of the custard over the bottom of the prepared crust, smoothing it with the back of a large spoon or rubber spatula. Arrange enough banana slices (not quite one-third) in a tight, tiled pattern over the custard, pressing down with your hands to pack them firmly. Repeat the process to build a second layer, using ¾ cup custard and enough bananas to cover. For the third layer, spread ¾ cup custard over the bananas and top with the remaining bananas, starting 1 inch from the outer edge and working toward the center. Spread the remaining custard evenly over the bananas to prevent discoloration. Cover with plastic wrap and refrigerate until completely chilled, at least 4 hours or overnight.

4. In a medium bowl with an electric mixer on high speed, whip the remaining 2 cups cream until soft peaks form. Add the remaining 2 teaspoons granulated sugar and the vanilla extract and continue to whip until stiff peaks form.

5. With a sharp knife dipped in hot water, cut the pie into 10 equal slices. Transfer to dessert plates. Fill a pastry bag fitted with a star tip with the whipped cream and pipe onto each slice.

6. Right before serving, drizzle each slice decoratively with the warm caramel and chocolate sauces, sprinkle with chocolate shavings, dust with a little confectioners' sugar, garnish with fresh mint, if desired, and serve.

YIELD: 1 (9-INCH) PIE, 10 SERVINGS

Select bananas that are ripe but still firm so that they hold their shape when sliced and pushed into place.

•

The pastry cream needs to be very stiff (the reason for the addition of cornstarch and why the pie needs to be chilled completely before serving) so that the pie will slice cleanly.

•

For that last layer, be sure to cover the bananas completely with pastry cream; otherwise they will turn brown.

graham cracker crust

1¼ cups graham cracker crumbs (9 to 10 crackers)

¼ cup granulated sugar

¼ cup (½ stick) unsalted butter, melted

1. Preheat the oven to 350°F.

2. In a medium bowl, combine the graham cracker crumbs and sugar, and mix well. Add the melted butter and mix well. Press the mixture into a 9-inch pie pan. Top with a 9-inch aluminum pie pan and, with a circular motion, press the crust tightly into the pan, so it comes fully up the side of the pan. Remove the aluminum pie pan.

3. Bake the crust until browned, about 25 minutes. Let cool on a wire rack for 10 to 15 minutes before filling.

YIELD: 1 (9-INCH) CRUST

chocolate sauce

½ cup half-and-half

1 tablespoon unsalted butter

8 ounces semisweet chocolate chips

½ teaspoon vanilla extract

1. Heat the half-and-half and butter together in a small, heavy-bottomed saucepan over medium heat until bubbles start to form around the edge of the pan; do not let it come to a boil. Remove the pan from the heat.

2. Place the chocolate and vanilla extract in a medium heatproof bowl. Add the hot half-and-half mixture and let sit for 2 minutes, then whisk until smooth. Serve slightly warm, or keep in an airtight container in the refrigerator for several days. Let come to room temperature or warm it briefly in the microwave before using.

YIELD: 1½ CUPS

caramel sauce

¾ cup granulated sugar

2 tablespoons water

½ teaspoon fresh lemon juice

½ cup heavy cream

2 to 4 tablespoons whole milk

1. Combine the sugar, water, and lemon juice in a medium, heavy-bottomed saucepan and cook over medium-high heat, whisking until the sugar dissolves. Once it has dissolved, stop whisking and let the mixture come to a boil. Let it continue to cook, without stirring, until it turns a deep amber color, 2 to 3 minutes; stirring the syrup at this point can make the sugar crystallize. Watch closely to make sure it doesn't burn.

2. Very carefully add the cream (the hot sugar mixture will sputter when the cream hits it), whisk to combine, and remove the pan from the heat. Add the milk, 2 tablespoons at a time, until the sauce is smooth, velvety, and thick enough to coat the back of a spoon. Let cool to room temperature before serving with the pie. (The sauce will thicken as it cools.) It will keep in an airtight container in the refrigerator for up to 3 weeks. Let it come to room temperature or warm it briefly in the microwave before using.

YIELD: GENEROUS ¾ CUP

portuguese custard tartlets

All I can say is "Yum!" I learned how to make these tartlets at my first job. They are very popular, and I can't go long without a fix. I'm very lucky that there is a large Portuguese community in Newark, New Jersey, so I can take a short road trip from New York City to buy some from one of the bakeries there. They are simple to make at home (particularly when you use frozen puff pastry) and oh so good. The filling is almost like a pudding.

1 (14-ounce) package puff pastry, thawed according to package directions

½ vanilla bean, split in half lengthwise

1½ cups heavy cream

¼ teaspoon finely grated orange zest

6 large egg yolks

¾ cup granulated sugar

1 tablespoon cornstarch

Confectioners' sugar, for sprinkling

1. Lightly butter 18 standard-size cupcake or muffin wells.

2. On a lightly floured work surface, roll the puff pastry out to a thickness of ⅛ inch or less. Using a 5-inch cookie or biscuit cutter, cut out 18 circles. Fit the puff pastry circles into the buttered cupcake wells, cover the tins with plastic wrap, and refrigerate while you make the filling, at least 30 minutes and up to 1 day in advance.

3. In a small, heavy-bottomed saucepan, scrape the vanilla bean seeds into the cream, then add the bean and orange zest. Bring to a boil over medium heat, cover, and immediately remove the pan from the heat. Let the cream steep for 30 minutes.

4. Preheat the oven to 425°F.

5. In a medium bowl, whisk the egg yolks, granulated sugar, and cornstarch together until thickened and pale yellow. Whisk in the steeped cream, then strain the mixture through a fine-mesh strainer. Set the filling aside while you blind-bake the tartlet shells.

6. Place a cupcake liner inside each pastry-lined cupcake well. Add pie weights or dried beans to the liners and bake until the pastry is set around the edges, 6 to 8 minutes. Remove the tins from the oven, then carefully remove the cupcake liners and pie weights and return the pastry shells to the oven until

the bottoms of the shells are opaque and slightly firm, about 2 minutes longer. Remove from the oven and lower the oven temperature to 350°F.

7. Divide the custard filling evenly among the pastry shells, about 2 tablespoons per shell. Bake the tartlets until lightly golden and the custard is set, 20 to 25 minutes. Remove from the oven, let cool briefly in the tins, then transfer the individual tartlets to wire racks. Serve the tartlets warm or at room temperature, sprinkled with confectioners' sugar. These can be made up to 1 day in advance and stored at cool room temperature.

YIELD: 18 TARTLETS

cinnamon & spice deep-dish
apple pie

I love apple pie and had to include my own take on it for this book. This particular combination of apple varieties is key to the final texture and flavor of the pie. The Granny Smiths provide tartness and crispness, while the Galas are there for sweetness and to knit the filling together, as they will break down and intermingle.

Double Pie Crust (recipe follows)

2 pounds Gala apples (about 4)

1½ pounds Granny Smith apples (about 3)

1 tablespoon fresh lemon juice

¾ cup plus 1 to 2 tablespoons sugar as needed

3 tablespoons all-purpose flour

½ teaspoon ground cinnamon

¼ teaspoon freshly grated nutmeg

⅛ teaspoon ground allspice

¼ teaspoon salt

¼ cup (½ stick) unsalted butter, cut into pieces

1 large egg yolk

1 tablespoon heavy cream

1. Preheat the oven to 500°F.

2. Roll out one piece of the dough on a lightly floured work surface to an 11- or 12-inch round. Transfer it to a 9- or 10-inch deep-dish pie pan, gently fitting it into the pan. Trim off the excess dough. Repeat with the remaining piece of dough but transfer it to a parchment or waxed paper–lined baking sheet. Refrigerate both until ready to use.

3. Peel, core, and cut the apples into ¼- to ½-inch slices and toss in a large bowl with the lemon juice.

4. Combine the ¾ cup sugar, flour, spices, and salt; sprinkle over the apples and toss until well combined. Transfer the apples to the pie shell. Dot the top with the butter. Cover with the top pastry, trim the overhang, and crimp the edges to seal.

5. In a small bowl, whisk the egg yolk and cream together. Cut 4 slits in the top of the pie, brush the egg wash on top, and sprinkle with the remaining 1 to 2 tablespoons sugar. Set the pie on a parchment-lined rimmed baking sheet to catch any drips and place on the center rack. Reduce the oven temperature to 425°F and bake for 25 minutes.

6. Rotate the pan and reduce the oven temperature to 350°F. Bake until the crust is nicely browned and the juices are bubbling, another 45 to 50 minutes. Set on a rack and cool at least 4 hours before serving.

YIELD: 1 (9- TO 10-INCH) PIE, 8 TO 10 SERVINGS

double pie crust

2⅔ cups all-purpose flour

2 tablespoons sugar

½ teaspoon salt

¾ cup (1½ sticks) cold unsalted butter, cut into ¼-inch dice

¼ cup vegetable shortening or lard

½ cup ice water

In a medium bowl, combine the flour, sugar, and salt. Add the butter and shortening, and cut it into the flour with a pastry blender, a fork, or your fingers until the mixture resembles coarse crumbs. Sprinkle in the ice water while continuing to blend. Press the dough into a ball, and work it with your hands until it just comes together. The dough might seem slightly dry, but as it rests, the flour will continue to absorb liquid—don't add any extra liquid, or your crust will not be flaky. Divide the dough in half, shape each piece into a ball, then flatten each piece into a disk and wrap in plastic. Chill the dough at least 20 minutes or up to overnight before rolling.

YIELD: 1 (9- TO 10-INCH) DOUBLE PIE CRUST

Don't cut a fruit pie that has just come out of the oven. All the juices are bubbling hot and will drain out of the pie if you do.

•

For maximum flakiness, chill all the crust ingredients. Don't cut in the butter too much—small pieces in the dough add flakiness. And once you start adding the water, be careful not to overwork the dough or the crust will end up being tough.

mile-high icebox
chocolate–peanut butter pie

I am a huge Reese's Peanut Butter Cups guy, and I love them frozen; when I opened Emeril's, there had to be a pie on the menu with that taste. Since that original version, there have been multiple re-imaginings of the recipe, each one pushing the flavor level yet another notch higher. For this book, I wanted something truly over the top.

I set myself two challenges: First, amp up the chocolate. Second, I wanted to make this pie gluten-free so that my daughters Jilly and Jessie could enjoy it, too.

Despite the multiple components, this is an easy recipe—bring it to your next potluck and your friends will think you're a culinary rock star! Just be sure to give each layer enough time to chill completely. It also freezes well for up to two weeks. Defrost it in the fridge overnight before serving.

PEANUT BUTTER CRUST AND COOKIE GARNISH:

1 cup granulated sugar

1 cup creamy homogenized peanut butter

1 large egg, lightly beaten

**CHOCOLATE–PEANUT BUTTER
CREAM CHEESE LAYER:**

1 cup chilled heavy cream

1 (8-ounce) package cream cheese,
at room temperature

3/4 cup confectioners' sugar, sifted

3/4 cup creamy homogenized peanut butter

1/2 cup semisweet chocolate chips, melted
(see Essentials, at right) and cooled to
room temperature

2 teaspoons vanilla extract

PEANUT BUTTER–WHIPPED CREAM LAYER:

1 (.25-ounce) package (2 teaspoons) unflavored powdered gelatin

2 tablespoons plus 2 teaspoons water

2 cups chilled heavy cream

1/2 cup confectioners' sugar, sifted

1/2 cup creamy homogenized peanut butter

1 teaspoon vanilla extract

GANACHE:

4 ounces bittersweet chocolate, finely chopped

1/2 cup plus 1 tablespoon heavy cream

GARNISHES:

Sweetened whipped cream (optional)

Bittersweet chocolate shavings
(about 2 cups, optional, see page 268)

1. Preheat the oven to 350°F.

2. In a medium bowl, combine the ingredients for the Peanut Butter Crust and stir with a wooden spoon until smooth. Press 1 cup of the mixture evenly into the bottom of a 9-inch springform pan and bake just until set, 13 to 15 minutes. Remove to a wire rack to cool completely.

3. Using the palms of your hands, roll the remaining peanut butter mixture into a 3/4-inch-diameter log. Cut the log crosswise into 1/2-inch-thick disks and place them on an ungreased cookie sheet about 1/2 inch apart. Using a fork, press on each round to form a crosshatch pattern. Bake until lightly browned around the edges, 10 to 12 minutes. Cool slightly on the sheet, then transfer the cookies to a wire rack to cool completely.

(continued)

To measure peanut butter without it sticking, coat the inside of the cup with cooking spray; the peanut butter will slide right out.

•

To melt the chocolate, microwave it or melt it in a heatproof bowl set over simmering water.

•

The recipe for the peanut butter cookie dough will make more cookies than you will need—enjoy the rest as is.

4. Make the chocolate–peanut butter cream cheese layer. In a small bowl using an electric mixer on low speed, begin to whip the cream; once it starts to thicken, increase the speed to medium-high or high and whip until stiff peaks form. Refrigerate until needed. In a medium bowl, beat the cream cheese and confectioners' sugar together on medium speed (no need to clean the beaters) until smooth. Add the peanut butter and melted chocolate and beat until well combined, scraping down the side of the bowl as needed. Using a rubber spatula, fold one-third of the whipped cream into the peanut butter mixture to loosen it up a bit, then gently fold in the remaining whipped cream just until the mixture is smooth and uniform in color. Spoon the mixture into the springform pan and smooth evenly over the crust with an offset spatula. Refrigerate, uncovered, until firm, about 1 hour.

5. Once the chocolate–peanut butter layer is set, make the Peanut Butter–Whipped Cream Layer. Combine the gelatin and water in a small heatproof bowl and set aside to soften about 5 minutes. Bring a small pot of water to a boil, remove from the heat, set the bowl of gelatin over the hot water, and stir until the gelatin is completely dissolved. It's important that the gelatin still be liquid when you add it to the whipped cream, so leave it over the hot water until you need it.

6. In a medium bowl, whip the cream with the confectioners' sugar (use clean, dry beaters) until stiff peaks form. Add the peanut butter and vanilla and, with a whisk, combine until the mixture is uniform in color. With the whisk, mix in the liquid gelatin. Using a rubber spatula, quickly transfer the mixture to the springform pan. Smooth it evenly over the cream cheese layer with an offset spatula. Refrigerate, uncovered, until firm, about 2 hours.

7. Once the Peanut Butter–Whipped Cream Layer is set, make the ganache. Place the chopped chocolate in a small heatproof bowl. Bring the cream to a rolling boil in a small pot. Immediately pour the hot cream over the chocolate; let sit undisturbed for 1 minute, then stir the mixture until smooth with a small whisk or rubber spatula. Pour the chocolate over the chilled peanut butter–whipped cream layer and spread gently and evenly over the top with an offset spatula. Refrigerate, uncovered, until firm, at least 1 hour and up to overnight.

8. To unmold the pie, wrap the outside of the springform pan with a kitchen towel warmed with hot tap water and run a thin kitchen knife around the pie to loosen it from the side of the pan. Gently remove the ring. If necessary, smooth the outer edge of the pie with an offset spatula. Pipe whipped cream rosettes around the edge, one for each slice, if desired, then lean a peanut butter cookie against each rosette. Finally, fill the center with the shaved chocolate. To serve, slice the pie into 12 wedges, running a thin, sharp knife under hot tap water and wiping it dry before each slice.

YIELD: 1 (9-INCH) PIE, 12 SERVINGS

making chocolate shavings

I filled the center of this pie with shaved chocolate. If you want to take it entirely over the top, frost the side of the pie with whipped cream and press more shaved chocolate against it all the way around; I decided not to do that because I love the look of the layers.

To make shavings, run a vegetable peeler along the edge of a thick block of chocolate. If you have a thin bar of chocolate, you're better off grating it on the largest holes of a box grater. For smooth, pretty curls, the chocolate should be at cool room temperature—too cold and the chocolate will crack, too warm and it will be a melty mess.

chocolate genoise with
chocolate buttercream and raspberry filling

When I became chef at Commander's Palace, it didn't have a well-developed dessert menu and creating one became a priority. Aiding me in this challenge was Lou Lynch, known as Mr. Lou. I originally hired Mr. Lou, who had just retired from the Army, to work on *garde manger* (cold appetizers) but it turned out that his genius was in desserts. He became my pastry chef at Commander's and later was my first pastry chef at Emeril's. This genoise was one of my first collaborations with Mr. Lou, and many of the desserts in this chapter were Mr. Lou's creations. A genoise is very different in texture from the cake most Americans are familiar with—insanely rich (it contains 12 eggs), it's also light and airy because you whip those eggs until they have tripled in volume. This is a cake that should be made the day before you plan to serve it so that the layers have enough time to soak up the raspberry syrup.

Softened unsalted butter, for greasing

1½ cups cake flour, plus more for dusting

½ cup unsweetened Dutch-processed cocoa powder

2 tablespoons cornstarch

¼ teaspoon baking soda

12 large eggs

2 cups granulated sugar

¼ cup (½ stick) unsalted butter, melted

Raspberry Syrup (page 272)

Raspberry Filling (page 272)

Chocolate Buttercream (page 272)

½ pint fresh raspberries, for garnish

Confectioners' sugar, for garnish

1. Preheat the oven to 350°F. Grease 3 (8-inch) round cake pans with softened butter. Line the bottoms of the pans with parchment paper, then grease the parchment with butter. Dust the bottoms and sides of the pans with flour, tapping out any excess.

2. In a small bowl, sift the 1½ cups cake flour with the cocoa powder, cornstarch, and baking soda.

3. In a large metal heatproof bowl, whisk the eggs and granulated sugar together with a balloon whisk. Fill a medium pot one-third of the way with water and bring to a gentle simmer over medium heat. Set the bowl over the pot (make sure the bottom of the bowl does not touch the water) and whisk vigorously until the egg mixture has thickened and tripled in volume, about 10 minutes. You must whisk the entire time to keep the eggs from curdling. If at any point it seems that the mixture is cooking too quickly, remove the bowl from over the pot and whisk the eggs until they cool a bit, then return the bowl to the heat.

4. Once the eggs are thickened, remove the bowl from the heat. Sprinkle one-third of the flour mixture over the eggs and gently fold into the batter using a large rubber spatula. Repeat with two more additions of the remaining flour. Once the flour is incorporated, drizzle the melted butter around the edge of the batter and fold in gently.

5. Divide the batter evenly among the prepared pans and bake them on the center rack until the cake begins to pull away from the sides of the pans. Do not open the oven to check the cakes before 20 minutes. When checking at 20 minutes, open the door slightly and peek in (see Essentials, at right).

6. When done, remove the cakes from the oven and set aside on greased wire racks to cool for 5 minutes, then invert the cakes onto the racks. Unmold the cakes, then reinvert them and let

(continued)

DO NOT use a cake tester when baking a genoise cake. This type of cake is very sensitive to deflation, which is why you should not open the door to check on its progress until 20 minutes have passed— the loss of heat from the oven because of the open door could cause the cake to fall. The cake pulling away from the pan is your cue that the cake is done.

cool completely. Once the layers have cooled, trim the tops with a serrated knife to form an even surface, then cut each layer in half horizontally. Generously brush one side of each layer with the Raspberry Syrup, using all of it.

7. To assemble the cake, place a layer on a serving plate or 8-inch cake plate. Spoon 3 to 4 tablespoons of the Raspberry Filling in the middle of the layer and spread it evenly over the top. Set another cake layer on top. Spoon about ¼ cup of the Chocolate Buttercream in the center and spread it evenly over the top. Continue to build the cake in this way, alternating the filling and buttercream. Once the final layer is on top, apply a crumb coat to the cake (see opposite). Refrigerate the cake for at least 10 minutes to allow it to set, then frost the top and sides generously with the remaining buttercream. For the best flavor, cover and refrigerate the cake overnight.

8. Right before serving, arrange fresh raspberries on top of the cake in an attractive pile and lightly dust with the confectioners' sugar.

YIELD: 1 (8-INCH) 6-LAYER CAKE, 10 TO 12 SERVINGS

raspberry filling

1½ pints fresh or frozen unsweetened IQF raspberries

¾ cup plus 2 tablespoons water

¾ cup granulated sugar

2 tablespoons cornstarch

1. Combine the raspberries, ¾ cup of the water, and the sugar in a small saucepan. Bring to a boil over medium heat, then reduce the heat to low and simmer until the raspberries have broken down completely, about 20 minutes.

2. Strain the mixture through a fine-mesh sieve set over a bowl. Use a flexible spatula to press the berries against the sieve to extract all of the juice. Discard the seeds. Transfer the juice back to the pot (no need to clean it) and bring to a simmer.

3. In a small bowl, whisk the cornstarch and remaining 2 tablespoons of water into a slurry. Whisk the slurry into the raspberry juice all at once and continue to simmer until thickened, about 5 minutes longer. Remove from the heat and let cool completely before using. This will keep in an airtight container in the refrigerator for up to 1 week.

YIELD: 1½ CUPS

raspberry syrup

¾ cup water

½ cup granulated sugar

¼ cup raspberry-flavored liqueur, such as Framboise or Chambord

Combine the water and sugar in a small saucepan; bring to a boil over medium heat, stirring until the sugar dissolves. Remove from the heat and set aside to cool. Stir in the liqueur.

YIELD: 1 CUP

chocolate buttercream

This is a smooth, velvety icing that is not overly sweet. Buttercream is not the icing to choose if you're bringing a cake to a picnic. It is heat-sensitive and cannot go without refrigeration (or air-conditioning) very long without melting.

8 large egg yolks

1⅓ cups granulated sugar

½ cup water

1 pound unsalted butter, softened and cut into 2-tablespoon pieces

8 ounces bittersweet chocolate, melted

1. In a stand mixer fitted with the whip attachment or in a large heatproof bowl using an electric mixer, beat the egg yolks on high speed until light in color and doubled in volume.

2. In a small, heavy-bottomed saucepan, combine the sugar and water and bring to a boil over high heat. Let continue to boil until large bubbles break across the entire surface and the mixture reaches 240°F when tested with a candy thermometer. Immediately pour the mixture into a heatproof liquid measuring cup to halt the cooking.

3. Working quickly, and with the motor of the mixer running on high, pour the syrup down the side of the bowl into the yolks. Continue to beat until the bowl feels cool to the touch on the bottom.

4. Decrease the mixer speed to medium and add the butter one or two pieces at a time while continuing to mix. Once the butter is fully incorporated, stir in the melted chocolate. This can be refrigerated in an airtight container for up to 1 week. Before using it, remove it from the refrigerator, let it warm up to cool room temperature, and whip it until it becomes spreadable.

YIELD: 6 CUPS

applying a crumb coat

Here's a lesson I learned when I took a cake decorating class when I was a kid. To get a beautiful, smooth look when icing a cake, you need to start by applying a crumb coat.

The crumb coat is a very thin application of icing meant to plaster any loose crumbs to the cake. Take a small portion of the frosting and, using an offset spatula, apply it as thinly as you can to the top and side of the cake, covering the cake completely. Refrigerate the cake for at least 10 minutes. That will firm up the icing, sealing in the crumbs. Then you can apply the final coat of icing, working with a smooth, crumb-free surface. Try to use nice, even strokes when frosting the cake; having a spinning cake stand will make the whole process a lot easier.

chocolate sheba cake
with white chocolate crème anglaise

This is one of the first desserts I developed for Commander's Palace, with my sous chef Peter Olson. I was looking for a chocolate dessert that was light but still mousselike. Peter had experienced a dessert similar to this when he was in Paris, and after some experimentation, the chocolate sheba was born, and it soon became a best-seller. Because this will keep in the freezer for up to a month, it's a wonderful choice for entertaining.

1 cup pecan halves or pieces, toasted (see Essentials, page 227)

1 cup chilled heavy cream

1 pound semisweet chocolate, chopped

1/2 cup (1 stick) unsalted butter, cubed and at room temperature

10 large egg yolks

7 large egg whites

1/3 cup sugar

White Chocolate Crème Anglaise, (see opposite) for serving

1. Line a 9-inch round cake pan with plastic wrap so that it overhangs the top of the pan by 6 inches on all sides (you'll need two pieces of wrap to do this). Sprinkle the pecan pieces evenly over the bottom of the pan.

2. In a medium bowl with an electric mixer on high speed, whip the cream until stiff peaks form. Set aside in the refrigerator until ready to use. Wash and dry the beaters.

3. Fill a small pot halfway with water, and bring to a simmer over medium-low heat. Combine the chocolate and butter in a heatproof metal bowl that will sit on top of the pot without the bottom touching the water. Stir the butter and chocolate with a rubber spatula or whisk until melted, combined, and smooth. Remove from the heat. Add the egg yolks, one at a time, to the chocolate–butter mixture, whisking thoroughly to combine before adding the next one.

4. In a large bowl, whip the egg whites with the electric mixer (using clean, dry beaters) on high speed until soft peaks form. While beating, gradually add the sugar and beat the whites until stiff, glossy peaks form (do not overmix or the whites will dry out). Using a large rubber spatula, gently fold the egg whites into the chocolate mixture.

5. Gently fold one-third of the whipped cream into the chocolate mixture with the spatula. Repeat with the remaining cream, folding just until the cream is incorporated. Do not overmix.

6. Pour the mousse into the prepared pan over the pecans and fold the plastic over the top of the mousse. Wrap the entire pan with plastic wrap and freeze for at least 2 hours and up to 1 month.

7. To serve, unwrap the sheba and unmold onto a serving platter, pulling away the plastic wrap. Heat a long thin knife with hot tap water, wipe dry, and slice the cake. Repeat for each slice. Serve over a pool of White Chocolate Crème Anglaise.

YIELD: 8 TO 10 SERVINGS

white chocolate
crème anglaise

Classic crème anglaise is made even richer with the addition of white chocolate. When making crème anglaise, it is important to cook the custard just to the point where it sets; otherwise the eggs will scramble and the sauce will not be smooth. If you are unsure of yourself, you can use a thermometer—eggs will set around 160°F, but after 180°F they will be scrambled. On the other hand, if you don't cook the crème anglaise long enough, the sauce will be thinner than ideal.

3/4 cup heavy cream

3/4 cup whole milk

1/3 cup sugar

3 large egg yolks

3 1/2 ounces white chocolate, chopped (about 1/2 cup)

1 teaspoon vanilla extract

1. Combine the cream and milk in a heavy-bottomed 2-quart saucepan and heat over medium heat.

2. While the mixture heats, in a medium bowl, combine the sugar and egg yolks and whisk until well blended and pale yellow in color.

3. Once the cream and milk come to a simmer, remove the pan from the heat, add 1/4 cup of this hot mixture to the egg mixture, and whisk to blend. Continue in this manner until half of the milk mixture has been incorporated into the eggs, then pour the egg mixture into the saucepan and whisk to combine. Return the saucepan to medium heat and whisk vigorously until the anglaise begins to thicken, about 5 minutes.

4. Once thickened, remove from the heat and strain through a fine-mesh strainer into a clean bowl. Add the chopped white chocolate to the strained custard and whisk until the chocolate is melted and combined. Stir in the vanilla. Set aside to cool, then transfer to an airtight container and refrigerate until ready to use; it will keep for up to 1 week.

YIELD: 2 CUPS

Because the egg yolks are only just warmed by the heat of the melted chocolate and the egg whites used to make the meringue are uncooked, please use the freshest eggs possible.

triple coconut cake
with seven-minute coconut frosting

I love coconut, and when we decided we needed to include a coconut cake in this book, it had to be awesome. My fabulous test kitchen crew (Charlotte Martory, Stacey Meyer, and Kamili Hemphill) worked with me on this to make it perfect.

1 cup (2 sticks) unsalted butter, softened

2 cups sugar

3 large eggs, at room temperature

3 cups sifted cake flour

1 tablespoon baking powder

1 cup unsweetened coconut milk

1 teaspoon coconut extract

1 teaspoon vanilla extract

Seven-Minute Coconut Frosting (recipe follows)

2 cups natural coconut flakes, sweetened or unsweetened, toasted (see Essentials, at right) or untoasted

1. Preheat the oven to 350°F. Grease 2 (9-inch) round cake pans with butter or nonstick cooking spray. Line the bottom with parchment paper and grease. Lightly flour the pans; set aside.

2. In a large bowl using an electric mixer on medium speed, cream the butter and sugar together until light and fluffy. Add the eggs, one at a time, beating well after each before adding the next one.

3. Sift the flour one more time, adding the baking powder. Add it in thirds to the batter, alternating with the coconut milk and beating well after each addition. Beat in the extracts.

4. Divide the batter evenly between the two pans, and gently tap the bottoms against the countertop to get rid of any air bubbles. Bake until a cake tester inserted in the center comes out clean, about 30 minutes. Remove from the oven and let the cakes cool in the pans at least 10 minutes, then invert the pans onto greased wire racks. Remove and discard the parchment paper, then turn the cakes over and let them cool completely before frosting.

5. Set one layer on a cake plate and cover evenly with ¾ to 1 cup of the frosting. Set the other layer on top and use the remaining frosting to ice the top and side of the cake. Cover the top and side of the cake evenly with the coconut flakes (toasting is optional). This cake does not require refrigeration.

YIELD: 1 (9-INCH) 2-LAYER CAKE, 8 TO 10 SERVINGS

seven-minute coconut frosting
(For a tutorial, see page 278.)

1 cup sugar

2 tablespoons light corn syrup

½ teaspoon cream of tartar

Pinch of salt

⅓ cup water

3 large egg whites, at room temperature

1 teaspoon coconut extract

1. Whisk the sugar, corn syrup, cream of tartar, salt, and water together in a small, heavy-bottomed saucepan. Bring to a boil over medium heat (do not stir it) and cook, undisturbed, until it reaches 240°F on a candy thermometer, about 2 minutes; stirring can cause the sugar to crystallize.

2. Meanwhile, in a medium bowl using an electric mixer on high speed, beat the egg whites until foamy.

3. Once the sugar syrup reaches 240°F, immediately and carefully pour it into the egg whites, with the mixer running on high speed, away from the beaters to prevent splattering and possible burns. Continue to beat until the frosting is glossy and fluffy, about 5 minutes. Beat in the coconut extract. Use immediately.

YIELD: ENOUGH FOR A 9-INCH 2-LAYER CAKE

(continued)

To toast coconut, spread it over a parchment paper–lined baking sheet. Bake in a preheated 325°F oven until golden brown, 5 to 7 minutes. Check on it regularly to see that it is browning evenly and stir a few times. Sweetened coconut flakes will brown a little faster than unsweetened. Let cool completely before using.

making seven-minute frosting

Also known as Italian meringue, this beautifully glossy icing is made by whipping hot sugar syrup into whipped egg whites. It's incredibly stable and sturdy and you can shape it into peaks and twirls; it can even stand up to heat (this is the icing used for Baked Alaska). Have everything ready to ice the cake because the frosting must be used while it is still warm; it firms up as it cools.

1. In a heavy-bottomed saucepan, whisk the sugar, corn syrup, cream of tartar, salt, and water together, then, without stirring, heat the syrup to 240°F over medium heat. Success hinges on heating the syrup to the right temperature, so be sure you have a good-quality candy thermometer.

2. While the sugar syrup is cooking, whip the egg whites with an electric mixer on high speed until they are foamy.

3. As soon as the sugar syrup is the proper temperature, carefully pour it into the egg whites, with the mixer running on high speed. Pour it in away from the beaters to prevent spattering—hot sugar syrup can burn badly.

4. Continue to beat until the frosting is glossy and fluffy, about 5 minutes, then beat in the extract.

1

2

3

4

maple bourbon fudge

My mom used to make fudge, so I took those flavor memories and mashed them up with my love for maple syrup and bourbon.

2 cups walnut halves

2 tablespoons unsalted butter, plus more for greasing the pan

3 cups sugar

²/₃ cup whole milk

²/₃ cup half-and-half

¼ cup light corn syrup

¼ cup grade A maple syrup

¼ teaspoon salt

¼ cup your favorite bourbon

1. Preheat the oven to 350°F. Spread the walnuts on a baking sheet; place in the oven and bake until they start to smell toasty, about 10 minutes. Keep a close eye (or nose) on them. Pour the nuts onto a clean kitchen towel and use the towel to rub off the skins.

2. Line an 8-inch square baking pan with aluminum foil and grease with butter or nonstick cooking spray. Spread the walnuts evenly over the bottom. Fill a large bowl with ice water.

3. Place the 2 tablespoons butter, the sugar, milk, half-and-half, corn syrup, maple syrup, salt, and bourbon in a heavy-bottomed 4- to 6-quart saucepan with a candy thermometer attached and set over medium heat. Stir the mixture with a wooden spoon until it comes to a boil, controlling the heat as necessary to prevent it from boiling over, then allow it to cook without stirring, which can cause crystallization, until it reaches 238°F, 15 to 20 minutes.

4. Quickly immerse the bottom of the pot in the ice water and let it sit for 5 seconds. Place the pot on the counter and allow the fudge to cool, undisturbed, until the temperature on the thermometer drops to 115°F, 1½ to 2 hours.

5. Using an electric mixer, beat the fudge until it starts to lose its gloss and thickens, about 20 minutes. Quickly spoon the fudge into the prepared pan, spreading it as best you can with a wooden spoon or rubber spatula. Do not scrape down any of the fudge that clings to the saucepan—this will help prevent unwanted crystallization in the fudge. Allow the fudge to sit at room temperature to cool and set, at least 4 hours and up to 8 hours.

6. When ready to serve, invert the fudge onto a cutting board and cut into 1½-inch squares. Store in an airtight container at room temperature for up to 1 week or in the refrigerator for up to 2 weeks.

YIELD: 36 PIECES, 12 TO 16 SERVINGS

candy thermometer

Invest in a good-quality candy thermometer. Seven-Minute Frosting, the pralines on page 285, and fudge are all about heating the mixtures to the right temperature. Then the fudge has to cool to 115°F, which can take up to two hours. You cannot rush this—if you try to beat fudge before the temperature falls to 115°F, you will not get good results. Temperature is so important that I recommend you test your thermometer before starting to make sure it is accurate. Stick it in a pot of boiling water; if it doesn't register 212°F, you need to get yourself a new thermometer.

summer
berry crisp

Jazz Fest in New Orleans is the last weekend in April through the first weekend in May, which is the height of berry season in Louisiana—the strawberries and blackberries are in and the first crop of blueberries is being harvested. At the festival you'll find vendors selling berries in all sorts of ways, strawberry lemonade being one of the most popular. One of my longtime customers, Jim Fifield, former president and CEO of EMI, has been coming in from the West Coast for Jazz Fest for years, and he always has a food and wine pairing at Emeril's to celebrate his birthday. The one item that absolutely must be on the menu every year is a berry crisp.

2 tablespoons unsalted butter, cut into cubes, plus 1 tablespoon for the pan

1 pound fresh or frozen IQF blackberries (no need to thaw any of the berries if using frozen)

1 pound fresh or frozen IQF blueberries

1 pound fresh or frozen IQF strawberries

³/₄ cup granulated sugar

¹/₃ cup all-purpose flour

2 teaspoons vanilla extract

Brown Sugar Oatmeal Topping (recipe follows)

Whipped cream or vanilla ice cream, for serving (optional)

1. Preheat the oven to 375°F. Grease a 9 x 13-inch baking dish with the 1 tablespoon butter. Line a baking sheet with parchment paper or aluminum foil.

2. In a large bowl, combine the cubed butter, berries, granulated sugar, flour, and vanilla. Toss well to mix. Transfer the fruit to the prepared baking dish and cover with the oatmeal topping.

3. Place the baking dish on the baking sheet to catch any juices that may bubble over. Bake until the crisp is browned on top and the juices have thickened around the edges, about 50 minutes.

4. Serve warm or at room temperature with whipped cream or vanilla ice cream, if desired.

YIELD: 10 TO 12 SERVINGS

brown sugar
oatmeal topping

6 tablespoons (³/₄ stick) cold unsalted butter, cut into small pieces

1 cup all-purpose flour

1 cup old-fashioned rolled oats

³/₄ cup firmly packed light brown sugar

1 teaspoon ground cinnamon

¹/₂ teaspoon freshly grated nutmeg

¹/₄ teaspoon salt

Combine all the ingredients in the bowl of a stand mixer fitted with the paddle attachment and mix on low speed until the mixture is crumbly and coarse. (Alternatively, combine the ingredients in a bowl and, using a pastry blender, two knives, or your fingers, cut the butter into the dry ingredients until the mixture resembles coarse crumbs.)

YIELD: ENOUGH TOPPING FOR 1 CRISP

You can change this recipe up in several ways— first, you can make it with any combination of sweet berries you prefer, or use all of one kind of berry. Also, instead of preparing this in a baking dish, you can bake it in individual ramekins.

white chocolate
bread pudding
with macadamia caramel sauce

At one of my first restaurant jobs in Massachusetts I got turned on to bread pudding. Later, when I went to Commander's Palace, there was bread pudding on the lunch menu, and we served bread pudding soufflés in the evening. This is the perfect indulgence to offer friends and family at the holidays.

4 cups heavy cream

4 cups whole milk

18 ounces white chocolate chips or chopped white chocolate (about 3 cups)

8 large eggs

3/4 cup sugar

2 teaspoons vanilla extract

1/2 teaspoon salt

1 (12-ounce) loaf day-old French bread, about 30 inches long, torn into rough pieces (toast if fresh to dry out)

1/2 cup (1 stick) unsalted butter, melted

Macadamia Caramel Sauce (recipe follows), for serving

1. In a large saucepan, heat the cream and 2 cups of the milk together just to a bare simmer. Remove the pan from the heat and add the chocolate chips. Set aside, undisturbed, for 1 to 2 minutes, then whisk until the chips are completely melted.

2. Preheat the oven to 350°F.

3. In a large bowl, whisk together the eggs, sugar, vanilla, and salt until thoroughly combined. Whisk in the remaining 2 cups milk, then slowly whisk in the hot cream–chocolate mixture, 1 cup at a time, until completely incorporated. Add the bread, gently

pushing it down into the liquid. Set aside until the bread is completely moistened, 5 to 10 minutes. When mixing, take care to stir gently so as to not break up the bread pieces.

4. Brush the bottom and sides of a 9 x 15 x 3-inch baking dish (such as a lasagna pan) or 2 (10 x 10 x 2-inch) baking dishes with some of the melted butter to coat. Spoon the bread mixture into the dish(es) and drizzle the remaining butter over the top. Bake, uncovered, until the bread pudding is puffed and set in the center and crispy and deep golden brown on top, 1 hour to 1 hour and 10 minutes.

5. Remove from the oven and let cool slightly before serving. Serve with the warm Macadamia Caramel Sauce spooned over the top.

YIELD: 16 TO 20 SERVINGS

macadamia
caramel sauce

2 cups sugar

1/2 cup water

1 1/3 cups heavy cream

3/4 cup (1 1/2 sticks) unsalted butter, cut into pieces

1 teaspoon vanilla extract

1 cup chopped toasted macadamia nuts (see page 54)

1/2 teaspoon sea salt

Follow the steps for making Macadamia Caramel Sauce on page 284.

YIELD: 3 3/4 CUPS

(continued)

DO NOT shortcut the soaking of the bread. Let it soak until the egg and cream mixture has thoroughly penetrated all the bread. You want the bread to be spongy. That sponginess will transform into a light and puffy interior when it bakes.

283

making macadamia caramel sauce

Use this tutorial as a reference when making any kind of caramel sauce. The steps are the same, short of adding the nuts.

1. It's important that you use a heavy-bottomed saucepan, otherwise you run the risk of scorching. Combine the sugar and water and bring to a boil over medium-high heat. As the sugar melts, swirl the pan occasionally, just until the sugar completely dissolves. From that point on, do not stir the mixture; doing so can cause the sugar to crystallize. Cook the sugar syrup until it is a deep amber color, as shown here.

2. Turn the heat off and very carefully pour the cream into the syrup; it will immediately bubble up and can cause the very hot syrup to spit and spatter—melted sugar is hyper-heated and can cause bad burns.

3. As soon as you finish pouring in the cream, add the pieces of butter and vanilla.

4. Stir the mixture until you have a smooth sauce, then stir in the nuts and salt. You can use immediately or let cool and refrigerate.

toasted pecan pralines

Learning how to make a praline properly was a priority when I became chef at Commander's Palace. The job of teaching me fell to Floyd Bealer, the morning chef, who told me, if you don't know how to make a praline in New Orleans, you're in trouble! You can find all different flavors of pralines throughout the city, but I like the original the best.

¼ cup (½ stick) unsalted butter, plus more for greasing sheet

1 cup firmly packed light brown sugar

¾ cup granulated sugar

Pinch of salt

½ cup heavy cream

2 tablespoons light corn syrup

¾ cup pecan halves, toasted (see Essentials, page 227)

1 teaspoon vanilla extract

1. Line a baking sheet with aluminum foil and grease with butter. Set a small serving spoon nearby—you will need this in easy reach when you are ready to portion out the pralines.

2. Add the ¼ cup butter, both sugars, salt, cream, and corn syrup to a 2-quart heavy-bottomed saucepan with a candy thermometer attached to it and bring to a boil over high heat, whisking until the sugars dissolve. Continue to cook, without stirring, until it reaches 246°F, about 3 minutes; stirring can cause the sugar to crystallize.

3. Remove the pan from the heat and allow it to cool, undisturbed, for 4 minutes. Add the pecans and vanilla, and, using a wooden spoon, beat the mixture vigorously until thickened and the nuts are suspended, about 2 minutes. Working as quickly as you can, portion the pralines with the spoon onto the prepared pan. Let cool completely before serving. Store pralines individually wrapped in waxed paper in an airtight container. These are best served the day they are made but will keep for up to 2 days. After that, their smooth, shiny surface will become more granular, although the taste is just as delicious. Crumbled "old" pralines make a great topping for ice cream!

YIELD: 12 PRALINES

pralines & humidity

Pralines are sensitive to humidity. Sugar attracts water, so if you make them on a rainy day, your pralines will end up sweaty. If you have the option, make them on a day when the humidity is lower, or switch on your air conditioner.

j.k.'s chocolate soufflés

At Commander's Palace, one of my great customers was John Kushner, or J.K., a New Orleanean through and through. When he came, he would always insist that the meal end with this soufflé. When I opened Emeril's, I put J.K.'s Chocolate Soufflés on the menu in his honor. This is easier than a classic soufflé. Serve them straight out of the oven.

2 teaspoons unsalted butter, softened

1/2 cup granulated sugar

8 ounces semisweet chocolate, finely chopped

4 large egg whites

3 large egg yolks

1/4 cup Grand Marnier

Pinch of salt

Confectioners' sugar for dusting

Chocolate Grand Marnier Sauce (recipe follows), for serving

1. Preheat the oven to 400°F. Grease 4 (6-ounce) ramekins with the butter and sprinkle the bottoms and sides with about 1/2 teaspoon granulated sugar each. Place the ramekins on a baking sheet.

2. Add the chocolate to a heatproof bowl set over a small pot of simmering water (don't let the bottom touch the water) and whisk intermittently until melted. Remove the bowl from the heat.

3. In a medium bowl with an electric mixer on high speed, beat the egg whites until frothy. With the mixer running, add 1/4 cup of the granulated sugar and continue to beat until stiff peaks form.

4. Whisk the egg yolks into the melted chocolate, one at a time, then add the Grand Marnier, salt, and remaining granulated sugar. Using a whisk (a balloon whisk, if you have one), gently fold the whipped egg whites into the chocolate mixture one-third at a time until thoroughly blended.

5. Divide the chocolate mixture evenly among the ramekins, filling each to within about 1/4 inch of the rim. Bake until they are puffed and somewhat firm, about 20 minutes. Remove from the oven.

6. To serve, place a ramekin on each of 4 small plates and sift confectioners' sugar over the tops. Allow each guest to break the top of their soufflé with a spoon and pour in the warm Chocolate Grand Marnier Sauce.

YIELD: 4 SERVINGS

chocolate grand marnier sauce

2/3 cup heavy cream

5 teaspoons Grand Marnier

2 teaspoons granulated sugar

Pinch of salt

2 ounces semisweet chocolate, finely chopped

1. Add the cream to a small, heavy-bottomed saucepan and set it over high heat. Add the Grand Marnier, sugar, and salt. Whisk in the chocolate and bring to a boil, whisking constantly.

2. Remove from the heat and serve warm. If you make this ahead, let it cool, then store in an airtight container in the refrigerator for up to 2 weeks. Warm gently in a double boiler before serving.

YIELD: ABOUT 1 CUP

The bowl and beaters you use for whipping egg whites must be very clean. Even the smallest trace of grease will keep the egg whites from whipping properly. Use a metal or glass bowl since plastic tends to hold onto grease even when "clean."

Everyone must be ready at the table when you present a soufflé. No scurrying for utensils, coffee, or after-dinner drinks.

champagne
mint granita

Serve this frozen ice as a palate-cleansing course or with a cookie as a refreshing dessert after a big meal. No machines needed; this is made the old-fashioned way, in the freezer, scraping it periodically.

³/₄ cup sugar

1 cup fresh mint leaves (preferably spearmint if you can find it or grow it)

3 cups brut Champagne or other dry sparkling wine such as Prosecco

¹/₄ teaspoon finely grated lemon zest

1 tablespoon fresh lemon juice

1. Place the sugar and mint in a food processor or blender and pulse until blended. Transfer the mixture to a medium bowl; stir in the Champagne and lemon zest and juice. Let the mixture stand for 10 minutes, stirring until the sugar has dissolved.

2. Pour the mixture into a 9-inch square nonreactive metal baking pan and place it in the freezer. Stir the mixture, pulling a fork back and forth through it every 45 minutes or so. The mixture on the bottom will tend to be more syrupy, so be sure to mix it up into the icier portions of the granita. Keep repeating the process until the granita has uniform flakes of flavored ice all the way through it, which will take about 4 hours. It won't be frozen solid; it'll be more like a slushy, with flakes of ice all through it. It will keep in the freezer for up to 2 weeks.

YIELD: 4 TO 6 SERVINGS

You can serve granita simply, in chilled dishes. For a more memorable presentation, hollow out an orange or other similarly sized citrus fruit (clementine, blood orange, tangerine) and fill it with the granita. Keep it in the freezer until ready to serve.

creating a cheese board

Cheese, wine, and bread are my Holy Trinity of the Table, and I often offer a cheese board instead of dessert after a meal. There are no hard and fast rules on choices, though I like to offer an odd number of cheeses, three or no more than five, choosing representatives from the different types of cheeses, from mild to funky:

- **Fresh**: Unaged cheese like chèvre and feta.
- **Soft-ripened**: These runny cheeses often have a rind formed by spraying the outside with a mold; they include Brie, Brillat-Savarin, and Camembert.
- **Semisoft:** These are creamy cheeses that don't have a rind, like Morbier and Port Salut.
- **Firm/hard:** These can range from mild to pungent and are firm enough to be grated; they include Cheddar, Edam, Asiago, Parmigiano-Reggiano, Fontina, and Pecorino.
- **Natural rind:** These cheeses form rinds without the addition of molds, like tomme de Savoie.
- **Washed rind:** These cheeses are bathed in a brine or other liquid such as wine to encourage the growth of a particular type of bacteria. These include époisses de Bourgogne and Reblochon.
- **Blue:** These cheeses are created by spraying them with a particular kind of mold. They can range in texture from creamy to firm and in pungency from mild to assertive. Types include Roquefort, Stilton, Maytag Blue, and Danish Blue.

Present the cheeses on a large platter, marble slab, or wooden board, and make sure each one has its own knife, so there is no mixing of flavors. Harder cheeses require a sharp knife. Let the cheeses sit at room temperature for at least one hour before serving; this is particularly important for cheeses like Brie that need time to soften. Serving cheeses directly from the refrigerator dulls their flavor.

Regarding what type of wine to drink with cheese, my only rule is that it's up to your own individual taste. My preference is red.

In addition to the cheeses, you can offer nuts (walnuts and pecans pair very nicely), grapes or slices of fruit like pear or apple (cut them right before serving and toss them with a little lemon juice to keep them from browning), crackers, slices of bread, and/or savory jam. I've included recipes on pages 294 and 295 for some of my favorite cheese board go-alongs, but you can find plenty of options in the supermarket if you don't have time for extra cooking.

my 9 favorite american-produced cheeses

1 **San Andreas,** a semifirm raw sheep's milk cheese from Bellwether Farms, Petaluma, California

2 **Green Hill,** a Camembert-style double cream cow's milk cheese from Sweet Grass Dairy, Thomasville, Georgia

3 **Pleasant Ridge Reserve,** a firm raw cow's milk cheese from Uplands Cheese, Dodgeville, Wisconsin

4 **Bay Blue,** a mild and mellow blue cheese made with pasteurized cow's milk, from Point Reyes, Point Reyes, California

5 **Red Hawk,** a washed-rind triple cream cow's milk cheese from Cowgirl Creamery, Point Reyes, California

6 **Kunik,** a triple cream cheese made with a combination of goat's milk and cream from Jersey cows, from Nettle Meadow, Thurman, New York

7 **Taupinière,** a soft-aged goat cheese with an ash coating from Laura Chenel's Chèvre, Sonoma, California

8 **Winnimere,** a soft raw cow's milk cheese from Jasper Hill Farm, Greensboro, Vermont

9 **Tillamook County Creamery Sharp Cheddar,** an aged Cheddar from Tillamook, Oregon

*Sugar & Spice
Mixed Nuts*

Balsamic Fig Jam

*Mixed Fruit
Mostarda*

sugar & spice
mixed nuts

If you can get ahold of Mexican chili powder, use it—it's got an extra chile kick!

1 large egg white	½ teaspoon ground cumin
½ cup sugar	½ teaspoon cayenne pepper
1 tablespoon unsalted butter, melted	½ teaspoon salt
1 tablespoon ground cinnamon	¼ teaspoon ground allspice
	1⅓ cups walnut halves
1 teaspoon chili powder	1⅓ cups pecan halves
	1⅓ cups natural almonds

1. Preheat the oven to 250°F.

2. In a medium bowl with an electric mixer on high speed, whip the egg white until it holds a stiff peak.

3. In a small bowl, combine the sugar, melted butter, cinnamon, chili powder, cumin, cayenne, salt, and allspice. Mix well so the spices are evenly distributed.

4. Using a rubber spatula, mix the nuts with the whipped egg white until they are well coated. Add half of the spice mixture to the nuts and stir to coat. Add the remaining spice mixture and stir well with the spatula, scraping down the side of the bowl.

5. Spread the nuts in a single layer on a baking sheet and bake until golden brown, fragrant, and crispy, about 1 hour, stirring every 15 minutes. Let cool completely and store in an airtight container at room temperature for up to 6 weeks.

YIELD: 4 CUPS

balsamic
fig jam

This jam is incredibly easy to make and will keep in the refrigerator for several months and much longer if you follow standard canning procedures (check out the website for the National Center for Home Food Preservation for the most up-to-date guidelines). I never bother to can it because this usually gets gobbled up before it can ever go bad.

1 tablespoon unsalted butter	½ cup water
½ cup finely diced red onion	¼ cup fresh lemon juice
¼ cup balsamic vinegar	1 teaspoon grated orange zest
4 cups fresh Black Mission figs, cut into quarters	4 cups sugar
	1 (1.75-ounce) package pectin

1. Melt the butter in a large, heavy-bottomed saucepan over medium-low heat. When it begins to sizzle, add the onion and cook until it begins to caramelize, 3 to 5 minutes, stirring as needed. Add the vinegar and cook for 1 minute longer, scraping any browned bits up from the bottom of the pan. Add the figs, water, lemon juice, orange zest, and sugar, and bring to a boil over high heat. Once boiling, sprinkle the pectin over the mixture and stir until dissolved. Reduce the heat to medium-high and continue to cook for 10 minutes. Skim off any foam that comes to the top.

2. Remove the pan from the heat and ladle the hot jam into sterilized canning jars with sterilized lids. Put on the rings and screw tightly shut. At this point, you can process the jars if you plan to shelve the jam; otherwise, allow the jars to cool and store them in the refrigerator for up to 3 months.

YIELD: 3 PINTS

mixed fruit mostarda

This is a delicious partner for blue cheese, especially a creamy blue such as Cambozola, but it's also good with aged Cheddar, Gouda, and Parmigiano-Reggiano.

2¹⁄₂ cups sugar

1¹⁄₂ cups dry white wine

¹⁄₃ cup water

1 tablespoon cider vinegar

2 tablespoons yellow mustard seeds

1 tablespoon Dijon mustard

3 bay leaves

1 teaspoon dry mustard (like Colman's)

¹⁄₄ teaspoon salt, plus more to taste

¹⁄₈ teaspoon plus a pinch of cayenne pepper

2 firm d'Anjou pears, peeled, cored, and diced

1 (7-ounce) package dried mixed fruits, quartered and/or cut into thin strips if large

¹⁄₂ cup dried tart cherries

1. In a large, heavy-bottomed nonreactive saucepan, combine the sugar, wine, water, vinegar, mustard seeds, Dijon, bay leaves, dry mustard, salt, and cayenne, and bring to a simmer over medium-high heat, stirring occasionally, until the sugar completely dissolves. Add the pears, dried mixed fruits, and cherries, and reduce the heat to medium. Cook, stirring occasionally, until the fruit is very tender and the syrup is thick and glossy, 40 to 45 minutes.

2. Let cool briefly, then taste and adjust the seasonings if necessary. Remove the bay leaves. Let cool completely, transfer to an airtight container, and refrigerate for at least 24 hours before serving. Mostarda will keep in the refrigerator for up to 3 months. Its flavor is best when served at room temperature.

YIELD: 2 PINTS

flatbread

A nice alternative to crackers.

1 (¹⁄₄-ounce) package active dry yeast

1 cup warm water (110° to 115°F)

1 teaspoon sugar

¹⁄₄ cup extra-virgin olive oil, plus more for cooking and brushing

2³⁄₄ cups bread flour

1¹⁄₂ teaspoons salt

Flavorings for garnish if desired, such as roasted garlic in olive oil, sautéed chopped onion, or chopped fresh herbs and olive oil

Coarse sea salt, for garnish

1. In a medium bowl, combine the yeast, water, and sugar, and set aside until it begins to bubble or foam, about 5 minutes. Stir in the oil and 1 cup of the flour with a wooden spoon. Continue adding the flour in generous ¹⁄₂-cup increments, stirring after each addition. Stir in the salt.

2. Transfer the dough to a clean work surface and knead several times with the heels of your hands, then shape it to form a ball. Return the dough to the bowl, cover with plastic wrap or a clean kitchen towel, and set aside in a warm draft-free place until doubled in bulk, about 1¹⁄₂ hours.

3. Transfer the dough to a work surface and knead a few times. Divide the dough into 8 equal pieces. Form each into a small ball and set aside on a baking sheet. Cover with plastic wrap or a kitchen towel and set aside in a warm draft-free place to rest for 10 minutes.

4. Flatten out each round of dough with your hands, then roll it into a thin 8- to 10-inch circle.

5. Set a griddle over medium heat and heat until it begins to smoke. Lightly oil the griddle and place a dough round on it. Cook until it begins to bubble, about 1 minute. Using tongs, turn the round to the other side and cook 30 seconds to 1 minute longer, just until it lightly browns. Set the flatbread aside and repeat with the remaining dough, re-oiling the griddle as needed.

6. Brush the flatbreads with oil and sprinkle with the flavorings of your choice. To serve, cut each flatbread into 8 to 12 wedges and serve warm or at room temperature. Store any leftovers in a zip-top plastic bag in the refrigerator. They will keep for several days; if you like, reheat them in an oven on low heat.

YIELD: 8 FLATBREADS

metric equivalents

The information in the following charts is provided to help cooks outside the United States successfully use the recipes in this book. All equivalents are approximate.

COOKING/OVEN TEMPERATURES

	Fahrenheit	Celsius	Gas Mark
Freeze Water	32° F	0° C	
Room Temp.	68° F	20° C	
Boil Water	212° F	100° C	
Bake	325° F	160° C	3
	350° F	180° C	4
	375° F	190° C	5
	400° F	200° C	6
	425° F	220° C	7
	450° F	230° C	8
Broil			Grill

LIQUID INGREDIENTS BY VOLUME

¼ tsp	=					1 ml
½ tsp	=					2 ml
1 tsp	=					5 ml
3 tsp	=	1 Tbsp	=	½ fl oz	=	15 ml
2 Tbsp	=	⅛ cup	=	1 fl oz	=	30 ml
4 Tbsp	=	¼ cup	=	2 fl oz	=	60 ml
5⅓ Tbsp	=	⅓ cup	=	3 fl oz	=	80 ml
8 Tbsp	=	½ cup	=	4 fl oz	=	120 ml
10⅔ Tbsp	=	⅔ cup	=	5 fl oz	=	160 ml
12 Tbsp	=	¾ cup	=	6 fl oz	=	180 ml
16 Tbsp	=	1 cup	=	8 fl oz	=	240 ml
1 pt	=	2 cups	=	16 fl oz	=	480 ml
1 qt	=	4 cups	=	32 fl oz	=	960 ml
				33 fl oz	=	1000 ml	= 1 l

DRY INGREDIENTS BY WEIGHT

(To convert ounces to grams, multiply the number of ounces by 30.)

1 oz	=	¹⁄₁₆ lb	=	30 g
4 oz	=	¼ lb	=	120 g
8 oz	=	½ lb	=	240 g
12 oz	=	¾ lb	=	360 g
16 oz	=	1 lb	=	480 g

LENGTH

(To convert inches to centimeters, multiply the number of inches by 2.5.)

1 in	=			2.5 cm
6 in	=	½ ft	=	15 cm
12 in	=	1 ft	=	30 cm
36 in	=	3 ft	= 1 yd	=	90 cm
40 in	=			100 cm	=	1m

EQUIVALENTS FOR DIFFERENT TYPES OF INGREDIENTS

Standard Cup	Fine Powder (ex. flour)	Grain (ex. rice)	Granular (ex. sugar)	Liquid Solids (ex. butter)	Liquid (ex. milk)
1	140 g	150 g	190 g	200 g	240 ml
¾	105 g	113 g	143 g	150 g	180 ml
⅔	93 g	100 g	125 g	133 g	160 ml
½	70 g	75 g	95 g	100 g	120 ml
⅓	47 g	50 g	63 g	67 g	80 ml
¼	35 g	38 g	48 g	50 g	60 ml
⅛	18 g	19 g	24 g	25 g	30 ml

subject index

recipe index

acknowledgments

The making of this book has been an incredible journey and one that is deeply personal to me. I am very lucky to be surrounded by such a great team at home, in my restaurants, and in all my businesses. My sincerest thanks go to:

My supportive family: Alden, EJ, Meril, Jessie, Jilly, Mom, Dad, Mark, Wendi, Katti Lynn, Dolores, Jason, Jude, John Peter, Steven, and Cherry and Kent Lovelace.

My culinary team who was instrumental in the creation and development of this cookbook: Charlotte Martory, Stacey Meyer, and Kamili Hemphill.

My Homebase team: Eric Linquest, Chris Wilson, Tony Lott, George Ditta, Craig Laborde, Carol Ripley, Susan Chatman Anderson, Jennifer Todd, and all of the dedicated employees at Homebase and at each of my restaurants.

Martha Stewart and all of my Martha Stewart Living Omnimedia associates.

My brand team: Paige Capossela Green, Julia Johnson, Melanie Summers, Eliza Howe, Dawn Lynn, Alain Joseph, Michelle Terrebonne Becker, and Maggie McCabe.

All my licensing and merchandise partners.

My committed team at William Morris Endeavors.

Emeril Lagasse Foundation Board Members and devoted team.

All of my associates at Time Inc. Books/Oxmoor House: Publisher: Margot Schupf; Editorial Director: Anja Schmidt; Writer: Pam Hoenig; Senior Editor: Erica Sanders-Foege; Creative Director: Felicity Keane; Art Director: Christopher Rhoads; Assistant Managing Editor: Jeanne de Lathouder; Executive Food Director: Grace Parisi; Food Stylists: Nathan Carrabba, Torie Cox; Assistant Food Stylist: Laura Arnold; Prop Stylist: Mary Clayton Carl; Executive Photography Director: Iain Bagwell; Photo Editor: Kellie Lindsey; Contributing Photographers: Cedric Angeles, Quentin Bacon; Photo Stylist: Mindi Shapiro Levine; Photo Intern: Caroline Smith